HOMING

HOMING

· · · *a memoir* · · ·

MARK LYONS

NEW DOOR BOOKS
Philadelphia 2019

NEW DOOR BOOKS
An imprint of P. M. Gordon Associates, Inc.
2115 Wallace Street
Philadelphia, Pennsylvania 19130
U.S.A.

Library of Congress Control Number: 2019941895
ISBN 978-0-9995501-5-1

For Jeane Ann, Jesse and Seth

CONTENTS

A NOTE ABOUT MEMORY AND DIALOG

I have included dialog in *Homing*, conversations that I participated in or overheard. How could I not include voice, so much of who we are, how we relate to each other? Of course, the dialog is not word-for-word transcription of those conversations—I did not have a tape recorder with me. But what amazed me as I reached back and gathered memories of conversations, some of which occurred more than fifty years ago, was the detail of their content as well as the voice, tone, inflection. I also vividly remembered the scene in which the conversations occurred—where we were, how people sat or stood, what they wore, the shapes of their mouths and eyes as they spoke. So I have no doubt: the dialog—its content and character—is true to the people who spoke, who participated in this story.

PROLOGUE: 1995

I WAS FIFTY-TWO and camping in the Adirondacks with my wife Jeane Ann and our sons, Jesse and Seth. After an exhausting day of packing and driving from Philadelphia, we arrived at Lake George, the first stop in our ten-day trip. We pitched our tents, and as JA and I made the fire and started cooking, the kids found a sand field where they could play baseball, then headed down to the lake. Jess was fourteen, very full of his teen-self—shoulder-length hair, tall and string-bean, fluid of body and speech. At ease with his world. As I sharpened marshmallow sticks, I watched him shake his dripping hair like a water dog, playfully harass his eight-year-old brother, and sit by the fire to read *A Hitchhiker's Guide to the Galaxy*.

In 1957 I was fourteen. The year my mother had her Nervous Breakdown. *Breakdown:* like a car that rolls to a stop, one last gasp of a cylinder. All systems seized. Ultimately, she was unsalvageable, beyond repair. 1957: the year that changed our family forever, that changed me forever. What did I remember about my fourteenth year as I watched my high-spirited son burn his tongue on a marshmallow, calling it *sweet napalm*? Mental hospitals and desperate night sobs from my parents' bedroom. Electroshock and the Black Dog. My mother wanting me to do unspeakable things. The ghost of Jimmy MacFarland. Rage. Escape plans. All in black and white.

Nothing else?

We set up our new camp at Heart Lake. The kids and I headed out for a grueling and exhilarating nine-mile hike of Algonquin Peak, up the front side, down the back. Forgotten faces and buried memories of my fourteenth year appeared behind white pines and granite boulders, whispered in the creek where we soaked our blistered

3

feet. *The pigeon coop. Baseball after three years of retirement. My first slow dance, the first breast I touched. The denizens of The Little Theater. Mexicans hiding under a eucalyptus tree.* Birds of America. *"The Shooting of Dan McGrew." Seven birds in one shot. The Pause That Refreshes. My day with Johnny Otis. Richie Cary and his Studee.* Memories that I repeated to myself over and over down the mountain, a mantra to a lost childhood. We returned to camp, where the kids regaled Jeane Ann with their hiking prowess, demanded sympathy for their blisters, and skipped stones on the smooth lake at dusk. In our Explorer I found a pen in the glove compartment, and the black vacation notebook we always carried with us to write down our bird, mammal, and amphibian sightings and annotated logs of our daily activities. I returned to our tent, zipped the fly, and begin my list: my fourteenth year.

Each day for the rest of our trip, two or three memories, buried for four decades, found their way to the surface, demanding my attention. I wrote them down, short notes, fragments. Then I took these seeds home and began to write. I wrote for four years, my list of lost memories growing, begetting other memories that kept multiplying themselves, filled with details, conversations, vivid scenes, unraveling emotions. I wrote frantically, afraid that the memories were transient, that they would disappear and leave me again with nothing but teen confusion, loneliness, and unanswered questions. I found many lost shards of myself and began to put fourteen- and fifteen-year-old Mark back together again.

The story, as I first began to write it more than twenty years ago, was about reclaiming my childhood. It was not about forgiving; it was about my suffering and rage, the sustaining power of private places where teen boys go, and how as an adult I was still caught in the orbit of my mother's dark gravitational pull. I was so focused on excavating the pieces of my own story and reassembling them that I could not really imagine my mother's story. My teen rage did not consider her pain—she was not a sufferer, she was a tyrant who imposed suffering on those who loved her, whom I had escaped to save myself.

I put my writing in a drawer for seventeen years. Enough.

In my seventies, with grown children, I returned to this story, unfinished business. As a parent, I cannot imagine a more profound grief than losing my children, knowing I had driven them away.

Revisiting these stories now, adding more chapters, I have searched for a way to imagine my mother's suffering and grief, to recompose the shards of her life. Ultimately, this story is about forgiving her. Or perhaps it is about forgiving myself for never having forgiven her.

SPRING 1957

Cast Party

On nights like this, being fourteen feels OK. I'm hanging around the cast party at our house following the final curtain of *The Solid Gold Cadillac*, and the whole cast and crew of the Downey Community Players are loosened up with alcohol, when Jimmy MacFarland starts chanting, "Let's hear Dan McGrew, bring on Lou!" Soon everyone is stomping in rhythm and pointing at my mother, chanting, "Dan McGrew! We want Lou!" With a swoop of her hand, my mother clears the magazines off the top of the coffee table in front of the long brown couch, ceremoniously kicks off her shoes, offers her hand to an idolizing fan, and dramatically takes her position atop the table. She looks down at the throng below her, brushes her hair out of her face, and waits for silence as the audience continues shouting "Dan and Lou!" Achieving the silence she commands, she motions to my father for her martini, which she raises to the ceiling, then clinks glasses with her audience. She begins. Deep round words roll up from her chest, take shape in her mouth, and fill the room like smoke rings:

> A bunch of the boys were whooping it up in the Malamute
> saloon;
> The kid that handles the music-box was hitting a jag-time tune;
> Back of the bar, in a solo game, sat dangerous Dan McGrew,
> And watching his luck was his light-o'-love, the lady that's
> known as Lou.

It takes ten minutes for my mother to recite from memory the fifty-eight lengthy lines of Robert Service's poem "The Shooting of

Dan McGrew." She punches the air with her hand to the rhythm of the words, lowers and raises her voice, shakes her head in despair, pauses to give her listeners time to react. The audience recoils with terror when the barroom door is thrown open by the near-dead intruder smelling of revenge, feigns rapture as the hairy half-crazed stranger plays softly at the piano, hisses at the treachery of the lady known as Lou, and bemoans the inevitable fate of Dan McGrew, *pitched on his head, and pumped full of lead.* Not sated with Yukon stories, the crowd demands the recitation of "The Cremation of Sam McGee," which my mother waves off as she steps down from the tabletop. Leave them always wanting more, she often says, referring to nothing in particular.

SIX YEARS AGO, when I was eight, my mother founded the Downey Community Players, which everyone calls The Little Theater. She has just directed and starred in *The Solid Gold Cadillac*, in which she played Laura Partridge, owner of ten shares of stock in a giant and corrupt corporation. Laura Partridge goes to a shareholders' meeting, brings down the bad guys, and saves the corporation. The Little Theater's audience went wild. Three nights a week for three months my mother went to rehearsals, directing and acting; and on weekends she and her favorite people drank beer and painted flats in our backyard. Now, after five performances, it's over. On the final night I watched her take a long bow, raise her hands to the air, clap in unison with the audience, clasp hands with her cast for one last bow, then march off stage right. No doubt: this is the world where she is happiest.

Mom says she always gets sad after closing out a play, when the curtain goes down and the house is dark. Cast parties are a way of putting the play behind you with a celebration, a kind of wake.

The party is populated by my mother's world of eccentric friends, small-time characters like those from the Damon Runyon stories she loves so much. At first glance they seem mostly like pretty regular people, next-door-neighbor types. But they transform into characters from a play when they enter the world of The Little Theater. There's Harry Cooke, married to Theresa, the bent and crippled lady who hobbles to every rehearsal with two crooked canes. Mom once told me that Harry runs around on Theresa, everyone knows it, even Theresa; but in fact he is really faithful to her, because he always returns home at night. Harry was a shower door installer until the booze got the best of him. After he was fired for shattering a truckload of glass, he pursued his real dream—to be a mortician. My mother thinks that is strange, since Harry seems happiest chatting it up with people over a couple of drinks. "Imagine Harry in his embalming room," she says, "telling dirty jokes to dead people, laughing like crazy about sex with a cadaver (*Well, they don't have to worry about losing their hard-on!*), slapping the dead person's thigh." Just recently, not long after he got his mortician's license, Theresa died. Harry is heartbroken, Mom says, and has quit running around.

My favorite theater people are Kay and John Dart. Mom says John is an *intellectual*: he has a whole room lined with books—literature, philosophy, mathematics, science—some in foreign languages, plus a deep red, worn oriental rug with black geometric designs, stained glass lamps, and a brown leather easy chair I get lost in. He has a bald head that he seems proud of, the way he strokes it from back to front with the palm of his hand, and a pipe with a curve in it that he lights up every three minutes. I like John because he really looks at me when he talks, trying to see who I am. Kay is big in all ways: a big head with big eyes, giant shoulders and arms that sweep you up and hold you gasping between her giant pillow breasts, a big mouth that bellows out stories and laughter between her sips of Scotch on the rocks, ice clinking against her teeth. Kay and John look at each other often, seem to know exactly where the other is, even when their house is full of people.

One night when we visited Kay and John it felt different. John didn't relight his pipe or look at me; he seemed worried about Kay. Kay wrapped her arms around her belly, as if she were trying to hold her breasts up, her head turned to the side, looking down at the floor. There were no jokes or loud laughs or discussions about Arthur Miller's new play. Kay and John went into the library, closed the door, and I heard Kay sob as loud as she usually laughed. Finally, they came out and hugged my parents good-bye. John ran his hand through my hair, Kay swallowed me with her breasts. We left for the long drive home.

"Mom, what's the matter with Kay and John?"

"It's their anniversary."

"If it's their anniversary, why aren't they happy?" I had this terror that they were divorcing.

"It's a different anniversary. Three years ago today they lost their children."

So I learned the story of Kay and John's kids, whom I never knew. They were three years old, twins, playing in the driveway. Kay thought they were in the backyard as she backed the car out of the garage. The terrible sound of two tricycles being crushed, then silence.

"Kay relives that moment every day of her life and can't forgive herself. Especially on anniversaries. John doesn't have the time to grieve, he keeps trying to make Kay feel it's not her fault, he keeps holding her up."

On our next visit to their magical house, I wanted to stay a little longer in Kay's suffocating breasts. John looked at me as always, and I didn't leave the chair next to him for the entire evening. I tried to imagine their house three years before, the sounds of two three-year-old boys; tried to imagine their sadness. I wanted them to know that I knew, to tell them I was sorry, but couldn't find a way. Coming home in the back seat of the car, it occurred to me that parents probably had all sorts of secrets, sometimes terrible ones. I listened to my parents chatting about the night, my father's hand resting on my mother's. Did they have secrets?

Eileen Sweet, another of The Little Theater people, is beautiful: a face filled with angles and shadows, blond hair and perfect breasts, she walks with long legs sliding through the air with her neck outstretched like a swan. She is "well off," my mother says, with a cabin in the mountains where The Little Theater holds its annual winter party and a house on the beach with a great bay window overlooking the waves. She's sad, too, divorced once, maybe twice; Mom says she chooses the wrong men, trying to find flash to match her beauty. She's almost forty, wondering if it might be too late to be happy, taking lots of pills, trying to find ways to get her life together. She has never acted in The Little Theater plays, but helps out by making flats, selling tickets, taking posters to local stores to put in the windows. Once I asked Mom why Eileen joined The Little Theater.

"Because this is one place she can just be herself. She doesn't have to be beautiful or sexy when she's painting flats. People here like her just because she's Eileen, not because she looks like a movie star. With us she doesn't have to be on stage. If someone in the group tried to date her, she'd leave in a minute."

Sometimes my mother seems terribly wise.

Leota Haas is the second spinster I know, besides my aunt. Nobody except my mother calls her Leota—she's always Leota Haas, or Miss Haas. "Nobody cares about the English language like Leota Haas," my mother says after one of their monthly visits, "and God protect the student who chooses to butcher it in her class." Maybe sixty, she is tall and stern, looking down over the top of her glasses with her hands perfectly still at her side, speaking with perfectly pronounced words that sound like a foreign language. She often travels to England, "so I can talk with people who know how to speak the King's English." She's never acted in The Little Theater plays, nor made sets. She occasionally prompts, but "only in the plays that have something to say." In her formality she seems like a foreigner in the midst of the drinking and loud laughter and hugging of the theater crowd. Once, Mom explained her presence: "When Leota Haas comes to The Little Theater, she crosses a line into a world which is exotic and a little sinful to her. She loves it. Leota is not just proper, she's passionate, too. There's passion in the theater. And language— even when we're all amateurs." Maybe Leota Haas is the most eccentric one of all.

"So, Mark, who's your favorite poet today?" Of course, I have no answer, and Leota Haas mumbles something about the tragedy of growing up without favorite poets. For a long time, I was intimidated by her gruffness; but I find myself hanging around in the living room when Leota Haas comes to visit Mom, listening to their discussions about Steinbeck and Hemingway and Shakespeare and Tennessee Williams. She always scolds my mother for wasting her time on those trashy whodunits with no literary value.

"So many great works to read in such a short lifetime, Phyllis, and you choosing to bed down with Hercule Poirot! You should choose your literature more wisely. There are no whodunits on the library shelves in heaven."

"Oh Leota, cut the crap. It's good to sleep around a little, it makes you appreciate the great loves in your life. I am married to John Steinbeck, I just have one-night stands with Agatha Christie." I think Leota Haas likes talking dirty with my mother.

There are many others in my mother's Little Theater: Irene and Harry Francisco, she with milky-white skin and an Irish accent, he with Italian gruffness; their passion is raising Pekingese lap dogs. The Roles, whom my Mom describes as "the dullest people on earth, but if you ever needed to count on someone, they'd be there." And of course Jimmy and Treva MacFarland and Ann and Bill Taylor, the best friends of our family, whom we met on La Villa Street, the *cul de sac* of stucco duplexes, the first day we moved to Southern California. That was way-back-when, in 1945, when I was three. Our three families moved from Oklahoma and Iowa and Michigan to follow our engineer fathers, who came to build planes after the War, finding work at Douglas, Lockheed, North American Aviation. Each family had kids about the same age, all boys. While our parents played cards together, or gambled in Las Vegas, or went to the horse races at Hollywood Park, or made plays, we kids played touch football, hung out at the new McDonald's over on Lakewood Boulevard, had marbles tournaments, swam in the public swimming pool, or hunted crawdads among the dikes of the orange groves. Once Donnie and Ronnie MacFarland and I discovered a World War I fighter plane in an avocado grove off Paramount Avenue, with torn cloth siding over wooden struts and ailerons that still worked when we pushed the pedals.

For six years our house has been filled with theater people, nailing frames and stapling canvas to make flats. After they add the coat of white primer comes the magic: painting the inside of the apartment for *The Glass Menagerie*, or the hillside scene for *Heidi* (I played Peter, got to push grandmother's wheelchair down the mountain), or the Boardroom for *The Solid Gold Cadillac*, or the spooky fireplace for *The Monkey's Paw*. People practicing their lines as they paint, threatening to quit their jobs as engineers or teachers or housewives and do summer stock in Provincetown (where's Provincetown?). The best times are the grunion hunts at the annual Little Theater beach party at our Sunset Beach vacation house—sixty drunken people trying to be silent on the beach at three o'clock in the morning, each with a lantern, waiting for the grunion scouts to come up on the sand, then return to the full-moon-lit sea. *Shhhh!* Covering one another's mouths in drunken silent laughter, *Shhhh! Don't make a sound or the scouts will send the fish elsewhere!* Then on the tallest wave of the fullest moon of the highest summer tide, tens of thousands of seven-inch silver fleeting fish slither out of moonlit water, catapult themselves up the steep sandy bank, establish their beachhead ten feet above the high-tide line, jam their tails into the sand, and deposit their eggs. All of that silver spectacle lasts less than twenty seconds, the time it takes for the next wave to come in and for the fish to hurtle back down the bank and disappear beneath the wave. The sound is incredible, maybe a million grunion at once flapping on the sand, the roar of the receding wave in the background. Then sixty drunken fishermen with a bucket in each hand leaping out of the shadows above the embankment, with shouts of pandemonium, like when the Yanks jump out of the foxholes and charge the enemy in World War II movies. People sliding on a moving floor of fish, sometimes three or four enemies of war in each hand, tossing them into buckets, amid hilarious laughter. Twenty seconds, and the surviving fish have escaped on the next wave. The bucket brigade lies spent, face-up on the sand beneath the full moon. When we are lucky, we get two waves of fish, enough to fill up ten buckets, maybe seven hundred grunion. Then back to the beach house for beer and soda and chips and laughter over gutting the fallen prey, which are no longer than five inches with their heads off. We all sleep in until eleven the next morning, then cook up the best, absolutely the best, breakfast ever: grunion fried in butter, browned with the crunchy tails still on, dashed with salt and pepper. I eat at least thirty, chased by fresh squeezed orange juice bought from the Sunset Beach corner store.

BACK AT THE CAST PARTY, it's time for charades. My mother hands Harry Cooke, from the opposing team, the quote, "Screwed, tattooed and stranded in Texas." Harry thinks for a few seconds, then gets down on his knees and acts like a carpenter with a screwdriver. Exaggerated twisting motions of his wrists and elbows, grimaces to show how hard he's working. My mother howls, "You can do better than that, Cookie!"

The Ghost Under the Bed

Late March, a cool Southern California Thursday evening, and I am alone with my mother. Michele, my two-year-old sister, has already gone to bed, and my seventeen-year-old brother Bill is out somewhere; he's never around. My father is away on business, Milwaukee or Denver, with plans to return tomorrow night. The windows are open and a slow breeze moves through our house, a few crickets chant, two owls argue over the night space. The orange groves have blossomed, and for a reason I have never understood, the sweet blossom smell is stronger in the evening when things cool off. Soon the bees will come, and the groves will become a quiet constant hum. My mother hunkers in her deep low chair situated in the corner of the living room, comforted by the pepper wood burning in the fireplace, her face masked behind her latest book. I sit at my grandmother's mahogany desk, which defiantly stands on three legs, writing a report on the conquest of Spain by the Visigoths. The flames in the fireplace ebb to coals, a signal: Mother folds the corner of her page over, switches her lamp to low-watt night-light, rises from her worn-out throne, and heads for the bathroom.

"Dear, I'm going to take off my face and turn in. Are you about ready for bed?"

"I'll be up for another half hour, got to finish this report." I am about to add, "and please stop calling me *dear*, I'm not a kid anymore," but opt to let it slide. The irritation in my voice can speak for me.

As she passes through her bedroom on the way to the bathroom, she freezes.

"Mark, I hear something . . . *shhhh* . . . hear? Hear? It's under the bed. There's something under the bed."

"Probably the cat."

"Listen . . . *shhhh* . . . hear? No . . . it's louder than that . . . listen. . . ." Her hands signal silence, like a concert conductor. "There's something under the bed . . . I think it's a person . . . Come here." She's whispering now, an urgent undertone.

"Mom, there's nobody under the bed . . . I don't hear anything . . . if it's anything, it's the cat, she always hides under there."

"Get a broom. There's somebody under the bed. Get a broom! *Quick!*"

I just want to finish my report, but her voice captures me. I am glad there is no one around to see me do this as I dutifully go to the back porch, pull the broom off the snaps, stomp dramatically into the bedroom to scare the "burglar," and sweep back and forth under the stained oak bed.

"See. Nothing. Nothing. Not even the cat. Can we go to bed now?"

"No, you missed a spot, there in the corner. Get down and look."

"Mom . . . c'mon . . . please. . . ."

"Look! Just look! Do it!" Terror in her voice. "*Do it now!*" A sensation, a quivering, settles on my shoulders, the first instance of my own undefined dread—not afraid that I'll find someone under the bed, but aware of that precise moment when I feel my mother begin to spin away. I turn on the overhead light in the bedroom, get down on my hands and knees, take a long serious look under the bed, turn my head from the headboard to the footboard, a dramatic sweep to demonstrate that I have carefully surveyed the entire floor of the bedroom.

"Nothing, Mom. Clean as a whistle. Really. Let's go to sleep."

"I can't sleep in this bed. There's someone there. I know it."

"Look, Mom." Taking her shoulders, I slowly lower her down to her knees. "Look. Nothing."

Trembling, she forces herself to look under the bed, flat on her stomach. Nothing. She sits up and leans against the bed, knees to her chest, eyes elsewhere. I expect her to be relieved, but now she is distraught, weeping, shaking out of control.

"It's OK, Mom. There's nothing. A creaky floor caused by the heat being turned off. OK?"

I hold her for an hour, cradled on the thick green rug, rocking until the trembling stops. She refuses to sleep in her bed, and I walk her to the couch in the den, find a pillow, cover her with a blanket, kiss her on the forehead.

"Everything is fine, Mom. I love you." I stay with her until her flitting eyes remain shut, her breathing deepens and slows, the grip on my hand relaxes. I take off my shoes and walk stocking-footed to my back bedroom, lie down in my jeans, and feel the damp current of orange blossom air move through the window at my head. My eyes are open for a long time, trying to replay the last hour, find some meaning. No words come for what I have witnessed, some fundamental change in my mother, a mystery. I hum to myself quietly, an aching mourning hum, for a loss that I feel but do not comprehend.

FRIDAY MORNING. I dress for school and stand on the floor heater in the living room to dry my hair, still wet from the shower. My mother sits in her chair, staring into the fireplace. "Bye, Mom, see you after school." No answer.

When I come home from school, she is still in her chair dressed in last night's nightgown. "Hi, Mom, I'm going over to Dicky Tostenson's to shoot some baskets, be back for dinner." Silence from a person who is such a talker, who always wants to know how my day went or tell me about a book I should read.

We don't eat supper. At nine o'clock my father comes home from the airport and Mom meets him at the door. High-pitched wounded-animal sounds, like when I came across a raccoon in the orchard, its two hind legs caught in a spring trap. "Mark, please go to your room, your mother and I need to be alone."

The dark is filled with foundation-shaking sobs.

EARLY SATURDAY MORNING: a flurry of phone calls, drawers opening and closing, the snap of luggage being shut. "Mark, please watch your little sister. There's lunch meat in the fridge. I'll call from the hospital."

I pull back the curtain and watch my father walk my mother to the car. He holds her elbow, keeping her erect as she shuffles. She's forty-four, but overnight has acquired the walk of a ninety-year-old. The doors of our new '57 Chevy close. The sound of tires on asphalt, then they are gone.

James

Michele is still asleep. Bill never came home last night; sometimes he stays over at his buddy's house. Dad left with Mom an hour ago, said he was taking her to some place called Edgemont Hospital. I head out to the backyard, check the grass. Dry enough. On my back now, hands and feet stretched out, I take off my red flannel shirt and use it as a pillow. It's already tee shirt weather. Forty feet above me are the twisted bark-flaked branches of the skeleton of our last standing pepper tree. Six years ago, we had five trees that shaded our yard, all over a hundred years old. This last surviving tree died in the fall, mother of them all, whose eight-foot-diameter trunk and rotted branches had been our fort, our lookout for marauding neighbor kids loaded with hard green oranges looking for a war. We would load our ammunition in a bucket or gunnysack—green olives, oranges, lemons, occasional apricots and plums—and haul it ten feet up to the crotch of the tree and stash it there, waiting for the enemy. If the day was boring, inevitably they would come. Usually two or three, sometimes four or five, mostly from Seventh Street, the next block over, sliding through the bamboo that separated the Gunthers' yard from ours, in stealth position with back and knees bent to forty-five degrees, slowly rotating on their heels from side to side as they moved forward, eyes sweeping, checking out enemy positions. We loved the power of watching them sneak through our backyard, oranges cocked in hand, extra ammo stashed in their World War II packs, thinking they were invisible. We had them in our sights, and they were oblivious. Finally, we could stand it no longer and opened fire. *Geronimo!* The civic fury of our block rained down on them in our backyard until they could regroup, scramble behind the olive or plum trees, and begin to return fire. Ultimately the battle degenerated into *Got you!/Did not!* arguments, which were never satisfactorily resolved because there were no wounds to substantiate our claims of a direct hit. Two years ago, we settled the problem by stealing a bunch of overripe pomegranates from old man Higgons' yard. *Fire! Bam! Splat!* and red pomegranate blood oozed through the white tee shirt of Ronnie Lobaugh. *A direct hit and don't say I didn't.* Last summer one of the fifteen-year-olds introduced a rock into the field of battle, which hit Dave Gunther's sister behind the ear (*What was she doing in the middle of the fight anyway?*), immediately ending the conflagration with tears and the shrieking of Dave's mother. As we retreated through the back fences, emptying our pockets of ammunition and praying our mothers would receive no phone calls from old lady Gunther, we somehow knew that the neighborhood wars would soon be history.

The tree is leafless now, a rheumatic skeleton against the shifting sky. Pepper tree branches form no pattern, unlike those of an oak or locust, and—being evergreen—are not seen naked until they die. Now, with the smaller branches stripped away by last winter's storms, all that remains of the skeleton are at most ten giant burnt-brown limbs angling upward to one hundred feet, giant twisted spaces between them. On a branch fifty feet above my head roosts a pigeon. Nothing special to look at: black back and tail, two white bars on the wings, a gray breast with a black neck, head phosphoresced with purples and greens, glass-orange eyes within a perfect black ring. At first glance your basic park pigeon, the kind we throw white bread to at lunchtime in school.

The bird leans off the branch, glides down ten feet, and then the sound: a powerful flap, like snapping the sheets before I hang them on the clothesline. Three flaps and a glide, then steady snapping flaps as the pigeon rises out of the girders of the tree and begins to circle. I close my eyes and listen to the wings beating the air. As the circle gets bigger, round and round, there's a whistling sound as the bird picks up speed. The orbit widens and the sound almost disappears, then gets louder as the radius shrinks, like turning the volume down and up again on the radio. Twenty minutes and forty laps later, the bird returns to the gnarled branch, beak open, tongue flicking in and out.

I call this bird James—I name all of my pigeons. He is the only pigeon I ever trained to be a racer. I am not sure why I picked him—someone may have said he's got that big muscular breast of an English Homer. First, I taught him to go through the one-way coop trapdoor, then let him fly with some of the older flock that already knew how to home. Then I took him to the yard next door and released him, then over to the Gunthers', down the block, over to the Presbyterian Church three blocks away, tossing him into the air, rushing home on my one-speed Schwinn to see if he could beat me, or if he would ever return. Then the real test: With a nail I poked some air holes in a rusted tin picnic box I found in the garage, then cut some old inner tubes into strips and made giant rubber bands to hold the box onto the rack on the back of my bike, and practiced some sharp turns to ensure it wouldn't fall off. I caught James after his morning feeding. It was time for his five-mile test. We rode down to South Junior High, with the big field that would give him more space to orient, to get his bearings. I put the kickstand down and opened the picnic box. James was a little spooked by all the unfamiliar space, but he cocked his orange eyes at me and the open sky, then pulled himself into the air. I watched the circle form, then expand, as my bird oriented himself. After three or four laps, just before going out of sight, he broke from the circle, almost as if by centripetal force, and headed east on a tangent for home. The race was on. I jumped on my bike, stood as I pedaled off the grass of the baseball field, and raced home down Lakewood Boulevard. Half an hour later, I dropped my bike in the driveway without putting down the kickstand and ran for the coop. No bird. Scanned the sky and listened for the beating. Nothing. Ten minutes more, still nothing. Had I pushed him too fast? Then the familiar orbiting whistle, louder and faster, tightening around the crooked tree. James landed on his branch, his tail silhouetted against the sky. I lay back on the warm damp ground and watched until he glided down to the trapdoor, entered, dipped his beak in the water trough, and pointed it to the sky to let the water trickle down his throat.

My first pigeons were a gift from Richie Cary, when I was eleven—three years ago now, when we were both in sixth grade. Elmer and Oscar. As with all of his gifts, neither of us realized or acknowledged it at the time. Richie lived in a secret kingdom on two run-down acres on La Reina Avenue, behind Our Lady of Perpetual Help School. His garage was stashed with old doors and windows, hard rubber wheels, bent and nicked tools hanging from hooks in the ceiling beams and nails on every wall, shallow pans of gasoline to clean parts, used oil filters, odd-sized engine cylinders, an electric table saw, a drill press, a greasy lathe, piles of lumber resting on pegs protruding at an upward angle from the back wall, smells of oil and solvents and paints. All baked by the sun coming through the west window over the efficient work bench covered with vises and bolt-filled cans. Under a torn canvas tarp in the back corner was Richie's prize: a '49 Studebaker Starlight coupe with a bullet nose, spaceship headlights, and rounded rear windows. The Studee's engine was on the concrete garage floor, upside down to expose the cylinders, bleeding oil. Pistons, pulleys, and belts and other unnamed parts in unmarked boxes. Richie's plan was to have his Studee ready to roll by the time he was fifteen and able to drive.

After I watched Richie remove the fan belt from his engine, we began the ritual that was part of every visit, the part I waited for. We walked through the back door of the garage to the barnyard of sheds and pens, kicking cans and an upside-down rake out of the way in the path dotted with sun, and surveyed his animals: ground-feeding Rhode Island Red and White Leghorn chickens with fresh eggs and chicks, plus two geese—one on death row, getting fattened up for the Fourth of July. Baggy-skinned rabbits, one doe with hairless bunnies ("How can anything so ugly get so cute?"), a chinchilla, a pair of hang-tit goats milked every morning. We raked the chicken coop and goat pen, then shoveled the steamy pyramids of rabbit manure under the hutch into the wheelbarrow, got a running start through the weeds behind the sheds, and flipped it over, shit flying against the cinder-block wall in the back corner. Then we sat on upturned feed kegs and scraped the droppings from the crevices of our soles with a pointed twig.

Every visit to his house, Richie had something new to show me. This time he took me past the goat pens to a clearing, and stood me in front of an old rabbit hutch whose top had been cut out to add a second four-foot level covered with ¾" mesh chicken wire. He unlatched the wire door of the lower level, stretched through the opening on one knee into the darkness of the roofed section of the cage, reached into a nest box overflowing with straw, and carefully backed out. In his left hand he cradled a pure white pigeon with a black beak and gray cere, and stroked the curve behind the bird's neck. He nodded permission to my hand hovering to do the same. We walked into the sunlight behind the cage.

"Watch." He tossed the bird into the air. The bird fell maybe half a foot before realizing it was free, and with one powerful magnificent stroke of the wings it was airborne, rising in a straight line at sixty degrees until it was twenty feet above the telephone wires. Then it began the circle that still mesmerizes me three years later. I watched, rotating as if the pigeon and I were attached by a string.

"Let's get the eggs, he'll be back in twenty minutes." Richie and I collected seven red-brown and four white chicken eggs and carried them to the refrigerator on his back porch, then returned to wait. Soon the pigeon whistled down to the coop, cocked its head in four directions to check for marauders, pushed the wire flap of the trap-door on the second level of the fly pen, and settled down into the shadows of its nest.

Just after Thanksgiving I asked Richie if he had any baby pigeons I could buy. A couple would be fledging in two weeks, enough time for me to build a pen. Elmer and Oscar, seventy-five cents each, a birthday present to myself.

Now I have thirty-six birds, eight of them descendants of Elmer and Oscar. They live in luxury housing I built for them last year: a six-by-twelve-foot coop with lapped redwood siding, with nest boxes and perches, a fifteen-by-twelve-foot fly pen with a porcelain sink for swimming, a trapdoor in the roof for my pigeons to return after doing their afternoon sky laps.

James has finished his training laps and glides down from the pepper tree to the top of the coop. I'd better go check on Michele, explain that Mom and Dad will be back later on.

Dancing Shoes

The year I got Elmer and Oscar, I also played shortstop. On the field I felt like a dancer, and my body and I were friends. I practiced my dance moves for hours against the chimney of our house, firing a baseball against the bricks, catching the rebound. I would begin with the center bricks then aim for a brick a little farther to the left or right, forcing myself to stretch for the ball. One more brick at a time until I was completely off balance, extended on one foot. Then snatch the ball and find the motion: back foot planted, pivoting as I swept the glove and ball to my throwing side, firing the ball at a one-foot square drawn with chalk on the chimney. Practice makes perfect. And I pretty much was, for eleven.

I saw Mr. Jamison only two times. Two small encounters to him, I'm sure; but I never forgot him. When I was eleven, he watched me play shortstop in tryouts for the Downey Junior Athletic League's first season. Five fielded balls and five swings at the plate, then we were scored from ten to one, the *tens* being future all-stars and the *ones* being the poor guys who couldn't catch yet. Our names were divided by rank into ten hats, and the coaches took turns picking from each hat, so that the teams would have an even distribution of good and bad players.

Five balls: first a hard low grounder right at me to find out if I can keep my glove on the ground and bring it up to follow the ball on the hop; then a grounder far to my right to see if I can move to my back-hand and make the pivot to first; a line drive that looks like it is going over my head, to measure my reflexes; then a deep pop-up thirty feet behind second base. And finally, the shot: a scorcher over the top of the pitcher's mound toward second base, two bounces and it will be in the outfield. The Move, my chimney move: running to my left, three crossovers of my legs, reaching down to grab the ball off my toe just before the second bounce, with my right foot extended back and above my shoulder for balance, one step to stand and recover, then turn, rotate, cock, and fire sidearm to first. One motion.

After the tryouts, one of the scorers in a red baseball hat says, "Hey, kid, got a minute? Your name's Mark, right? I'm Mr. Jamison. Where'd you learn to play ball like that?—you've got a great move to your left. I'm not supposed to tell kids, but you're in the *ten* hat. So, I noticed you're wearing tennis shoes—you'd have even more range if you wore cleats. Do you have any baseball shoes?"

"No, I wear these tennis shoes, they're comfortable." As much as I loved baseball, I never had asked my parents for some real baseball cleats.

"Nothing feels better than a good pair of broken-in sneakers, but baseball shoes are designed for comfort. Listen, I've got a son who has outgrown his cleats, had to buy him a new pair this season. Old ones are just sitting around in the garage. Might fit you. Like to try them on?"

So we arranged the fitting: the next day, Sunday afternoon at two. I knew he would be on time. When I heard a car pull in our driveway,

Mom was in her chair reading her Agatha Christie whodunit, Dad on his couch reading his sports page. The bell rang, and I nervously went to the door.

"Who's there, Mark?"

"Just someone from the baseball tryouts. Wants to show me something."

I didn't invite Mr. Jamison in, somehow wanted him to myself. I brought out a clean pair of white cotton socks, with double red stripes at the top. Mr. Jamison and I sat in the sun on the red tile porch steps, talked about how the teams would be chosen by the coaches next weekend. I kept staring at the crack in the tile that looked like Nevada. I took off my high tops and looked to him for a sign.

"So, want to try these on? They're pretty ragged looking, but they're broken in and the leather will be good with a little work. Cleats just need to be sharpened."

Mr. Jamison unrolled the top of a brown paper Vons Markets bag, reached in with hairy arms, and pulled out the shoes by the heels. I had never held a pair of baseball cleats before: paper-thin leather, they used to be black, I could tell by the leather under the laces on the tongue; but now they were mostly scuffed brown and powdered with diamond dust. One shoelace had been broken and retied, the tongue was crackly stiff, the sole lining of the left shoe unglued and curled. But there were no holes. I wondered what position they had played.

"Shall we?" Mr. Jamison took the shoe cradled on my thigh and nodded at my right foot. My leg extended itself hopefully. He then inserted two long fingers into the shoe, loosened the laces, pulled the tongue back, and reached for my foot. I closed my eyes as I felt my pointed toes settle into the shoe. My foot explored the space inside as I held my breath and imagined a fit. *Please*, my lips mimed.

"Seems just a little loose. Why don't you try walking around a bit?"

I put on the other shoe and found the grass. Ran five strides, bent my knees and side-stepped to the left, then to the right, body turning in the shortstop motion. Dance shoes. The heel rode up, the toes caught the grass.

Too big.

"Got a second pair of socks? Often ballplayers wear two pairs to cut down on blisters." I think Mr. Jamison wanted the shoes to fit as much as I did. But two pairs of socks still didn't fill the space. He looked at the shoes hanging on my feet, shook his head, and nibbled at his right lower lip.

"No, they're just a little too large. You know, my son's thirteen, and a pretty big kid. I'm sure they'll fit you maybe next year. Want to hang on to them?"

"That's OK. They'll fit some other kid. I can get some."

He wrapped the lonely shoes back up in the paper bag and extended his hand.

"I'm sorry about the shoes. They'd've loved to play shortstop with you. Good luck, keep working hard and you'll be a fine ballplayer someday. Maybe I'll see you playing in the league this summer. Or in the All-Star game."

"Thanks." That's all I could say. I watched him cross the lawn to his dusty four-door Mercury with the bat bag in the back seat. My eyes closed, I listened to the car door clunk shut, the driver's side window roll down, the ignition rev, the three distinct sounds of shifting gears, then nothing. I felt a great sadness—not because the shoes didn't fit, but because he was gone. I turned and went back into the house.

"What was that about?" Dad peered over the top of the sports page.

"Nothing. The coach had some old baseball cleats, thought they might fit me."

"Did they?"

"No. I'm too small."

My father's head disappeared behind his newspaper.

I walked through the living room to the kitchen, out the back door. I opened the door to my pigeon pen, and six birds cautiously stepped out, looked both ways before taking to the air, then settled on the long horizontal branch of the pepper tree. I checked the nest boxes; another pair of squabs was on the way.

I never saw Mr. Jamison again, though I'm sure he knew my disappointment when the shoes wouldn't fit. Maybe he understood, too, the hunger I felt for the attention he gave me, how he noticed how much I loved the dance. By the end of that summer my body had betrayed me, the grace and joy of the move to the left, the perfect pivot and spring-action throw disintegrated to pursed wheezing with shoulders tucked to my ears. The rush I felt when I saw the ball leave the bat howling toward me turned to frozen terror and dropped pop-ups, bungled easy two-hop grounders. After being thrown out yet again trying to steal second base, I stood on the bag, bent at the waist with my hands on my knees, gasping for air.

I stopped dancing and became an asthmatic.

Attack(ed)

I have third period gym, all ninth graders. We are lined up in our red gym shorts and white tee shirts when Mr. Sharpeless, the gym teacher, announces that today is timed sprints in the hundred-yard dash. They do this every spring. Sharpeless takes this all very seriously: a whistle, starter's gun, stopwatch, a log to mark the times. He's an ex-Marine. *I am going to whip these kids into shape. We are a nation of pussies.*

It's one of those bad days for me, when I wheeze every time I exhale. Sharpeless is not sympathetic. "Just run through it, Lyons, you won't pass gym unless you take this test." I am the last to run today; the other kids have headed back to the gym. I hate this. Running makes me feel most out of control; there is a demon inside my lungs cranking down my windpipes until I am helpless.

"OK, Lyons, let's make this quick so I can go to lunch." A little panicked, I tell him that I am wheezing, ask to run another day. "Running is good for asthmatics, Lyons, expands their lungs. You don't want to be a cripple, do you?"

He's one hundred yards away at the finish line. First the whistle, to tell me to get ready, then the puff of smoke and the smack of the gun. I go. The first twenty yards aren't so bad, maybe this will be a good day. Then the dreaded feeling that I hate, the tightening in my chest. I open my mouth to try to get more air in—it goes in easily, but slowly leaks out, making piercing sounds like air that seeps out of a balloon when you pinch its neck. I crane my neck to try to get more air in and out. I hear the echo of Sharpeless through the fog. "Keep your damn head down, Lyons, and pump those arms, this isn't a beauty pageant!" All I see are the two white lines of the runner's lane. I fix on the *clop clop* of my gym shoes on the dirt, try to forget my breathing. "Only forty yards, Lyons, now let's see your kick!" I am sure that I've almost completed the run, how can I run forty yards more? My neck muscles are bulging, trying to pump more air out, my diaphragm sucking. I am a machine with a leak somewhere. Fucking Sharpeless, I hate your ass. I hate my body. I am a wild-eyed wounded animal, cornered. "Twenty yards more, Lyons, dig deep!" I have this hazy fantasy that my momentum will carry me the last twenty yards, or that I am tall enough to fall over the finish line from here. I can't get any air out, so just hold my breath. Suddenly it is silent as I stop gasping for air and I hear my heart, like the single piston on Richie Cary's Briggs and Stratton lawn-mower engine. I close my eyes and command my legs to keep moving, running in a fog toward a cliff. I have a suffocating pain in my chest and feel the blackout coming. A thunderous click in my ears as Sharpeless pushes down on the stop-watch. I open my eyes to catch the light blue of his denim pants as I crumple to the ground on my hands and knees, stomach contracting, retching for air. I can't stand the humiliation of being on the ground after running a hundred yards. I grab the chain-link fence, pull myself up, stand hunched over, hands on my knees, mouth wide open, gulping in air that slowly leaks out, hocking up thick white phlegm.

"Twenty-four point two seconds. A little faster than a snail, slower than a turtle. Enough for you to pass gym and let me get some lunch."

Sharpeless writes the time down in his log and heads for the locker room, his white tee-shirt with rolled-up sleeves tight around his biceps. His back is to me now, so I ease myself against the fence and slump down until my butt is on the warm ground. The empty field is a cage. I spend my lunch hour there, propped against the fence, slowly lowering my knees from my chest, feeling my lungs relax and my windpipes loosen, tasting the miracle of air. I close my eyes and sleep in the sun.

Thanks for Checking In

My mother has returned home after being at Edgemont Hospital for eleven days. As soon as people heard she was back, the phone began to ring off the wall. Leota Haas, Harry Cooke, Eileen Sweet, John and

Kay Dart, the Taylors and MacFarlands, the Franciscos, the Roles—
her theater people, her friends, checking in.

Mom nods to Dad: *Pick up the phone.*

"Oh, hi, Eileen. Thanks for calling. She's right here, just a second." He starts to hand the receiver to my mother, but she shakes her
head. My father persists, pointing to the receiver, whispering to my
mother *take it*. She stares into the fireplace.

"I'm sorry, but Phyl can't come to the phone right now. Yes, she's
doing better, should be back on her feet in a week or so. You bet—
I'll tell her you're thinking of her. She'll get back to you in a few days.
Thanks, again."

The phone rings five or six times more. Each time, my mother
sits in her chair and nods *no* to my father, who continues to assure her
friends that all is well.

My father: the guardian at the gate.

I am not sure how I know this, watching my mother in her chair,
eyes focused inward like a blind woman who has stopped looking.
How when she shakes her head, *No*, she is saying *No more of that, of
who I have been.* I don't understand any of this, but I have this terrible
fear: I will never see The Little Theater people again.

First Pubie

My thirteenth year was tough. I was obsessed by my height, or lack of
it. I was by far the shortest kid in my class—no, in school. No more
than four feet seven, in eighth grade. Skinny, about eighty wheezing
pounds.

Worst of all was gym. Manhood time. I was the only kid in eighth
grade with not one strand of pubic hair. Strip, put on your jock and
shorts, go out to the field and do the boy gym thing, return, strip,
shower, dress. Plenty of opportunity for my classmates to see the
naked truth: Lyons has no pubies. I don't remember anyone pointing
and laughing, no comments—how did they pass up this opportunity
for cruelty? Nothing was said, but that didn't stop my sense of humiliation as I wrapped my wan and pathetic body in a towel as soon as I
could, spent two minutes in the communal showers, then rewrapped.
But I knew: they knew. And that was important to all of us.

That summer, as usual, our family spent two weeks at Sunset Beach. One day I came back from swimming, went to the outdoor shower at our beach house, and dropped my swim pants to wash off the sand. Lo! There it was: pubic hair #1, an inch long, blond. I ran it through my fingers, carefully so as not to dislodge it. Definitely mine.

I dried off and went into the house. Dad and Bill were down at the beach. Michele, a year and a half, was asleep in her crib. Mom was reading. I called her into my bedroom, "I have something to show you."

She sat on my bed, and I dropped my shorts. Being naked in front of my mother was no big deal—everyone in our house walked around without clothes as we changed out of sandy swim trunks or dried off after a shower.

"See: there, right there at the base."

She cradled my penis and balls in her hand and touched my first man hair, then stroked the hair on my head.

"Our little guy is becoming a man."

We both were very proud. I went for a walk on the beach.

Slow Dance

"The easiest way to sweep a girl off her feet is on the dance floor," my mother advised me shortly after I turned fourteen. "A girl figures if you can dance you can do anything."

I liked the idea of a girl thinking I could do anything, whatever that meant, so this spring I heeded my mother's counsel and enrolled in Mrs. Schaefer's Thursday night social dance class, held in the junior high cafeteria. In ten weeks, I more or less have learned the waltz, cha-cha-cha, box step, and swing; but they seem like old-fogy dances not designed for 1957-model kids. Ballroom dancing, parents call it. Not the kind of dancing I imagine going on at Marcia Bryant's pool parties, to which I have never been invited.

On the other hand, I have met my first girlfriend at Mrs. Schaefer's, so maybe Mom was right. At first, my attraction to Ann Hegardt was purely practical: she was the only girl in the class shorter than I, so I automatically went to her when Mrs. Schaefer taught us the etiquette of asking a girl for a dance and ordered us to practice. I assayed

Ann's height and found it to be satisfactory—meaning my four feet ten inches would not be unsatisfactory to her. Then I noticed she was kind of cute. Cute: not sexy with big blossoming boobs like Ginger Bilder, not slinky and aloof with perfect long red hair like Janie Pearson, not effervescent everybody's-friend-popular like Patti Thomas; but not pimply or homely or pathetic either. Cute: I liked looking at Ann Hegardt, but it was not impossible to take my eyes off her. She wasn't going to win any beauty contests, but her looks weren't going to get in her way either. Sort of like me, except it was OK to be a short girl.

"Dancing is the work of the Devil"—that's what my Seventh Day Adventist friend David Pederson said when we switched on *American Bandstand* one afternoon at his house. He changed the channel before I had a chance to ask what he meant, but in Mrs. Schaefer's I began to understand, as I anticipated the end-of-class slow dances with Ann Hegardt. (I think Mrs. Schaefer always had the last dance be a slow one, so we would keep coming back.) I noticed things about Ann that were new to me: the shampoo smell in her hair, the softness of her forearm as we returned from a spin in our waltz, a brush of her cheek. Nor did she seem eager to let go of my hand when the music stopped. Occasionally when we danced at the end of the evening, I got those embarrassing hard-ons bragged about in gym, and I tried to hide my pleasure by bending twenty degrees at the waist and shuffling like an old man to the metal folding chairs on the rim of the dance floor.

Somehow it did not feel awkward to ask Ann to go to a movie, so last night Dad chauffeured us to the Meralta. We held hands in the dark, petting each other's palms. I couldn't imagine kissing her, or trying; and she didn't seem to be waiting for me to make a move, a relief. The magic of touching a girl kept me awake all night, lying in bed eyes open, afraid if I fell asleep the sensations would abandon my hand.

Still filled with pleasure this morning, I enter the living room to find mother in her chair, the bamboo scratching sound of Dad raking grass outside. I claim my spot on the floor furnace, heat waves radiating up my pajamas. Mom looks up from her book.

"So did you have a nice time last night?"

"Yeah, it was fun."

"So what did you do?"

"You know. We went to see *The Incredible Shrinking Man*."

"Right. That must have been scary. Did you hold hands?"

"Yeah." I look down at the floor furnace and shift my weight to my right foot.

"Anything else?"

"No, Dad picked us up and brought us home . . ."

"No. I mean did you do anything else besides hold hands?"

"*Mom* . . ."

"You know, like kiss, or kiss in any kind of special way?"

This does not feel right.

"Or did she touch you anywhere, you know, anywhere really private? You know . . . that happens when a boy and a girl get close, it can happen to anybody. It can happen really fast."

I feel a sense of danger—this is all new territory to me. And dirty. I feel dirty. What has just happened? How can I stop this conversation?

My mother cocks her head. "Well . . . ?"

I shake my head. "I gotta go, I told Richie Cary I'd be over at eleven to work on his engine."

I retreat to my room, dizzy. I bend over, my head between my legs, take some deep breaths. I put on my mechanic's jeans, covered with grease and oil, and make my getaway on my bike.

Richie's got the Briggs and Stratton engine dismounted from a trashed lawn mower he picked up at Old Man Brunner's repair shop. This is the part I love best, how Richie patiently explains pistons and crankshafts and carburetors and shows me what tools to use. His secret world, magic to me. He hands me a socket wrench and instructs me to remove the cylinder head. I love the feel of the wrench ratcheting as I crank my wrist. He holds the block as I extract the piston and unbolt the crankshaft. He shows me how to unclip the rings, and we put the piston in a pan filled with gasoline.

"I've never held a piston in my hand," I say to Richie.

"Pretty cool, huh? Wait until we've got new rings on her and slip her back into the block. This baby's going to purr like a kitten."

I wash my hands off in the cool gasoline, grease swirling like lava and disappearing down the drain in the middle of the garage. Richie's looking like he wants to chat.

"Say, didn't you have a date with what's-her-name last night?"

"Yeah, name's Ann."

"So, how'd it go?"

"OK. She's OK." I don't want to say anything to anybody about Ann Hegardt. "Want some help shoveling your rabbit shit?"

"I got a better idea: let's make some CO_2 rockets." So Richie teaches me to use a lathe to convert a foot-long 2"× 2" pine block into a fuselage with a pointed head, the rocket body. Then we use a drill press to hollow out a ¾" cylinder in the fuselage for the CO_2 cartridge. Next, we make three slits along the sides of the fuselage and glue in triangular wings we've cut from a tin coffee can. We take a red brush and paint our names on our rockets, and go out to the grassy mall next to the hutches. Richie has made a special launcher—you drop the rocket down a slot, where the cartridge is punctured by a nail. I kiss the head of my rocket and drop it down the slot. *WHOOOOOOSH!* It takes five seconds for the cartridge to shoot off all of its fuel, and the rocket disappears in the orchard behind Richie's house.

I have not forgotten this morning's conversation with my mother. It's five o'clock, and I'm hoping Mrs. Cary will invite me to supper. She does. Saved. I assure her there's no need to call home, my parents know where I am. We have homemade peach ice cream for dessert. I want to spend the night.

The lights are out in our house, Mom and Dad have taken to going to bed early. I pee in the bushes by the driveway so that I won't have to go past their bedroom on the way to the bathroom. I leave my shoes on the porch steps, carefully open the door to my bedroom, edge across the floor, and slide under the covers. Tonight, I will not replay memories of Ann Hegardt's soft hands.

Land of the Gimps I

Sharpeless and Mr. Hershey, the athletic director, are talking to each other as I lock up my gym clothes. Mr. Hershey motions me over and asks me to go upstairs to his office with the glass windows overlooking the locker room and showers. I like Mr. Hershey, he's a teacher, not a drill sergeant.

"Have a seat, Mark. Listen, I want to tell you about a gym program that's starting next year in high school, think it'd be good for you. It's for kids who have one type of physical condition or other, who might do better if they weren't in regular gym. They're going to have a special P.E. class for you kids, help you get your strength up, work within your limits." He is trying to be so careful as he tells me that I need to be in a dreaded class for kids with "special needs."

Handicapped. He's talking handicapped.

What if he's right?

The next week a tour is arranged for me and some other Special Kids to visit Downey High School, where we'll be going next fall. I look around as we stand in the weight room off the main gym. I know some of the kids.

Frank Wechsung, tall and lithe.

"What're you here for?" I ask.

"Rheumatic fever. Heart shit."

Lee Hammil smiles and tells me he has leukemia. I wish I hadn't asked.

And a mean-looking kid from the other junior high school, Henry Onereski, whose right leg is bent and drags behind him as he motors on two crutches. Henry has a goatee. I'd heard of him before; the story goes he beat the shit out of some kid with his crutch.

A pigeon-toed kid has a twisted mouth and one eye that doesn't move; nobody can understand him when he talks.

Next to me in line as we get weighed is a pale kid with oozing acne and grotesque gray gums that cover his teeth.

"Epilepsy, 'n you?"

"Asthma." I try to sound casual, like I really don't belong here.

Some kids look so sick you don't want to ask. Does Mr. Hershey really think I'm a cripple like these kids? They enroll me in the class for next year, assuring me that the other kids in school won't even know.

Welcome to the Land of the Gimps.

Night Sounds I

I awaken to night sounds, Mother and Father shuffling about the house. Whisperings. Medicine cabinets opening and closing. Dad's low voice, trying to calm. Mom's voice, rapid, high-pitched. *But I can't sleep. Sure you can, try to lie down, just close your eyes, I'll be here beside you.* A moan. Silence. He's walking away, she's chasing after him. *Bill! Please! I can't! Just one more pill, one more. I'm sorry, you've already taken three.* Sobs. *Just one more, I won't ask for more. You'll be fine, just give the medicine time to work.* More scuttling sounds, Dad mumbles something. Mom shrieks, wild, desperate. *I can't do this, Bill! I'll tell! Fine. You'll be fine. I can't! Try to sleep. I'm begging you. I swear, I'll tell! I mean it! Bill! I'll tell!* Medicine cabinet opens and shuts. Clacking of pills in a bottle, like cicadas.

Tell? What's there to tell?

Finally. Silence. Mom has won the battle of the pills. Here in the dark, I know: this is who we have become.

Out my window the sky is turning light. I find a way to fall asleep.

Night Sounds II

It says four a.m. on the clock next to my bed. I stare at the ceiling, a tinge of tightness in my chest. Then wait, breathing, breathing, listening for the wheeze. In and out. So far OK, I try to go back to sleep. Then the heaviness, a light weight sitting on my breastbone. I sit up and open the window for some fresh air, prop my pillow against the sill. There it is, the first wheeze, like a tiny animal in my lungs crying to get out. Now the pressure begins, a constriction, a band twisting around my chest. I sit then stand then sit then lie down, trying to find a position that will let the air out. I take a hot shower to try to relax the muscles in my throat and chest. The hot humid water loosens up the plugs of mucus in my airways and I hack it up and spit it down the drain. My chest burns from sucking air and pushing it out, *suck push suck push*; exhaling takes four times as long as inhaling, like breathing through a one-way valve. The pitch of my breathing gets higher and thinner. Inevitably the panic comes, the terror that soon it will all stop, there will be no more air. Full wheezing now, bent over, my hands on my knees, the only sound is sucking and blowing, like a bad bagpipe. All the noise I make wakes up my mother. "Here, take another ephedrine," she says. But I've already taken two pills, and they just make me shake with tremors, my heart puttering like the tappets on Richie's Studee engine. "Just relax! Just relax!" my mother almost demands. "Relax!" But there is no relaxing, only panic. When she sees the terror in my eyes, she says, "OK, I'll have your father take you to Dr. Steere's for a shot of epinephrine, as soon as his office opens."

In the car with Dad, my wheezing drowns out the engine. I stumble into Dr. Steere's office. Five minutes after my shot, a quiet, full breath. My shoulders relax, I close my eyes and listen to the sweet sound: exhale/inhale. No hitches, no whistles, no rasps. This miracle of air. I vow to myself I will never take breathing for granted. But of course I will, until the next attack.

Dr. Steere puts the glass syringe and needle on the sterilizer tray and says, "Here, you might want to try this, something new that just came out. An inhaler, sort of like an epinephrine mist." He teaches me how to push down on the canister and breathe in at the same time, two puffs when I need it.

The next night, sometime before sunlight, I wake up wheezing, tight. Here we go again. I reach for the inhaler on the windowsill. One puff in, hold it for five seconds, then out. Repeat. In the dark I wait. And listen. And feel the movement of my chest. It's relaxing. Within two minutes the whistling disappears, my chest is no longer tight. I breathe quietly, silently.

I cry, or want to. In my hand I hold the possibility that I will no longer be a gimp.

Spring Training

I haven't touched a ball or glove for three seasons, since I was eleven—the year my asthma started and my body said *fuck you*. No way was I going to give my wheezy puny body another opportunity to humiliate me on the baseball diamond. Wednesday afternoon, three years after my last game, I come out of gym class and see a notice on the bulletin board:

BASEBALL TRYOUTS
EAST JUNIOR HIGH SCHOOL TRAVELING TEAM
MONDAY, APRIL 17, 2:30
CORNER DIAMOND

I go home and do something without thinking too much. I close the door to my bedroom, go to my closet, open a taped storage box, and pull out my baseball glove, flung there in frustration and confusion the day I quit baseball. Wilson Duke Snider Pro Model four-finger. Still fits, I haven't grown that much. I unscrew the cap to an old bottle of neat's-foot oil and begin: eight drops in the palm of the glove and on the web, a bead down each finger. The oil heats up as I work it in, softening my hand as well as the leather. I close my eyes to finger invisible cracks, add more neat's-foot and rub until I can't feel them. I find a hardball with one red thread dangling from a seam and pop it into the pocket of the glove. Then wind a belt around the glove two times, wrap it in a newspaper and hide it under the bed.

I get up early, when the house is still asleep. I unwrap my mummified glove with a perfectly formed pocket, imprint of a nine-inch hardball, and ease out the back door. It feels familiar and a little exhilarating to throw a ball against the brick chimney, the clean hard echo as it bounces back. After an hour I've gained some confidence, so I find some old chalk and draw a square covering eight bricks. My chest tightens and wheezes seep from my mouth. I take a break for two swigs on my inhaler, my constant companion tucked in the right rear pocket of my jeans. I work another hour on grounders, stretching my range to right and left.

Saturday morning. I take twenty dollars out of my cigar box savings account, bike down to Salter's Sporting Goods, and buy a pair of baseball cleats.

I tell coach Hershey I play second base—secretly my arm doesn't feel strong enough for shortstop. All week fungoes, infield practice, bunting, hit and run, double plays, relays from the outfield, base stealing. I'm not that bad, I feel OK at second base, the range and throws fit the limits of my body. On the weekend I wash my practice uniform in bleach. More workouts with the chimney.

Eighty kids came out for a team of twenty, and I expect to be cut early. Coach Hershey is sort of quiet, not a shouter, a no-nonsense guy who wants to be a principal someday. I'm sure he's wondering what the hell is this kid whom I've enrolled in the high school special needs gym class doing on my baseball diamond trying to beat out a bunt? I sense that he likes the fact that I am here, trying to keep up. I make the first cut. Then the second. I did not expect this.

The final cut will be posted tomorrow on the gym bulletin board. At night I stare at the ceiling, pipe dreams about after-school practice, traveling with the team for away games. It was a dangerous idea, this decision to try out. You were better than you thought you could be. Good enough to hope, but not good enough to make it.

I walk to school through the orange groves, their dikes filled with irrigation water, arrive at 7:30, go to the gym bulletin board. Nothing is posted. Fucker Sharpeless, hands on his hips, tells me the final roster won't be up until after sixth period. He knows something. All day in class the fantasy teases me. Finally, sixth period ends and I walk to the gym like it doesn't matter. Kids huddled around a piece of paper tacked to the bulletin board, fingers underlining names, shouts of *Yes!* Some silently turn away. I wait until they're gone, then start at the top of the list with my finger. Nothing. It's not alphabetical, but by first pick. My finger continues, looking for an *L*. This was a bad idea.

#20: Lyons, M.

#20: The last player to make the cut. Nobody around. I go to the last row of lockers, out of sight, straddle the bench, suck on my fist. I will be lucky to play in a single game. Johnny Mullens is clearly the better second baseman, but I'll wear a uniform and practice every day.

I am not a cripple.

Play Ball

Today we play Lakewood, almost the end of the season. I haven't played in a single game, but somehow don't mind, I still get pumped for practice. It's a home game, a sunny spring day with the baked grass smell of fresh-cut baseball field. Coach Hershey is walking behind me with his clipboard in his hand.

"Hey, Lyons, I'm starting you at second base today. Be ready." He says it casually, but I know he knows what it means to me.

I automatically reach for my asthma inhaler stuffed in my back right pocket. It's not there. I am a little panicked, then remember I probably left it in my street clothes in the locker. Take a deep breath. I run back to the gym, dial the combination, search my pants. Not there. Search my jacket. My book bag. Not there. I am taking short and shallow breaths. I remove everything from my locker and search it, putting my shoes, my shirt, jacket, pants, back in one by one. Not there. Repeat the process one more time. *Shit!* I feel the tightness start in my chest and know I will be wheezing soon—it always happens at the moment when I realize I'm caught without my inhaler. I'll have to tell the coach I can't play.

One last shot . . . I put a nickel in the pay phone outside the coach's office and call home. Bill is there.

"You left your asthma shit at home? So, what do you want me to do about it?"

Here we go again—my eighteen-year-old brother toying with me, setting me up for a put-down. What do I want? I want him to offer to bring the medicine to me at school. I hate him for making me ask. I want to shout *Forget the goddamn medicine, I don't need you!* But I am really wheezing now, and realize that today I do need him, so I tell him how much I would appreciate it if he could drive the medicine over to the game, I will be his friend forever.

"I wish I'd never learned to drive. OK, buddy, you owe me big time."

"Thanks. Really."

"So, when do you think you're going to grow up and get your shit together, start taking care of yourself. You're fourteen, you know. Act it."

"Yeah . . ."

"I'll meet you at the fence by first base in twenty minutes."

As soon as I know that I'll have the medicine, my lungs loosen, my breaths become more measured. I take second base for infield practice. Ten minutes later Bill pulls up outside the fence in Dad's cream and green Chevy, gets out of the car like he's climbing off a horse, and leans against the chain-link fence. He holds the inhaler like it's a cigarette. I trot over to the fence, trying to act like I'm only saying hello to my brother, and he slips me the metal and plastic lifesaver.

"Thanks, really. I'm starting today." I try not to sound excited; I know that he would find a way to make that feel asinine.

"Good for you." I can't tell if he means it or he's saying *Big fucking deal.*

"Second base." I want him to say *Mind if I stay and watch awhile?*

"Well, I'm outta here. See ya." He's not staying, the asshole's going to make me ask.

"You want to stay and watch a while, a couple of innings maybe?"

Goddamn it, why did I ask him? Fuck, I did it again. He looks at his watch, glances up Woodruff Avenue, brushes the corner of his mouth with his index finger, taps his heel, bends down, plucks a piece of grass and sucks on it.

"Nah. I brought you your damned asthma medicine. Got stuff to do."

PLAY BALL! And I do. My defense shines: Nice move to the left on a grounder heading for the hole, clean throw to Jenks at first. Sweeping tag on a kid trying to steal second. Then the best: a hard one-hopper to Steve Ferraro at short, he underhands it to me at second, I pivot and throw to Jenks, catch the runner by a step. The ump's thumb goes up: double play. Yes! I strike out twice, but that's OK, I haven't faced a real pitcher in three years. Sitting on the bench after being replaced by Mullens in the fourth, listening to the sounds of infield chatter and the ball smacking the catcher's glove, watching the shadows settle over the pitcher's mound, replaying that double-play pivot and throw, I feel at home.

Dialing Up Ferlin

I'm glad to be graduating from junior high and playing summer ball. I look pretty sharp in my cap and gown, and gaze out for my family as I march down the aisle. Dad, Michele, no surprise that Bill's not here. Where's Mom? Maybe she went to the bathroom. As people's names are called and they pick up their diplomas and shake Principal Lancaster's hand, I keep looking out to see if my mother has come.

After the ceremony, I ask where Mom is. Dad is having trouble looking at me.

"Something came up, she couldn't make it. She wanted me to tell you she's really sorry."

"Is she back in the hospital?"

40

"No, she's home, with Jeannie." Jeannie is the practical nurse who stays with my mother when my father is at work or away. Mother has decided that she can't be alone, ever. Enter Jeannie, the only person from the outside who steps foot into our house.

"Well, if she's home, why didn't she come to my graduation?"

"She just couldn't . . ."

"I don't get it, Dad. She's home, she should be here. It's my graduation!"

"I know, Mark. She couldn't make it. She just couldn't."

That's it? *She just couldn't?* Dad has become my mother's messenger, making excuses for her, covering up. I look at the wall, trying to keep myself from shouting, accusing—not cool to make a scene in front of my classmates. I don't want to humiliate my dad any further, I can see he's barely hanging on, exhausted. Last night was another rough one, being chased around by Mother begging for more medicine. My hangdog father: every day he seems more wrung out, eyes half open, walking with a kind of shuffle to Mother's tune. To keep the peace, I sit on my rage.

We go to the Ironwood Restaurant to celebrate.

"We have a present for you, I think you'll like it."

And I do. It's the newest thing: a black GE transistor radio, about four by six inches. Runs on batteries. Maybe three kids in school have one. *Oh yeah.*

When we come home, Jeannie says my mother is asleep, she'll be on her way.

"Goodnight Dad, thanks for coming to graduation, the radio too." I go to bed and hold my new transistor radio up to my ear, volume down low. Then turn the dial until KPOP 1020 comes in clear. *Love Is Strange. I'm Walkin'. Little Darlin'. Searchin'.*

Bitchin'.

The gift. When the night sounds come, my mother begging and howling, I can reach over and pick my transistor radio off the windowsill, dial up KPOP, and hold it to my ear. Then crank up Ferlin Husky singing *Gone.*

SUMMER 1957

Curly Hair

A morning ritual my mother and I have shared since first grade: after breakfast, I take a shower, dry my hair with a towel, get dressed, and get my book bag. Then I sit on the floor between my mother's legs with my back to her, and she brushes my hair. She loves my curly hair. "Promise me you'll never cut it," she says; "your curls are your most handsome feature." As I sit on the floor she brushes my hair and curls it over her fingers, primping and patting. A tap on my shoulder, the signal that she's done. "Give me a kiss and get out of here," she says, and I am off to school.

Last year, in eighth grade, I started making noises like I wanted to brush my own hair in the privacy of the bathroom.

"Come on, it's the only time we really have together before you head off to your busy world." She seemed to be pleading. I felt like I was abandoning her, and relented. The hair brushing continued.

A year later now. When summer's over, I'm starting high school—new school, new people. Time for a new look. I go down to Bob's Barber Shop.

"The usual?" asks Bob.

"No, I think I'll have a butch, not too short." Like it's no big deal.

"A butch? We're never too old to change . . ." For the first time Bob uses electric clippers instead of scissors. Curls fall to the floor. Twenty minutes later, I look two years older. *Indeed.* I buy a jar of red Butch Wax.

When she sees my hair, my mother says, "You have broken my heart."

Birds of America

This morning on my walk up the driveway to get the *L.A. Times* I almost step on an egg, dew-covered, noticed by me at the last second because of its contrast with the asphalt. It's topped off at one end, the jagged exit hatch pipped open from the inside without the help of the parent. The first test of survival: if the baby bird doesn't have the strength to break out of its egg, it dies. After the hatchling has given birth to itself, the parent bird will clamp the eggshell between its beak, fly a safe distance from the nest, and drop the shell in an open space—to prevent marauders from finding the nest and eating the chicks. The empty shell is almost an inch long, washed a very pale blue then dabbed with thin brownish-red blotches, almost like paint drippings. Using my fingers as tweezers, I remove the eggshell from the asphalt and lay it in the flattened palm of my left hand.

"Mark, can I look at the front page?"

"I didn't get the newspaper, sorry."

"But I thought you were going outside to get the paper. That's what you were going to do, isn't it?"

"Yeah, but I found something."

"Wish you'd found the paper. Is it out there?"

"Yeah, at the end of the driveway." As I close the French doors into my bedroom, Dad slides on his slippers, ties the cord hanging on his bathrobe, and heads down the driveway.

I lay the jagged shell on a sock, climb up on the chair, and take down a book from the shelf: *Birds of America*, with paintings by Louis Agassiz Fuertes, the most famous bird illustrator since Audubon. His paintings are almost like *Candid Camera*, catching birds as they prune themselves or dig in the sand for an insect or fight over a space on a branch. Not at all like birds stuffed in some museum. I thought about writing him once to ask him how he learned to draw, but I think he may be dead. More than eight hundred glossy pages filled with information about feeding and nesting habits, migration, winter and summer colors, ranges, species and families, chapters on building bird blinds for photography, life histories of the great American ornithologists. A wheel in the glossary lists all the orders of birds, from the least intelligent to the most intelligent. Pigeons are in the middle, between quails and hawks—not too bright but not too dumb. How did they figure that out? A test? If a pigeon can home 500 miles in two days, it must be pretty smart. Better than I could do.

Plates number 1 through 5 are my favorites: one hundred eight life-size color photographs of birds' eggs. There my egg is: #19 on plate 3. No doubt, an oriole. Dumb bird, trying to decoy me away from its nest with an empty egg shell. I already know where the nest is, hanging like a long woven basket from the top of the sycamore tree in the front yard.

Birds of America II

The first time I held *Birds of America* I was twelve, two years before my mother crashed. It was the day after Halloween, when Dicky Tostenson had cut my head open with a tin can. Mom yelled like crazy at Dicky as blood trickled down my temple, "Get out of this yard and don't come back, I don't know what's gotten into you kids!" She finally listened to me explain that it was a mistake; Dicky and I were just playing, bashing each other with two dummies that we had made and dressed with old clothes to scare the trick-or-treaters the night before. Only we forgot that we had used tin cans to stuff the legs of the dummies. Dicky was allowed back in our house, and he observed from a distance as a Band-Aid was applied to the cut.

My mother and I often used minor injuries like this as an excuse for me to stay home from school, so the next morning she suggested that she and I take the bus to L.A.

The bus ride always seemed much longer than it actually was because it passed through so many foreign worlds. Up Firestone Boulevard we first crossed over the dusty Los Angeles River bed lined with cement dikes that never contained water, then we passed the South Gate Drive-In where the high school kids went to make out. I tried to imagine myself there sometime, wondered what I'd do. Then, as we turned north through Watts, black people began to get on the bus; in East L.A. brown people speaking Spanish and carrying big paper bags climbed in. As we crossed over the Downtown Bridge the yellow, orange, and black Southern Pacific Express snaked into the Mexican Art Deco train station, crisscrossing tracks in the switchyard.

Japanese and Chinese passengers got off at the Chinatown stop; most of the Black and Spanish travelers deboarded in the garment district and at the factories near the natural gas tank farm where giant containers magically rose and disappeared into the ground. Others got off and entered the back doors of restaurants and department stores in the shopping district, the end of the line.

I always played a game on these bus rides filled with at least five languages, a variation on *Name That Tune*. I'd close my eyes and listen, trying to figure out what language the passengers were speaking. *Pwes CO-ha-lo, eye-ben-DEE-tow, DAY-ha-may-SO-la, kay-O-ra-tee-EN-es.* That was an easy one, with the sing-songy rhythm: Mexican. Someone talking with sounds like *-oto* and *-hashi* and *-kana*—definitely Japanese. Someone else in Spanish, but not quite—Filipino? A guy speaking English, long drawn-out words, then he says *you-all*—Alabama?

The first time I heard somebody talking Spanish was one early Saturday summer morning when I was eleven, after buying pigeon feed from the granary along the railroad tracks. I decided to do some exploring, take a different route home. I walked my bike behind some hoppers parked on a side rail and rode along the tracks past the school bus maintenance garage. As I turned down a puddled dirt path lined with knee-high weeds, I heard voices. No way that was English. There were three goats tethered to a log; a bunch of chickens and their chicks darted in front of my bike, a couple of scrawny dogs nipped at my tires. Dung smell and weird music with guitars and trumpets through radio static. Corn and orange twisty pumpkins in a weedy field, irrigated from an opened fire hydrant. Two kids kicked around a half-deflated soccer ball. A low-rider, chromed, pin-striped, and chopped. I looked into one of the tin-roofed pens, hoping to see a sheep or baby goat. A woman sitting on a mattress on the dirt floor with a baby at her breast stared out at me. I felt like an invader from another world. I nodded and gunned my bike as I hung a U-turn and never looked back.

Mexicans in Downey? Speaking Spanish? Living in an abandoned corral? I had not yet learned to ask questions that would help me understand the meaning of all this.

As we got off the bus my mother announced that she felt like buying some new towels and hose. "Why don't we go to May Company's first? Maybe I'll get some shoes that are more comfortable to walk around in. You want to pick out a new outfit, a shirt and matching pants?" My mother was about to begin what she called a shopping spree.

I felt a bit disappointed. I didn't really care much about clothes. Not yet.

"Can I pick out a book?" I usually didn't care about books either, but it beat standing around in Women's Wear.

"Sure. I'll tell you what, I'll drop you off at the Books section, and come pick you up in half an hour. What do you have in mind?"

"What do you mean?"

"What book are you going to pick out?"

"I dunno. I'll just look around."

On my own at the library, I always headed for the nature section. Most of the books at May Company were for kids—great pictures, but not a whole lot of information. It was easy to find my bird book: it was bigger than the others, over two inches thick and twelve inches high, with a pair of red-tailed hawks on a green and white cover: *Birds of America*.

My mother found me in the corner of the Books section behind the sale table, cross-legged on the floor, elbows on my knees, bent over the book on my lap.

"Where the hell have you been? I've been looking for you for fifteen minutes. Didn't you hear me calling?"

"I was reading. This is what I want."

My mother checked the book price on the flap. "Twenty-five dollars!" I hadn't looked at the price. "Is it really worth twenty-five dollars?"

"More."

She hefted the book with both hands. "Well, if you paid by the pound it would definitely be worth it. Will you really read it? This isn't a kid's book."

"I've already read the first thirty pages. *Please*. This is the only thing I want. If I bought clothes it would cost that much."

"Don't tell your father, he'll have a conniption. We'll have to tear the price off the cover flap or we'll both be in big trouble." We both enjoyed this secret, a harmless conspiracy against my father.

The book was so heavy we decided to put it in a locker and return for it at the end of the day.

"Chicken Fricassee please, with gravy on the mashed potatoes. And Thousand Island on the salad."

"I'll take the same, except can I have Blue Cheese?"

Mom and I had lunch at Lowry's Restaurant in downtown L.A., where men in ties did business and shoppers went once a year. Amid the clank of silver against white china, the waitress asked me directly for my order without looking at my mother, a sign that I was growing up. I recognized the brown busboy, now in a starched white coat buttoned to the neck, who took directions in Spanish—he was on the bus this morning. Were they called bus boys because that was how they got to work? I wondered how he felt waiting on white people who would get on the bus with him at the end of the day loaded with packages. A waterfall ran behind pink and lavender and green plastic strips on the wall, lit from behind. The water crashed into a pool on the floor, a constant sound like the waves at the beach. We ate slowly and a little politely, talking like two adults. I felt like we were on a date.

"You know that Fuertes means 'strong' in Spanish? The painter of your bird book is Louis the Strong, maybe that's why you like him so much."

"I wish I could draw. All of my bird sketches look like they were run over by a car."

"It takes a lot of practice and patience. I bet your friend Louis Fuertes couldn't draw very well when he was twelve. Then he must've decided that's what he wanted to do, and probably practiced five hours a day. Say, how about a movie? If we leave in ten minutes, we can catch *Ivanhoe*, it's playing at the Paramount."

"How do you know?"

"I just know. Come on, finish your ice cream so we can get out of here." As my mother called for the check, I realized that she had been planning this, that *Ivanhoe* was a surprise.

I did not want *Ivanhoe* to end. It was the perfect story, good guys vs. bad guys, the knights vs. the scoundrels, with love the prize for the winner. I was sure that the bad guys had control of the situation, that evil people would win out because they were willing to do anything; the rules of honor would bring about the self-destruction of the people I was rooting for. The situation seemed hopeless, then somehow in the end the good guys won, because they deserved to. That's what heroes were, no? As Mom and I left the theater, the final scene, the joust to the death, kept resonating in my mind: hoofbeats kicking up mud, the terrifying clang of the ball and chain against metal shield, the snap of broken lances, Ivanhoe on the ground with his shoulder ripped open, weaponless. De Bois-Guilbert, all evil and greed, moving in for the final kill. But somehow Ivanhoe rose up to save himself, to save honor. I replayed that final scene one more time, the moment when Ivanhoe used his last ounce of strength to grab the chain and yank Bois-Guilbert off the horse, the moment when hope was rewarded.

"Well, what do we have here?" My mother had definitely moved on from the movie.

"What're you talking about?" I felt a little annoyed, still replaying *Ivanhoe.*

"*Fine Artists Materials.* Looks like an art store to me. Why don't we wander in?"

"What for?" I was tired, impatient, not wanting my mother to make me guess what she was up to. I just wanted to go home.

"You'll see. Where's a salesman?" My mother cocked her head over the shelves and down the aisles to find help. "Oh, there's one. Excuse me, sir, my son here is interested in some oil paints and a pad of canvas to paint on. Do you have something that's a beginner's kit, not a toy? You know, something that will get him started."

I looked at Mom and shook my head in mock disbelief. She handed me the package of oil paints, brushes, thinner, and canvas.

Sometimes my mother really knew me.

Going home on the bus dead tired, Mom asleep with her head back against the seat, mouth open, bouncing to the rhythm of the street. On the return trip the migration pattern was reversed, packed with color and foreign languages and packages when we began, squeezing out people as we passed through Chinatown then East L.A. then

Watts and Compton, finally leaving just white passengers to drop off across from the Downey courthouse. Sitting next to my sleeping mother, I looked out the window and thought about how the day happened because Dicky Tostenson rapped me over the head with a Halloween dummy. If Dicky hadn't come up with this great idea to hang dummies from the pepper tree to scare trick-or-treaters, and if the trash men hadn't done their pickup the day before, forcing us to stuff the dummies with tin cans instead of newspapers, and if Dicky hadn't gotten silly challenging me to a dummy duel to the death, I wouldn't have ever gotten that cut on my head. Without the cut, Mom and I wouldn't have taken off the day to go to L.A.: no *Birds of America*, no lunch at Lowry's, no *Ivanhoe*, no oil paints. One of those days I would never forget, because some tin vegetable cans happened to be in the right place at the right time. I felt lucky, it was just luck that this all happened.

I felt a bit frightened, too. Like my life was out of my control. Good things happened, but I didn't make them happen. Could I stop bad things from happening to me? Bad things? Like what?

The bus unloaded the last of the other passengers, leaving me and my mother alone for the final leg home.

"Mom, Mom. We're home. Time to wake up." I gently nudged her shoulders as we pulled up to the Downey courthouse. We stumbled down the aisle holding our packages by their strings, thanked the driver, and stepped down to the sidewalk. Dad stood by our car across the street, waiting for us.

Nest Egg

Sunset Beach. We're here for our yearly June vacation, in a blue clapboard house peeling from the salt, the waves a constant rhythm in our ears. Our family memories seem to be organized by a calendar of summer vacations, as if we use our time together at the beach to collect the memories of the previous year and fix them, a family photograph: the year of the summer vacation after Dad changed jobs, the summer vacation after Mom and Dad founded the Downey Community Players, the summer after Michele was born, the summer Bill was almost hit by a car that plunged into the lagoon where he was swimming, the summer of the all-time grunion run, the summer I found my first pubie, the summer of my parents' twentieth anniversary. This is the summer my mother returns from the mental hospital.

My mother has been home for two weeks now. She wanted to cancel our beach vacation, but Dad convinced her it would be good for her spirits. Our beach house has a white wicker chair in the corner of the living room, its back to the bay window that faces the ocean. Dad found a TV dinner table in a closet and parked it next to her chair, for her whodunits and coffee and cigarettes. Mom doesn't go outside to sun herself anymore and refuses to visit beach friends we've made over our last ten vacations. She won't even go to her favorite restaurant, Sam's Seafood, for swordfish to celebrate their anniversary. The big bash annual Little Theater Party and Grunion Run has been canceled; visitors are not welcome. My mother has become a hermit whose daylight life is filled with simple routines divided with by-the-clock doses of medicines. Reading an old Agatha Christie, asking Dad to warm her coffee, lighting a cigarette, playing solitaire, eating her sweet roll or sandwich from a paper plate, rocking back and forth until her eyes close and she slumps. Then she checks the clock, asks where her medicine is, Dad fetches it, and the Agatha/coffee/solitaire/food/rock/slump/sleep/medicine cycle starts over again. She goes to bed early now, sometimes before the sun sets; then Michele and I may toss sea shells into a hat or play indoor basketball before I read her a story. My brother occasionally comes down for the day; it's a short drive from his apartment in Long Beach. He's gained a little weight—he works all night in a doughnut shop.

Most nights I awake to the sounds I hate: the shuffling, desperate begging, denials, until my father's voice weakens and breaks. Now I hear something new: my father quietly sobbing as he gives in to my mother. Then the sound of medicine bottles being sorted, a glass being filled from the tap, gulping of pills on the back of her tongue. Two defeated shadows scuffle down the hall to the bedroom. Silence. Dad gets up at six a.m., starts coffee, lines up Mother's pills on the TV table, sneaks out to get an *L.A. Times* to read before his day starts, reads the front page and chugs one more gulp of coffee as Mom shouts *Bill!* . . . *Bill!* from her bed, *Bill!!* . . . *I need my pill!* A variation on the medicine ritual that now defines their lives, her new morning pill—some kind of upper to jump-start her from the drowsiness of last night's three a.m. trip to the medicine cabinet. She takes it before she can get out of bed.

Mornings I try to get Dad to play catch in the sand or challenge him to a cribbage match in the sun, but he finds reasons not to play, mostly says he can't leave Mother alone in the house. *Well, can't she come and sit in the sun? Well, she doesn't seem to want to do that, I know it would be good for her, I'll ask her.* He goes into the house and doesn't return, I know she has said no. Mom is afraid to come out of the shadows, and she and Dad have made a pact that he will stay in the shadows with her.

Tuesday, we've been here four days. I've been diving under the nine-foot high-tide waves, and after fifteen minutes am shivering uncontrollably, a reminder of how skinny I am. I dry myself off and come into the house to fix my favorite sandwich, mustard between slices of white bread. My parents are sitting in the living room, like maybe I walked in on a conversation. "HiDad, HiMom, anyone want some Coke? I'm getting myself one from the fridge." No answer. "*Hello? Anybody home?*" Silence. I try to make eye contact with my mother, but she won't look at me. I look over at my father. "What's up?"

"*Please . . . ,*" Dad says with an urgent tone, though he doesn't raise his voice.

"Please what?"

"Mark, I think it's best that you go outside or to your room."

"Outside? I just came inside. Why should I go back outside? And my room's dark." I'm trying not to sound angry; but, then, I don't care if I sound angry.

"Bill . . . *please* . . ." My mother's voice has a tinge of terror in it. She still won't look at me.

"Mark, I need you to leave the room. Now." My father's *Now* is quiet and firm; no doubt, it's an order. Pleading, too.

No way do I want to be sucked into this scene. "OK, just let me get a sandwich and a Coke. I'll eat it outside." In thirty seconds, I slap together my sandwich, toss the yellow-bladed knife into the sink, and uncap a Coke. I slam the screen door behind me to let them know I'm tired of this shit. I doubt they notice.

It's about 3:30 now. Late enough for shadows, but still hot enough to take off my shirt. My favorite time of day. I head north up the beach, the diffuse sun on my left still too high to be a ball, a slight breeze picking up off the water. I move down the slope of beach to the hard surface of cold sand left by the receding tide, check my back pocket to be sure I have my inhaler, and break into a slow trot, feeling the wet sand suck at my feet. I tuck my tee shirt into the back of my trunks. Past the brown-shingled house of Nellie and Chuck Fitz, friends of my parents, whose daughter Sandy tried to kiss me last summer (almost the summer of my first kiss, but by the time I figured out what she was up to she changed her mind). Past the light blue water tower landmark with *Sunset Beach* painted in four-foot-high red letters visible from the peak of Highway 101 in Belmont Shore. Past Eighth Street, which runs across the Pacific Coast Highway to the lagoon where I catch turtles, past the sign pointing to *Sam's Seafood Family Dining at Its Best*. I stop: I have never been this far up the beach. New territory.

I keep walking, another mile or so. The sun slips behind some finger clouds, the air turns cool, I put on my tee shirt. Beyond the last beach house are monstrous gray smokestacks that jut out of the sand, the tallest coughing up white smoke that turns pink, rises, disappears. I am a little spooked, like I'm about to cross an invisible border to another country. Where am I? I almost turn back, a return to familiar landmarks, then sight a ten-foot-high chain-link fence, topped by rusted barbed wire, that runs from the Pacific Coast Highway a half mile up to my right, across the beach in front of me, and disappears into the water a hundred yards offshore. I approach the fence cautiously. Maybe it's a prison wall, danger on the other side. I look for guards, careful not to touch the wire, it may be electrified. Then a peeling white plywood sign with black stenciled lettering announces:

NO TRESPASSING
GOVERNMENT PROPERTY
US NAVAL AIR STATION
NO TRESPASSING

I eye the colossal smokestacks through the fence: U.S. Navy destroyers, cruisers, one mammoth sleeping aircraft carrier. I recog-

nize them from my father's World War II magazines I found in a
barrel in the garage with cartoons about Japs with drooling teeth.
The naval shipyard. Two hundred yards from the fence, the shore
between the giant ships and me is lined with eight-foot-diameter
gray steel spheres, stacked like cannon balls in old Civil War photos—the buoys which were used to string anti-submarine nets up and
down the coast during the War. The *rrrrrrr-chunk—rrrrrr-chunk—
rrrrr-chunk* of a giant crane loading wooden netted crates onto a navy
cruiser—probably headed for U.S. occupation forces in Korea. Waves
lap at the chain-link fence, the sun takes shape as it begins its descent
into the sea, still thirty-five degrees from the horizon. There are no
people, no one to see me. I tap the fence with gritted teeth, leaning
away: it's not electrified. I pry a three-foot-long two-by-six driftwood
board with sea-etched grain out of the sand, and dig along the bottom edge of the metal fence, above the tide line where the sand is soft
and dry. The board isn't very efficient, so I get down on my knees and
paddle the sand between my legs with my hands, a dog looking for its
buried bone. It takes five minutes to excavate a passageway under the
fence to the other side. Lie on my back, drop my head into the hole,
ease my arms under the fence and grab it from the other side, lower
myself down now, slowly curving my body so my back matches the
contour of the bottom of the hole and my chest doesn't scrape on the
metal prongs of the fence. I catch my kneecap on the fence as I push
myself clear, a two-inch scratch that will leave a scab.

I slide behind an old driftwood piling deposited on the upper sand
by the high tide. The piling is snapped off at the base, half covered
with black hairy mussels, some open revealing orange-pink flesh, a
trace of fish-rot in the air. I gaze out over the metal and sand and
water to make sure that no one has seen me. A tugboat moves up the
channel on the other side of the buoys, its deep bellowing horn signaling something to the dock. The gray navy ships have taken on a
pink tone, reflecting the sun. For a long time, I just crouch there in
the cover of the piling, surveying this new territory parcel by parcel,
alert to details, objects, colors, sounds. Piles of driftwood jammed
against the jetty that forms the channel, bent pipes and wire jut-
ting out of the sand like a no-man's land. Yellow and green and clear
shards of glass from shattered bottles surround the base of a metal

oil drum on which sits a beer bottle with its neck missing; probably used by someone for target practice. Thirty-foot leafy strands of salt-stinking seaweed cooking in the sun, stranded by the high tide. No footprints. It looks like nobody's been here for twenty years.

Then the scolding screech I recognize from my ten summers at the beach: a herring gull shadow appears on the sand, followed by the snapping of wings as the bird comes into view and settles on a hummock thirty yards in front of me. The seagull seems aware of the presence of a yet invisible intruder, and nervously turns its head around 180 degrees, scanning the area with orange eyes. The bird then walks directly to a place in the sand, a crevice, eases itself down, and carefully arranges something beneath its breast with its yellow beak. Everything in order, the gull again surveys the surroundings and, finding nothing changed, sits motionless, still uneasy, listening.

I have unearthed a seagull nesting ground.

A bird's nest is my favorite find. During breeding season, I secretly follow our yard birds in flight, beaks full of twigs or worms or insects, and discover where they nest: the finely woven oriole baskets hanging from the sycamore tree, the starlings and blackbirds sqawking in the fronds of the eighty-foot palm tree in the corner of our yard, the screech owl in the hollow of the crab apple tree along the back fence line, the mud nests of robins and straw nests of mourning doves in the old thick spruce in the front yard. English sparrows in the flaming oleander bush, mockingbirds in the apricot trees, mud houses of barn swallows under the eaves of the garage. I know where the birds nest at our old elementary school—recess discoveries—and I've found the secret nests of the birds who inhabit the belfry of the Presbyterian Church where I play football on the front lawn and occasionally visit services, especially if Ann Hegardt is feeling religious that week. Crows nest in the evergreens that are windbreaks for the orange grove I walk through on the way to school, where the orchard smudge pots are foundations for kestrel nests, the irrigation dikes homes for kingfishers. Phoebes nest high in the mimosas, near the trunk, on the golf course where Dad and I play pitch and putt. And now I discover that seagulls nest at the far end of Sunset Beach, way past the water tower, beyond the chain-link fence, an hour from any swimming beach that I know.

I slowly rise from my hiding place behind the broken piling, and the seagull instantly lifts straight up into the wind, squawks loudly to draw my attention, glides point-winged wide-tailed past me, alights on a rock twenty yards down shore. The gull screeches frantically as I walk deliberately toward its shallow nest. Now it takes off from the rock and circles fifteen feet over my head, threatening, flapping its wings loudly, feigning dive-bombs, trying to drive me away. I carefully sink to my knees to inspect the clutch of four eggs. The bird can no longer endure the threat to its clutch and swoops down, beak aimed at my head. I tumble over on my side to avoid the attack, sand on my cheek as the bird arches up into the wind, readying for another assault. In a crouch I scuttle to my piling, sideways like a crab, and watch the bird circle the nest twice and nervously settle.

A sad feeling, that this is my one encounter with this hidden place where most likely I will never return. I need a souvenir from this beach, something to take with me so I don't forget, something that will make it easier for my memory to return.

An egg.

In all of my discoveries of active nests I have never touched them or their contents, afraid that the birds will desert their eggs. My plan is to find an abandoned nest—no interference with nature there. I come to a small rise with occasional tufts of sharp spiked grass, a young dune, behind which I hear chaotic squawking and flapping of a hundred gulls air-bound: a nesting colony. Before the gulls have a chance to group themselves and organize an attack, I slither down the slope of the dune and quickly find what I am looking for: a deteriorated nest, with no bird scat and one discolored egg barely visible beneath unkempt twigs. The egg is stone-cold, definitely not being incubated. I grab the egg with a handful of sand and snapping sticks, turn and charge over the dune, pursued by winged shadows. The birds become silent as the intruder disappears.

Panting in the shadows of the piling, I inspect my prize. I shake it, hold it up to the sun, tap it, look for cracks, smell it, heft it in my palm, feel its surface with my cheek. A keeper.

The sun is an orange ball, an inch above the horizon, as I locate the passageway under the chain-link fence. First, I reach under the fence with my left hand, carefully placing the egg on the other side on top of my tee shirt. I lower myself down into the hole, pull my-self up on the other side, and shake the sand out of my shirt before putting it on. Make a plow of my hands and fill the passageway with sand, casually place some driftwood and twigs over the hole for cam-ouflage, and return to my egg. As I start back up the beach, I turn to look through the fence beyond the parched and peeling *No Trespass-ing* sign. Looking for things to remember, like taking photos when you say good-bye.

I AM GLAD to have a long walk home, more than an hour back down the lapping low-tide beach, the sun-ball now sunken below the hori-zon, orange and pink flames in the sky. The breeze has settled down, waves quiet and flattened. My ten summers at the beach have been filled with great discoveries: the red tide with the phosphorescent sand exploding when stomped, beached hammerhead sharks sucking air, thrashing when touched with a stick, a barracuda arching on the end of Dad's fishing line cast from the shore, manta rays gliding on the blue-green sea surface, abalone shells with their chips of mother-of-pearl. Digging for soft-shelled sand crabs, learning to swim in the safety of the lagoon across Highway 101, to dive under the crash-ing waves or to ride them two hundred feet to shore. The turtles and heron rookery I discovered with Chick Fitz, brother of Sandy who almost kissed me, when we waded neck-deep into the marshy back-waters beyond the lagoon. Flying fish and the spumes of the whales migrating south for the winter seen from the bow of the boat bound for Catalina Island. The world of crabs and insects and shellfish car-ried in the roots of giant kelp ripped from the bottom of the ocean in a recent storm, the fleeting captive tide-pool world of urchins and anemones and minnows. Learning to tell time by the tides. The magic of the grunion hunt and the great feast that followed. But the egg is my own find, a jewel snuck across the border. I'm making plans for the egg.

We've Missed You Folks

I come in the back door of our beach house. "HiMom, HiDad, I'm home."

"It's almost dark, what've you been up to?" My mother sounds sort of normal.

"Just went for a walk up the beach." I have the egg bootlegged behind my thigh as I head for the kitchen. "I'm starving . . . what's for dinner?"

"I think your Dad's calling out for pizza."

"Can't we go out? I'd love some clam chowder and fish from Sam's." Always worth a try, but I know what the answer will be. I have become resigned to being trapped at the beach house with my mother this vacation, no ventures to places that have become part of our summer family rites.

"Not tonight, maybe sometime . . ." Dad running interference.

I've decided how to preserve the egg. I will poke a hole in each end and blow out the contents, like they do at the Natural History Museum. First, I run tap water over the stained shell, and buff it with the pot scrubber, bringing out the gray-white color that hides it so well in the sand. Then I rifle through the utensil drawer and find what I am looking for, a metal skewer used for shish kabobs. Now begins the surgeon's work, tap-tapping on one end, making a tiny hole, then chiseling away bits of shell, until I have a hole about one-eighth inch in diameter, revealing the inner membrane of the shell, still intact. I repeat the procedure on the other end as carefully, and now am ready to puncture the membranes and blow out the yolk and egg white.

"What's going on in there?"

"Just looking at an egg."

"You want scrambled eggs and toast for dinner? We could whip up some instead of calling out . . ." Dad, the cook.

"Whatever, I'll feel like eating in a few minutes . . ." Now the delicate procedure, as I place the skewer in the center of the hole I have made in the shell, then gently apply pressure to the membrane.

POW! The egg explodes in my hand.

"What's that?" Dad hollers out, a little alarmed.

"Oh, nothing, I just dropped something."

"Be sure to clean it up." My mother is in on the conversation.

"What's that god-awful stink?!" My father's keenest sense of relating to the world is through his ample nose, and I've been found out.

"I don't smell anything, what stink?" I scramble to put the shards of eggshell and hardened rubbery yolk in a paper lunch bag, hiding the evidence.

"Oh my god, Mark farted, he farted a big one!" my brother chimes in. I didn't even know he was here. "Smell that, smell it! He's going to kill us all! Abandon ship!" Sister Michele laughs; *fart* is a new word in her two-and-a-half-year-old vocabulary.

"What in the hell is that stink?" My father is no longer alarmed. He's furious, stomping into the kitchen. He makes me show him the contents of the paper bag, getting his face close to inspect the contents. I open it up a slit, and Dad reels backward, overwhelmed by the sulfur dioxide fumes. My mother, father, and brother stampede for the front door as the fumes waft through the entire house. One of them grabs my sister by the hand; she is laughing and doesn't want to leave the scene. Dad stands out on the porch banging on the window, "Get that goddamn thing out of there, get it out of there, right now! Don't just stand there! Move!"

"OK, OK. I'll get it outside." I'm enjoying this, the chaos created by the egg. I exit out the back door, dig a hole in the sand beside the house, deposit the bag with its exploded contents, and affectionately pat the sand over it with my bare feet. I look up to see my entire family staring at me from a safe distance. Dad tries to enter the house, but quickly pulls back.

"No way we can go in there for a couple of hours, the smell's unbearable. The windows are open so a cross-breeze will eventually blow that stink out of there."

"I'm hungry, it's almost eight o'clock," I say, curious as to how my family is going to solve this problem.

"Let's go to Sam's, I haven't been to Sam's since last year," my brother suggests. He, too, misses our annual trip to our favorite restaurant.

"That's not such a good idea," my father says, looking at my mother, signaling that he will protect her, not make her be the disappointing one.

"Why not? Really, why not?" my brother and I ask simultaneously. We both know exactly why not, but secretly have agreed to push the limits, to ignore that Mom "gets too nervous in public to go out."

"Sam's! Sam's!" chants Michele.

"Oh hell, Bill, let's go." This is my mother speaking, and we look at each other, eyebrows raised a bit. Can this be happening? A small victory in the making. For us all.

Something I thought I would never have again: our family seated in our favorite maroon Naugahyde semicircle corner booth at Sam's, next to the giant aquarium filled with coral and small sharks and brilliant colored fish from the reefs of Australia. First, Mom orders her Manhattan, Dad his martini; Bill and I get strawberry daiquiris, hold the alcohol; a Shirley Temple for my little sister. Then come the sourdough bread and clam chowder, Mom and Bill take the Manhattan style, Dad and I the creamy New England stuff. Caesar salad covered with Parmesan. *Boys, don't eat too many breadsticks, it'll spoil your appetite.* We carefully scan the menu as if we are trying to decide among irresistible delicacies, but our appetites are totally predictable: Mom gets the prime rib dipped in horseradish, bloody but not cold if you don't mind; Bill sucks on a dozen giant shrimp, then eats the tails crunch by crunch; Dad delicately cuts his inevitable stuffed flounder and looks at each forkful before he puts it in his mouth; Michele nibbles on a Sam's Super Burger; and I peel off layers of my swordfish broiled in butter and lemon sauce. We are all a little giddy at being here again; talk turns silly, sometimes reminiscent.

"Boys, remember the time your father caught that octopus off the Seal Beach Pier, which promptly proceeded to slither itself to the edge of the pier and hurtle thirty feet down to freedom in the surf when no one was looking? Nobody really believes that story, at least nobody in their right mind . . ."

"Or the time Bill Taylor passed out on the beach in the middle of The Little Theater grunion hunt and nobody noticed? It wasn't until two hours later, three o'clock a.m., back at the house, that Ann realized her husband was missing and we had to send out a search party to find him flat drunk in the sand without a care in the world, then rig up a blanket to carry him back."

Then the standard desserts: fresh-baked strawberry shortcakes loaded with real whipped cream, all around. Another cup of coffee, a trip to the bathroom with underwater scenes painted on the wall. The real Sam drops by our table to say hello.

"We've missed you folks. How is everything, how come we haven't seen you more often this year?"

Nobody seems in a hurry to leave.

As the evening deepens, I begin to feel as if nothing has changed, we are back to who we have always been. It was just a nightmare: the ghosts under the bed, my mother's empty stare into the empty fireplace, the prison of her chair, the whispered phone conferences with doctors, my father's half-hearted explanations telling callers that Phyllis is not quite ready to see people yet, the deadly night sounds. No. This, our dinner at Sam's, is real, is who we are, the end of the bad dream.

The Green Room

Late July. Mom returned to Edgemont Hospital the week after our Sunset Beach vacation, her second visit. She misses us kids. We haven't heard from Bill for a while, I'm not even sure he has a phone in his new apartment. Dad decides Michele might be frightened by the hospital, so we drop her off at Jeannie's. So that leaves me. The drive to the hospital is silent, except for KFWB News Radio announcing the traffic delays and weather and ocean temperature.

My first visit to a mental hospital—Dad did not warn me. On two glass doors, square black letters announce *Visitors Waiting Room*. The rubber air seal on the bottom squeaks as Dad and I push the doors open simultaneously and enter. "Wait here," he says, "I'll go check with the nurse to find out where your mother can meet us." He nods at the guard in blue at the inner doors that say *Patient Area, Authorized Personnel Only, All Others Must Obtain a Pass*. The guard slips an orange card into my father's palm, they seem to know each other. Then Dad disappears behind the curtained glass doors. I try to peer through to see Mom, but the curtain is too dense, like gauze. Only hazy shadows move in the bright hallway on the other side. The guard says it might be a while, why don't I have a seat, they'll call me when my mother comes.

Tan Naugahyde chairs with skinny wooden arms and legs line the edges of the waiting room. Perfectly clean aqua-green tiles cover the walls up to the ceiling, reflecting fluorescent lights, echoing footsteps on the gray linoleum floor. I sit, elbows on my knees, chin resting on my palms. Staring at the floor, my eyes trace the repeating diamond patterns. Smell of antiseptic in the air. Footfalls betray their owners: shuffles that belong to future patients on their way to Admissions, *tock tock tock* of nurses marching on their rounds to dispense medications. Rolling squeaks of tennis shoes, a visitor or an orderly. Two pairs of shoes emerge from opposite sides of the waiting room and snap to a stop. Then whispers, a doctor talking to a family member. The intercom requests that Dr. Alivari please report to the nurse's station in B-4, announces that visiting hours end at five o'clock.

This could be a bus station. Or a prison.

A shadow appears on the floor in front of me. A very small voice, like there's only one vocal cord, a squeaky monotone.

"Hello, son. Please take me home. I'm so lonely here. Please take me home."

I stand up. She has tied her arms around my neck, her face buried in my shoulder. Sobbing.

"*Please* . . . Please take me home. I can't stand it, I can't stay here anymore."

My arms wrap themselves around her shoulders, a reflex. This body feels different to me, too frail.

It's not my mother.

"Margie, come on Margie, we have to go back to your room. This isn't your son Johnny." Two orderlies gently peel Margie off me and lead her shuffling back through the gauze door. My shoulder is wet. The door clicks shut electronically, a clean metallic sound. I have to sit down. I hear nothing, like the volume has been turned off. Out-of-focus figures move about in slow motion.

"Mark. Hey . . . *Hey* . . ." A familiar hand on my shoulder, gently nudging me as if waking me. Dad's voice and hand, reassuring in this land of strangers.

"Where's Mom?"

"She's inside."

"When can we see her?"

"She's pretty upset, feels she's not up to seeing anyone today."

"I thought that's why we came out here, she wanted to see us." I mean me.

"Next time. She's real shaky right now, it'd be best if she had some time to calm down. You know she loves you, she just doesn't want anyone to see her this way. She'll be home soon, really, you wait and see. She says to be sure to tell you she misses you." He half-smiles in that way which says I'm sorry, there's nothing I can do. Defeat and sadness.

I feign disappointment. I don't want to see my mother in this place.

We leave through the double doors, I stumble on the rubber mat. Turn left on the sidewalk, head for the asphalt parking lot. We walk, left-right, left-right, eyes front. I wonder if Dad notices that we are in formation. The path is lined with jacarandas, and a slight haze of pinpoint purple blossoms filters the sun.

A tapping sound, at first very soft, then louder. I look to my left. Rows of large square windows, and in one the curtains have separated. The face of my mother framed by the yellow lace, her right hand frozen in a wave, her lips not moving. Like a photograph. I want to go to the window, but don't. I wave weakly and keep on walking. I try not to look back.

I hate car rides when nobody talks. Dad doesn't even play the radio to hide the silence.

Jajerkoff?

The house is empty, nobody home. I have to pee. I hate it when I have to pee, the moment of truth. I unzip my pants, spread my feet a little as if digging in to swing at a fastball, pull out my penis, and stare at the wall. Hold my dick between thumb and first finger of my right hand, as if it were something I found on the floor. First a dribble, then a full stream, the only sound in the house. So far, I'm doing OK, just keep concentrating on the aqua-blue knickknack shelf screwed to the wall above the toilet: Pearlman's Shampoo for that hard-to-manage hair, a yellow bar of shower soap with a braided cord, Pond's moisturizing cream in a squeezable bottle, two sandpaper nail files, an extra roll of toilet paper.

The stream starts to peter out, like turning off a faucet, intermittent drops. My bladder is empty, but there is still some dribble in my penis, so now I have to shake it. Focus on the wall, don't think about the shaking. There is only the wall. The sound of pee drops shower-ing the lake of the toilet bowl. *O shit it's happening.* In two seconds, my prick goes from this wrinkled floppy thing to a six-inch pulsat-ing cigar, exploding with sensation as it fills up with blood. Now I am crazy, rubbing it back and forth between my thumb and forefinger, starting to arch back on my heels. The Pond's tube stares me in the face, placed there by some demonic force: *Use me.* I squeeze some of the white cream into the palm of my left hand with a *splurt*, slosh the stuff all over my dick, and move my left hand back and forth back and forth, a piston in a cylinder. In about ten strokes I am done, almost falling over backward, dizzy as I shoot all over the upraised toilet seat.

I have lost the battle again. I could probably do better if I didn't have to pee. But one has to pee.

It began early this summer when I was pedaling up Cherokee Drive to get an ice cream over at Domenico's, and Rodney Gaines screeched up to me on his bike, turning a one-eighty on the asphalt.

"Hey, Lyons, how ya *been*, how ya *doin'*?" The joker was already mocking me.

"OK," I said, not looking at him, hoping to discourage conversa-tion. I didn't like Rodney Gaines, he was one of those kids who were always trying to be tough, his hair slicked back in a greasy duck-butt, the kind of asshole who hung out with the rich kids who pretended to be bad. Levi cuffs creased and tucked under. A hard box of Ches-terfields rolled up in the sleeve of his white tee shirt. I was sure he thought I was one of those goody-goody kids who never smoked.

"Say, Lyons, j'ever jerkoff?"

"Ever what?"

"JERK OFF." He said it very slowly, his mouth carefully forming each word as if talking to someone who was deaf or retarded.

"What's that?" I was feeling a little retarded.

"What's that? You know, when you whip out your prick and rub it until you shoot jizz. Beat your meat. Rub your rod. Diddle your dong. Or as Ivan Jackinoff, the famous Russian poet, says: 'Hum 'til you cum.'"

"Oh. I didn't hear you. Sure."

"Sure what?" Rodney didn't believe me.

"Sure I do."

"Sure you do *what?*"

"You know . . ."

"No. No, I don't know." The inquisition.

"You know . . . jerk off." That's the first time I had ever used the term. I didn't say it with much authority.

"Yah? How often?"

"Couple times . . ."

"Couple times a *what?* A hour? A day? A week? A month? In your goddamn life?"

"A day." I was embarked on a pure lie, there was no turning back.

"A day? I'm impressed, Lyons. *Twice a day.* Didn't think you had it in you."

I had to get out of there. "I gotta go, see ya." I stood up on the right pedal of my bike, pulled up on the handlebars, and took off, not looking back.

That night I lay in bed, trying to remember how Rodney Gaines had described jerking off, something about rubbing your prick until you cum. So, I began the practice that became my obsession. At first I tried rubbing my dick against the inside of my covers, knees bent at different angles to try to get just the right contact. But that technique left the tip of my penis raw, like I had used sandpaper. I experimented until I found the perfect solution: hand cream. After working out the kinks in the process, I began to spend much of my time figuring out when and where I could continue these experiments, seeing how fast I could come (22 seconds), or how slow (2 hours and 14 minutes), learning to almost cum, starting to pulsate then backing off, then revving up again.

Now, six weeks later, it's clear: I have become addicted. I jerk off everywhere, no places are sacred: the Meralta theater; the Pep Boys, where I fix the flat tire of my bike—Manny, Moe, and Jackoff; the rec center where we play our baseball games; the stacks of the Downey Public Library; the sanctuary of the First Presbyterian Church.

Out of control, I am consumed with guilt. I consider stopping altogether, but realize no way, it isn't going to happen. OK, then: I can jerk off once every two days. Four times one week, three times the next. In moderation. For half a week I succeed, then meet my temptation in the bathroom while peeing and give in—already four times this week. That's OK, a little backslide is nothing to get upset about, back to once every other day. Then twice on Thursday. This is harder than I thought it was going to be. Time for some punishment. Because I have broken the rule, I have to wait *three* days until the next time. Two days later I fall again, and this time decide on *four* days of fasting. Peeing, or walking home through the orchard, or bored and alone after school, the dreaded sensation starts in the base of my penis, which swells up and demands my attention until I finish. When I'm done, I feel terrible, guilty, hating myself, then mete out another punishment. At each infraction, I tack on two more days of abstinence to the days that I have already been fined. By August 1, I am up to twenty-seven days before I can jerk off again. I am hopelessly in debt.

I sit on the front porch, feeling defeated. I cannot win this battle with my prick. How do people get anything done? Nobody jerks off as much as I do, they must have found a way to control themselves. I could never ask anyone how, that'd be a question that would spread through school faster than the rumor about Yvonne von Gulker getting pregnant by her bible camp counselor. Which she didn't.

Library Offers Amnesty to Book Delinquents

September 1—Downey Librarian Mrs. Kelly Anderson announced the Annual Library Amnesty Week. All delinquents who have books overdue may bring in the books during this week without being fined. No questions asked.

There on the front page of the *Downey Leader* I have my answer. *Amnesty.* A period when all debts are forgiven, and you begin over with a clean slate. So I grant myself a one-time jerk-off amnesty, the debt of twenty-seven days erased. Now I can start over, back to once every two days.

A week later, and I'm back in debt, required to wait four days before resuming my secret activities. But, of course, I can't wait four days, and the abstinence debt continues to grow.

Time to modify The Plan: every Sunday night I will grant myself jerk-off amnesty. Every Monday morning I will start the week over with a clean slate. Perpetual amnesty renewal. Of course! My life feels normal again, in control. I pump up the tires on my bike, hop on, and head down to the Pep Boys to get a new bike light.

Anna's Hummingbird

August, an early Saturday morning, before it gets too hot. I have begun to enjoy these mornings when Mom is in the hospital and my father is not rushing off to work. Friday nights, after Michele has gone to bed, Dad and I usually turn on the TV and watch *Your Hit Parade*, with Snooky Lanson and Gisele MacKenzie. Then we go to bed and sleep through the night, no ghosts, no sounds. The mornings are not frantic, with Dad arranging pills and breakfast for Mom, me looking for a place where I can't hear the sounds. This morning is peaceful, Dad reading the sports between slow slurps of black coffee in the window sunlight, my little sister still asleep. Crows insult each other on the dew-wet front lawn. Sitting together in silence, I want to ask my father if he would like to do something together, but don't know what we would do. In an hour he will leave for the hospital after dropping Michele off at Jeannie's. I watch him enjoying his sunlight and newspaper and decide to let him be; these mornings are among the few times he has to himself. I wonder how much he misses Mom, if he resents having to put down his sports page. How many of his daily trips are duty? In sickness as in health.

Michele comes out of the bedroom, rubs her eyes.

"Come here big girl." She climbs up on my lap. I open the comics section and read to her from *Little Lulu*. She giggles, as if she's gets the joke. I fix her some Sugar Pops, help her put on some shorts and a tee shirt. "Play catch with me before I have to go to Jeannie's," she pleads. At two and a half, she's talking up a storm, as my mother says. She goes to her bedroom, returns with her four-inch beanbag, and we head out to the front yard. We start our toss at four feet, then after three catches in a row we both take a step back. Now we're at twelve feet, a record. Michele can't stop clapping her hands for more. "Damn, girl, you are good!"

Dad shakes the car keys. "OK, kids, time to go." Michele begs for one more toss, we take two. She climbs into the car, a bit hangdog. None of us likes this moment.

The car drives off, and I return to the empty house, somewhat lost. What to do with my summer Saturday?

A knock at the door, a tall stranger I have never seen before, dressed in khaki for Saturday morning lawn-cutting.

"Hi, I'm looking for a Mark Lyons—I think his first name is Mark."

"Yeah, that's me."

"Hi, I'm Tom Simpson from Dolan Street, next block over. I understand you like birds?"

I shrug and open the screen door another eight inches.

"Somebody told me that you know how to fix birds up, in case they get hurt or sick or something."

"Sometimes . . ."

"Well, listen, I found this bird on my patio, I think it flew into our sliding glass doors, can't fly. I asked around about what to do with it and several people told me to take it to you, there's this kid on the next block who raises pigeons and seems to know something about birds. I wondered if you wanted to try and fix it up."

The tall stranger opens a cardboard shoebox, pencil-punched with air holes. All I see is wet cut grass. I look up at the guy, confused.

"There it is, in the corner." He points with a grass-stained finger.

There it is: wide-eyed, head turned upward and at an angle to the light: a hummingbird. Its left wing is unnaturally bent forward halfway up the leading edge. When I reach into the shadow of the box and run the wing between my thumb and forefinger, the bird doesn't struggle. A needle-like prick tells me that the main bone is broken, snapped on impact with the glass. This I know about birds with broken wings: they never fly again. Their wing bones are hollow and fill up with air pumped from their lungs when they fly, to make them lighter. It's impossible to line up the jagged broken ends of the tubed wing bones and hold them in place so they heal together. Most of the time the birds die of pneumonia, because germs get into the open bones and travel to their lungs.

"You want me to take him, see what I can do?"

"That'd be great, people say you're good at this."

"OK, though I'm not sure it has much of a chance. Never done anything with a hummingbird before."

"Well, thanks. Mind if I check back in a few days and see how it's doing?"

"Sure, I'm around pretty much every day. OK if I keep the shoe-box?"

As the khaki-backed stranger walks away I know I'll never see him again.

I have never held a hummingbird before, never been closer than twenty feet. According to *Birds of America*, this one's an Anna's Hummingbird, a male with a purple-red throat and forehead, a green back, dark wings. It's about three and one-half inches long, a little over two inches if you don't count the beak. I feel its heart, just a vibration in its chest, too fast to count. The heart runs about 500 beats a minute at rest, as fast as 1,200 per minute when the bird flies. Hummingbirds have always been magical to me, there is no other bird like them. They eat between one and two times their weight in nectar every day—how will I get enough food down this one to keep it alive? They are the only bird that can truly hover, even fly backward, not needing any wind to fly in place. Seagulls seem to hover, wings outstretched, flying in place as they drop clamshells on the beach, but they are actually using the wind to provide lift; without the wind they would drop to the sand like their clamshells. Hummingbirds hover in front of a flower by arcing their wings in a figure eight, changing the pitch of their feathers like a helicopter, beating fifty times per second. I try to imagine that. One-thousand-one: fifty beats. One-thousand-one: I can make maybe six beats with my fingers on my thigh.

Since Dad has left for the hospital, I have free roam of the medicine cabinet. Twenty amber plastic bottles with white caps, all labeled Rohrer Pharmacy. One tablet four times a day for anxiety, two pills as needed for sleep, take one upon awakening, do not take with alcohol, no refills, two refills, use only under the direction of a physician, expires 1/20/58, tiny red balls, gelatin capsules, blue flat footballs. I want to burn them all. There it is: two drops in each ear twice each day. The eyedropper for the swimmer's ear I had at Sunset Beach during our June vacation. I quietly unscrew the dropper from the bottle as if someone is in the house listening, and ease the medicine cabinet shut, a metallic click.

Knott's Berry Farm Clover Honey, Nature's Amber Secret, is stashed in the kitchen cupboard behind the Kraft Mac and Cheese and Skippy Peanut Butter. It's been there for at least four years, a gift from a visiting cousin: we are not a honey family. Two teaspoons of honey and two teaspoons of warm water, stirred with a toothpick, then sucked into the eyedropper, held up to the light to see if the color shows through the glass tube. No way the bird will ever drink out of this, I should put it out of its misery. This was a dumb idea. I keep the bird in a parakeet cage, abandoned when its blue and white striped occupant flew through our open back door and disappeared into the top of the pepper tree. I have decided not to name the hummingbird, just call it *bird*. I thought about calling it HB or Buzz or something, but hesitated about attaching a name to an animal that won't survive for long. Mr. Platow, my sixth-grade teacher, told us about how some tribes in Africa don't name their kids until they are two years old, because so many die before that. The kids aren't really part of the family until they have a name, so if they die before that there is no need to mourn. No name, no loss, no sadness. All of my pigeons have names and color-coded numbered bands on their legs, and I keep a three-by-five-inch file card on each one with all of their vital statistics: parents, date of birth, mate, first time trained to home, offspring, date died. The hummingbird will just be *bird*, no card.

I place bird on top of a yellow paper napkin in a shallow china soup bowl on the kitchen table. It's very calm, cocking its eye toward the light coming through the window, then at me. Then the eyes almost close completely, tiny gray eyelids. The bird is listless, maybe it's going to die sooner than I thought. I warm the honey-filled eyedropper between my hands and touch the tip to the needle point of bird's beak. Nothing. Try again. This was a bad idea. No name, just bird. No more Mr. Khaki Grass-man bringing dying birds to my doorstep on Saturday mornings. Don't interfere with nature, just let it take its course, Mom always told me when I cried after another failed attempt to save a wild bird. I squeeze the rubber on the dropper, a perfect drop of yellow honey water forms on the tip, unnoticed by bird. Here, bird, look—nectar—take it damnit or you will die. Not interested. One last chance: I deposit the drop on the tip of bird's beak; it tries to shake it off as if drowning. Finally, in a desperate effort to get the foreign stuff off, the bird's slivered black tongue appears for the first time and licks the beak clean. It just ate the honey. Another drop deposited on the needle black beak disappears, another, another. Now the bird is focused, waiting for more. Suddenly it puts the tip of its beak inside the tube of the dropper, about a quarter of an inch, and I see a most amazing thing: its serpent tongue beating back and forth inside the entire length of the dropper, extending almost two inches from the tip of its beak. The tongue is almost three and one-half inches long, curled up at the base of its beak like a New Year's Eve noisemaker. In five minutes, bird has emptied three droppers.

Every two hours I return to repeat the eyedropper ritual with the hummingbird, now craning its neck in anticipation as it watches me prepare the honey water and suck it into the glass tube. Three helpings and bird has filled its stomach, refusing to put its beak to the mouth of the dropper. Keeping this bird alive is going to be a project.

Sunday morning now, up at six to check on bird. Dad is awakened by the rattling of the honey jar in the cupboard.

"Jesus, what the hell are you doing up at this hour of the morning? Are you feeling OK? You're never up at six."

"I'm fine, just felt like getting up early, I'll get the newspaper."

This time I pick up bird with the crooked wing and stroke the bottom of its feet with the back of my left index finger. Its tiny claws naturally grab on, a perch. I alternate a spoonful of raisin bran cereal for myself with a dropper-full of honey nectar for bird seated on my finger. We have breakfast together. I skip baseball practice so I won't miss its two o'clock feeding.

Monday, the next step. Bird and I have the house to ourselves, Michele and Dad won't return until dinnertime. I walk around the house with bird perched on my finger; it's used to the motion, like being on a telephone wire in a gentle breeze. I wait until noon, after the sun has warmed up the nectar in the honeysuckle arbor along the driveway, then open the front door to expose bird to the air and light. Carefully I move along the red clay stepping stones to the arbor and ease my finger up to the orange wide-open mouth of a honeysuckle flower. The noon sun bakes the flowers, the sweet aroma of honey cooking. Bird has done flowers, it knows exactly what to do. Its body leans forward, cantilevered off my finger by its spread green tail, and its head and beak disappear into the mouth of the flower, withdrawing after it has drained the nectar. For a half hour we visit the various flowers on the vine. I learn when it is finished with one flower and wants to move on.

I have had bird now for two weeks, time to give it a name: *Bird*. We have our daily rituals. In the morning when the nectar in the honeysuckle is not yet sun-warmed, I feed Bird from the eyedropper. During the day we visit the sweet baked honeysuckle every two hours. This August is the first summer I have spent alone in an empty house—my sister scattered to Jeannie's house most days, my mother in seclusion at Edgemont, my father at work, my brother who-knows-where. So it's me, my pigeons, and my hummingbird. Bird has grown stronger on its Knott's Berry and honeysuckle nectar diet. When injured birds are sick and weak they are docile and tame, having no strength to fight or to survive, resigned to the mercies of nature, including humans. As they get their strength back, they begin to find their wildness again. Bird is starting to act restless, eyes dancing, occasionally needling my finger with his beak. A good sign. I try to tape the broken wing to its body, maybe it could set, but Bird struggles fiercely with unbalanced discomfort, rolling on its side trying to reach the tape with its thrashing feet. I carefully cut the tape with fine-pointed scissors and remove it. This isn't going to work.

Late afternoon, the last outside feeding of the day. I am on my toes, arms extending Bird to honeysuckle that we haven't reached before, almost to the top of the arbor. As I lower the hummingbird down, still licking the final nectar off the tip of its beak, I see the wildness in its eyes and know what is about to happen: Bird straightens its legs, spreads its green tail full width, leans forward slightly and leaps. Its right wing hums frantically, fifty times a second, while its left wing is motionless, and it crashes to the ground in a spiral. Like a helicopter shot down. Three times I pick Bird up, now wild with the idea of flying, and three times the leap and one wing humming, plummeting like a thing shot. The left wing is useless. It will never fly.

Another discovery about Bird: it has a voice, a tiny terrible *skeeskeeskeet* cry at the end of the leap as it plummets to the ground.

I arise early this morning as I have all month, up before Dad and Michele, to feed Bird. The most constant rhythm in my life this summer has been this daily feeding. I have spent more time with the one-winged Anna's than with my pigeons, or Richie Cary, or my Mother or Dad or sister, or playing baseball. Or jerking off.

The newspaper tells me it is the first week of September. I start school next week. As I mix the nectar for the dropper, I panic at the meaning of Labor Day: when I am in school, I will not be able to feed Bird every two hours, and if it goes without food all day it will die. A hummingbird's metabolism is not made for three meals a day. I know what Dad will say: put it out of its misery, it was not a good idea to start this project.

Dr. Stoddard is the veterinarian who has taken care of all of our cats and dogs for the last ten years, who taught me how to use anti-biotics and louse powder on my pigeons, and to insert my finger between their pelvic bones to determine their sex. He knows I have wanted to be a veterinarian for a long time. He always tells me what he is doing when he examines our pets: what he looks for in their eyes, where the heart and lungs are, what the normal temperature of a cat is, what ear mites and worms look like under a microscope, how to read a fracture on the X-ray, how you can tell how old an animal is. He has also put two of our cats to sleep: one when it got cat fever and went into convulsions; the other to relieve the punctured lung caused by the neighbor's '52 Buick. Today, the last day of summer, I ride up to his office steering my bike with my left hand, holding a small pencil-punched box in my right. It's late afternoon and his office is empty.

"Hey, Mark. What've you got in that box, the world's smallest chihuahua?"

I carefully fold back the flaps of the box, revealing Bird.

"Well, look at that! I've never held a hummingbird. What kind is it?"

"Anna's, a male."

"I can count on you to bring me a surprise. What's its problem?"

I run Bird's deformed wing between my fingers and touch the spiked broken bone as if it's a needle: "Broken wing. A sliding glass door. Think it can be fixed?"

"Boy, that's a challenge. Never took care of a hummingbird before. We'll see what we can do. How long ago"

"Almost a month." He's wondering why I took so long to bring it to him.

"We'll see. We'll try immobilizing it, tape its wing in place, see if it'll heal up. Bird's wings are tough."

I don't tell him about my failed attempt to tape Bird's wing.

"Hey, I'm working on a cat, spaying a female, want to come and observe?"

This is the first time that Dr. Stoddard has invited me to watch an operation. I feel like I am being initiated into a special club, invited to participate in the secret rituals of surgery, a privilege. The operating room is a bit disappointing, no green-tiled floors and intense mirrored ceiling lights and scrub suits and nurses handing over scalpels and clamps upon request like you see in movies. Rather, it's a small stainless-steel table bolted to the floor in the middle of a room cluttered with storage boxes and shadows. Clamped to the top of the table is a brown spring-controlled lamp that can move in three directions, like the light I use for studying. A small tray on rollers is covered with a paper towel and steel surgical instruments. Easy listening music comes through a speaker hung in the corner of the ceiling with a coat hanger.

"Come over and take a look, I'm about to sew her up."

At first I don't see the cat, because instead of being flat, the top of the table has been tilted so that it's about 60 degrees from the horizontal. The black and white cat is hanging upside down, belly facing out, hind legs strapped to the table with black cords, its eyes dead open, dry pink tongue hanging from a drooling mouth. The front legs are also stretched outward and strapped, an upside-down crucifixion. Dr. Stoddard sits in a stainless-steel chair in front of the suspended cat, its whiskered head between his knees. Then I notice the cat's shaven belly with the two-inch swollen pink incision starting to fold over. Dr. Stoddard inserts his two gloved forefingers into the incision and pulls back the skin and motions with his pointy clean chin for me to take a look. I put my hands in my pockets and bend over at the waist to get my anatomy lesson.

"I hang her upside down so that all of the organs fall away from her ovaries, makes it easier to operate without an assistant. See, here's her intestines. If you look down there you can see the spleen, there's her uterus. I already took out the ovaries, they're over there in the jar. Just gotta sew her up and we'll be done."

I realize I am not listening, just staring at the incision, the head of the unconscious upside-down cat hanging on the rack. The cat starts to spin, I'm about to pass out. A song seeps out of the speaker on the wall: *I'm gonna sit right down and write myself a letter, and make believe it came from you, buck-bye-yuh, buck-bye-yuh . . .*

"Hand me that suture material, OK?"

"Huh?" *I'm gonna write words oh so sweet, they're gonna knock me offa my feet . . .* I'm thinking Mom loves this song.

"That blue thread there on the tray, with the curved needle on the end, I need it to sew up the abdomen . . . Can you push the tray over so I can reach it?"

"Sure." *A lotta kisses on the bottom, I'll be glad I gottum . . .* I feel hypnotized by the cat, or is it the song? *Buck-bye-yuh, buck-bye-yuh . . .* She used to mouth the words to the song, circling me, in slow motion shaking her finger at me and winking.

"There, another cat's had her last litter. She'll be awake in an hour and eating out of her family bowl tomorrow morning. Funny how sterilizing animals is the bread and butter for a veterinarian. Maybe next time you can assist."

"Sure, great." *I'm gonna smile and say I hope you're feelin bettah, buck-bye-yuh.*

"Listen, let's make a deal about your hummingbird. Seein' as I have never had the opportunity to take care of a hummingbird before, I'll try to fix it up for free, see if we can't get it into condition to set loose. If in a week or so it's not getting any better, I'll put it down, so it doesn't suffer. Wild things shouldn't have to be caged."

I'm sure I look a little desperate, but mostly feel relieved.

"That's life, Mark. It isn't always pretty, or ends up like we want it to. But that's what is. If I have to put it down I'll use gas, he'll just go to sleep."

Riding home two-handed now on my Schwinn, one of those moments when you know you know something. I know two things: I'll never see Bird again; and I'll never be a veterinarian.

The house is still empty: no car in the driveway, Dad must be picking up Michele at Jeannie's. I head to the pigeon coop to check on my birds, close the trapdoor for the night. The nest boxes smell of bird-washed straw; the porcelain bath is stained black with olive pits from the overhanging tree; the tin feeder needs filling. Two scavenging English sparrows startle and flee through the steel-gray wire mesh. The males have settled into their night shift on the eggs, the females have eaten and bathed and taken their rightful place on the perches under the roof. I sit down in the dust of the fly pen, lean against the one-inch mesh that conforms to my back, lace my fingers behind my neck, rest both elbows on my knees. *I'm gonna sit right down and write myself a letter, and make believe it came from you, buck-bye-yuh-buck-bye-yuh* . . . The breeze of early evening massages my forehead and arms, the images and songs of the day begin to fall away. I feel anesthetized and slip into sleep.

FALL 1957

Kathy Fiscus

At seventy-five I still dream of Kathy Fiscus, who came into my life when I was six. Her memory continues to pursue me, reappearing in the middle of the night, then leaving me to nurse a quiet morning sadness. 1949: I was six years old. Early April, when one day was tee shirt and shorts hot and the next day sweatshirt and jacket cold. A Friday, Dad just home from work, he and Mom working their martinis in the living room, feet up, small talk, relaxed lines in their faces. Brother Bill came out of the bedroom and announced that it was six o'clock, time for the news. We hooked up our round-top Motorola to its jerry-rigged aerial, a clothes hanger suspended in the corner of the ceiling, turned the dial to the vicinity of 640, KFI-AM, and slid the aerial back and forth until the static minimized. Mom's right elbow on the arm of her chair steadied her drink; Dad rearranged the pillows on his couch, crossed his knees, lit up a Pall Mall, quietly exhaled. Bill and I stretched out on the floor. The News.

> This is the news at KFI-AM Radio. It's been four hours since three-year-old Kathy Fiscus disappeared down the fourteen-inch diameter uncapped well shaft in her neighbor's field in San Marino. Rescue efforts continue to move at a very slow pace, as the police and fire departments are afraid that the sandy soil will collapse the well and smother the child. A canopy has been set up over the opening, to protect her from the rain. Kathy's mother, Mrs. David Fiscus, just called down the shaft, "Are you all right, honey?" "Yes," the young child's voice quavered. "Is your head up or down?" "Up," replied Kathy Fiscus. Then she said, "Down." Then there was silence.

The news ended and we turned on the lights. "Three years old. I just can't imagine," my mother said. Nobody else spoke for a couple of minutes, then we got up. I left my dinner plate half full, canned peas and potatoes dispersed with my fork. Lying in bed, my room as dark as a well shaft. Was Kathy Fiscus crying out right now? Was she able to sleep? Did her parents talk to her all night, whispering down the well? Would she be alive when I awoke in the morning?

The next morning, Saturday, we turned on the news. KFI was broadcasting twenty-four hours a day from Kathy Fiscus's well. KTLA-TV was also broadcasting live from the shaft—the first time in TV history that a newscaster had left the studio and reported a breaking story live from the scene. But we had no TV, nor did any of our neighbors; we were stuck with our radio. The rescuers had brought derricks and bulldozers and cranes and had worked all night under floodlights donated by Hollywood studios. Firemen ran an air hose down the shaft. They were down to sixty-five feet. Still no Kathy. My parents went to the supermarket for food. I helped Dad pull weeds in the garden. Knocked on Dicky Tostenson's door to see if he wanted to shoot some hoops; nobody home. It was hot, I washed my face off with the hose. Threw some balls against the chimney. Tried to read a library book. Ate a mustard and white bread sandwich. Took a nap.

Saturday night, we all took our stations in the living room and turned on the news. They were down to eighty feet, digging around the shaft with backhoes. No sound from Kathy. All day long people began to gather at the well site—neighbors, friends, Seventh Day Adventists on their way home from church, teens detouring from a trip to the mountains. By nightfall, twelve thousand well-wishers, thrill-seekers, sightseers, gawkers, stood vigil or sat in their cars, some praying, some holding hands, some with cameras. The rescuers turned off the drilling machines and backhoes, afraid that the well would collapse. Lowered by ropes, they filled buckets by hand with mud, rocks. Kathy had not made a sound for twenty-four hours.

I went to bed as soon as it got dark. How could I sleep, knowing Kathy Fiscus was down that well? I wanted to go there, somewhere not far from me up in the foothills, and stand with all those people, waiting. Maybe she would feel our presence and know we were still digging, that we would find her. She would be OK. What was it like for her? Did she think she might never get out of that shaft? Did she cry? Was she hungry? What was it like for her mother and father, when did they let themselves know that they might lose her? What would that moment be like for Kathy?—*I am going to die.* No sound from Kathy Fiscus. I did not sleep.

Sunday night—fifty-seven hours after Kathy Fiscus fell down the well—our family resumed its vigil around the radio.

> After digging down one hundred feet, the rescue team finally reached Kathy Fiscus. A physician was lowered down the shaft, and has returned to the surface. He just announced that Kathy is dead, and apparently has been dead since shortly after she fell, from lack of oxygen.

There was a long silence on the radio. My father nodded to Bill, who turned the dial to Off. There in the dark of our living room, nobody moved for half an hour, Mom quietly sobbing in her chair, Dad on the couch, Bill and I on the floor, staring up at the ceiling. I went to my room, climbed into bed with my clothes on, pulled the covers over me. There in the dark, I understood for the first time: the world was not safe.

EIGHT YEARS LATER, almost to the day, it happened: my mother disappeared down her own well. Many rescue attempts were made, as she was brought to the surface, then slipped back down into her private abyss. Every time she was pulled up, there seemed to be less of her, as if she had left something of herself behind. She was never really to be found again.

At fourteen I began to carry an eternal vigilance: don't invest too much in anybody—they could disappear in a flash, without warning. Even now, decades later—when I am deeply in love with my wife, have two wonderful adult children who are thriving and a life full of writing and friends and work that connects me to communities I care about—I have paroxysms of fear: today I will receive the phone call that will change my life forever. For a few hours I walk around with a profound sadness, a sense of loss that is just around the corner.

When I was six, I suffered for Kathy Fiscus as I imagined her stuck in the shaft, crying to get out, wondering if her parents would reach her, save her. Then knowing, finally, that she was lost. Lying in bed I imagined that moment, and cried.

I never cried for my mother.

The Chair

We've had a hot spell, so my bedroom window is open, inviting in the smell of ripening oranges cooking on the trees. I start high school in two days, tenth grade. Not sure what that will bring, but it has to be better than junior high. It's another Saturday morning, an empty house. Our new order: Michele at Jeannie's, dropped off there by Dad on Friday night for the weekend. Bill wherever, down at his apartment in Long Beach that I've never seen. Mom at Edgemont, three months now, trying to get her engine running. Dad gone early to sit with her in the hospital. He will hold her hand as she stares out the window.

"I love you, precious one," he will say. He always says that.

She will look at him with eyes of a broken animal. "I know," she will say in a voice that reveals that his love may not be enough to bring her home. The first time I realized that my mother's sickness was not something that would go away like the flu was when I heard the change in her voice. She loved the sound of her own voice, a deep round musical sound, forming words perfectly, as if their meaning came from the enunciation. Throwing her voice, she called it, the way you do when in a debate or on stage. Speaking is like a good song—the music is as important as the lyrics. I grew up learning to never mumble.

In sixth grade she taught me about iambic meter.

"It's a secret of great poetry, a key to the human soul: ta-TA, ta-TA, ta-TA, ta-TA, ta-TA. Listen . . . it's like a heartbeat. Here, put your hand against your heart. There, feel it . . . ta-TA, ta-TA, ta-TA, ta-TA, ta-TA. Two-ROADS di-VERGED ina-YEL-low-WOOD . . . ta-TA, ta-TA, ta-TA, ta-TA, ta-TA. The rhythm of your heart. Shakespeare knew that, that's why we'll see his plays and read his sonnets forever."

She really said that. I was always uncomfortable when she talked about poetry or souls or shared one of her secret passions with me as if it should change my life. It felt a little embarrassing and hokey.

But secretly I felt proud that she knew all of this stuff other mothers didn't know.

"Being the engineer that he is, your father hasn't read a line of poetry in his entire life, except for the few poems I sent him when we were courting. And I'm not sure he read those. Order is his forte, not passion. I, on the other hand . . . If I have to make a choice, I'll take the chaos of passion. That's why we're such a good fit, your father and I. I fly around and bring him stories of what I have seen, and he clears off a landing spot for me when I need to rest. If you're lucky, you'll get both genes. My children are going to grow up appreciating the choice of words if it's the only good thing I do as a mother."

When she came home from the hospital for the first time last April, it seemed as if she'd left her voice there. Like a dog with a strong bark who has been beaten and dares only a whimper. Instead of resonating from her chest, the words got stuck in her throat and finally dribbled out of her mouth, weakly falling onto her lap. No rhythm, no meter, uttered instead of thrown.

I'm getting used to these mornings when I have the house to myself. The house isn't just empty, it has a weird silence, like watching a black-and-white movie on our Hoffman Easy-Vision with the sound turned off. Sometimes I feel like I'm making a jumpy 8-mm movie, my eyes the camera. Take a shot of myself in the bathroom mirror after a shower, Mr. Shorty Skinbones with some pimples that need popping. Zoom into the darkened paneled den that has become my new bedroom. Roll up the hall lined with copper-toned photographs of Mom and Dad in college, their eyes yet unsaddened. Turn right at the end of the hall into my parents' bedroom with the perfectly made unwrinkled bed, the site where my mother first discovered the ghosts hiding last spring. Open the door to the living room where our family spends most of its time together—when we're together. Dust particles hover like hummingbirds in the morning light filtered through the front curtains, and the hazy rays land on the couch where Dad usually sits, his skinny white legs crossed. An indentation in the middle pillow perfectly matches the contour of my father's butt. My camera pans from Grandma Birdie's three-legged mahogany desk and focuses on Mom's chair. It's private—off-limits to the rest of the family. Occasionally, one of us will dare to sit in the chair when she's not in the room; but when she enters, we automatically move to another site, deferring to the mistress of the house. Like a cat who has been caught on the furniture and leaps off without being told to. She dragged her chair west when we moved from Oklahoma in 1946. Filled with invisible sentimental value, it's an ugly homely beat-up slatted thing with hard square pillows that keep being turned over, flat wide arms, cherry-stained wood scarred with cigarette burns. The kind of furniture put on the curb for the Goodwill truck. A half-full cup of coffee sits on the right arm, cultivating green and gray velvety mold. Next to the chair is a metal folding TV table, Mom's portable medicine cabinet, supporting four amber plastic white-capped bottles and the telephone.

The chair used to be my mother's throne, where she sat and read her books, entertained eccentric people from The Little Theater, hooked up to the outside world through the telephone line. It was command central, where she directed the household, planned the next Little Theater production, talked to four or five friends each day on the phone. People wandered in, never knocking. At the end of the day she would call Dad at work to ask him to pick up some vermouth for their evening martini, and remind him that she loved him.

Now that she has lost her voice, Mother sits in her chair like a silent, defeated, caged bird. There in the corner, she takes an occasional sip of her coffee and stares into the fireplace, her head turned away from the room. Her coffee turns cold and she asks my father to warm it up. For maybe a half hour each day she reads a whodunit, four or five pages, before folding a page back and putting the book down. No more people walking in without knocking. No visits from Leota Haas to discuss the merits of Hemingway vs. Steinbeck; no counseling sessions with Eileen Sweet of the perfect breasts to talk about her boyfriend who still hasn't left his wife. My mother's throne room is empty.

With my imaginary 8-mm movie camera, I browse the fireplace mantel which holds some of the old books Mom loves the best, along with a few recent titles. The books rotate in and out of the overflowing shelves in the hallway and our bedroom, sort of her own in-house lending library. The mantel catalogs a mix of her favorite books of all time and her reading list for last year, before she began her pilgrimages to the mental hospital. *Spoon River Anthology* by Edgar Lee Masters, Rostand's *Cyrano de Bergerac*, *The Stories of Damon Runyon*, the *Rubaiyat of Omar Khayyam* ("'Omar the Tent Maker' in Persian," my mother informed me as if she had read it in the original language), *The Red Pony*, a western by Zane Grey, *The Marshes of Glynn* by Sidney Lanier, *The Collected Works of Robert Service*, two Book of the Month Club selections, the *Le Gallienne Book of English and American Poetry*, Volume XXVI of *Reader's Digest Condensed Books*, *Gone with the Wind*, something about Earl ("in like") Flynn, two Agatha Christie's for flavor, *The Snow Goose* by Paul Gallico.

The Snow Goose is one of the books Mom has tried to sell me on several times since I was twelve, calling it one of the secret jewels of the English language. "Just read fifteen pages and you won't be able to put it down. How can fifteen pages hurt you? It's by a sportswriter for Christ sake, only fifty-eight pages long and about a bird. Just read it, goddamn it!"

For the most part I have successfully resisted my mother's passionate pleas to read some of her literature, or any literature at all. To get her off my back I tell her OK, I'll read some at bedtime before sacking out, then take the book into my bedroom and slide it under the bed. A month later, when she isn't in her chair, I bring the unopened book back and slide it between her other volumes on the mantel.

I cook some cinnamon toast under the broiler, wash two slices down with cold milk, read the sports page. The Dodgers definitely are moving to L.A. next year and will play in the Coliseum until a new stadium is built. Carl Furillo and Pee Wee Reese, Don Newcombe, Sandy Koufax. I have never seen a major league ball game. Maybe on opening day Dad and I could go—but Mom would have to be in the hospital, or Dad wouldn't come. Maybe she could be in for just a short stay, a tune-up.

I don't feel guilty for this thought that I will never share with anybody.

Seven in One

Up until two days ago I had never shot an animal. Or met a wetback. Or touched a girl's breast. Now I have done all three, a month after starting tenth grade, a hundred thirty miles from home.

Ann Hegardt's father owns a citrus ranch inland from San Diego, just across the border from Mexico. He calls himself a nurseryman. He grows seedlings—oranges and lemons and grapefruits—until they reach about five feet, then sells them to big growers in Riverside County. Actually, he doesn't grow the trees, the hired hands do. Mr. Hegardt goes down to the ranch about once a month to "check on the operations," and sometimes brings along Ann and her older brother Rob, who's in college. Occasionally other people are invited. Saturday morning, five a.m., Rob and Mr. Hegardt ride in the cab of their green rock-pocked '52 Chevy pickup while Ann and I huddle with the sleeping bags and clanking new long-handled hoes and shovels in the back, eyes squinting to the wind as we cross through the dry brown passes of the inland mountains. The farthest I have ever been from home, a trip to a new world with this family that seems to like me OK.

Ann's mother has cancer, so she doesn't make these trips. Ann doesn't talk about it. I've only seen her mother once, a tiny pale figure in a white nightgown standing in her bedroom doorway whispering to Ann for a glass of water. I suspect her mother must be dying, but don't know how to ask. Ann has no idea that my mother has been at Edgemont for the last four months, since checking in after our Sunset Beach vacation. Not that I want to keep it a secret, I'm not even sure what I would be hiding. I don't know how to talk about my mother. Besides, how could people respond? Would I just announce it out of the blue?

"My mother's in the hospital."
"Oh, that's too bad. How long?"
"Four months."
"What for?"
"A nervous breakdown."
"Oh, that's too bad."
"Yeah. She'll be OK."
Really nothing to say.

The pickup left Highway 101 thirty miles ago. Now we're on Route 94 East, a thin number 2 pencil line of blacktop bordered with yucca and prickly pear cactus. Just past a cowboy town called Barrett Junction, the gears downshift and the truck veers hard right off the paved surface, rattles down an embankment, and heads into a sandy, tire-marked trail through the low desert. Sudden swerves of the truck to avoid craters and washes and boulders roll us over from side to side. We laugh in mock terror as if we will be thrown from the truck, and my arm slides around Ann's waist. Our bodies have been close when we slow-danced in front of the teachers at the Friday night sock hop, but never lying down. Completely covered with tan tasteless dust, we don't let go for fifteen more miles.

Ann and I sit up as the pickup begins to climb and snake around the low flat hills of the high desert—pink flowering plants, tall meaty cacti, and sandstone-layered arroyos. Our winding ascent continues for ten more miles following a dry creek bed lined with eucalyptus and oak, I recognize ten-foot miniatures of the pepper trees that shade our yard. The west-facing hills have become geometric, with perfect parallel lines: the orchards. As the truck jostles over an irrigation pipe, rear wheels spinning in the mud before grabbing hold, Ann points to a stucco box on the next ridge, their ranch house.

The pickup shifts to first and noisily grinds up the gravel drive to the house, and I see five shadowy barefoot figures knife through the citrus groves, dash across the road behind us, and dive into a corrugated shack hidden within the branches of an ancient avocado tree. I tap Ann on the shoulder and point to the disappearing shades.

"Wetbacks," Ann says, as if it is a vocabulary word she learned in English class, a word I should know.

"Wetbacks?" I have never heard this word, but it has a bad smell, like the time I heard Donald Spearman call somebody a *kike* on the playground.

"Illegals. Mexicans. They cross over the border to work, Dad hires them to take care of the groves. If they get caught, they get sent back. They saw our green truck and thought we were the immigration patrol. Their trucks are the same color. The workers have that hiding place there under the avocados. Whenever a new one comes over, the first thing the others teach him is where to hide when the authorities come. I keep telling my father he should paint our truck a different color."

"Do you know their names?"

"Just one, says he's Juan Antonio. The tall skinny one with the cowboy boots and sweaty straw hat, I think he's sort of the foreman. The others keep changing."

The four of us are exhausted by the dust and four-hour drive. We line up to take cold showers in the back shed and have a conversation-less dinner of spaghetti doused in Pepino's canned home-style sauce served on paper plates with a side of French bread. Ann's father and brother turn in, reminding us that we have to get up at five to set the irrigation pipes. "Turn the lights out before you hit the sack, and make sure the screen door's shut—the mosquitoes are still hatching in the ditches." Ann and I start for our neutral bedrooms, then realize we are alone. Suddenly we are not so tired. I am buzzed with sensations stirred up in the back of the pickup during the tumbling ride this afternoon, like a rash all over my body. Walking on our heels we creak the screen door open, the rusty spring hinges ratcheting in the dark, step out onto the porch and follow each other to the old green couch with cinder blocks for legs.

I am not sure how this all happens. Somehow, we both fall asleep, Ann's head on my lap—we've done a little making-out, as far as we dare to go. The last things I hear are something shouted in Spanish echoing up from the Mexican camp and an owl call that I can't recognize proclaiming territory in the eucalyptus stand above us. Maybe an hour later, night sounds silent, a chilling breeze wafts through the canyon and awakens me, not sure where I am. As I straighten up looking for a light source, I discover that Ann is holding my right hand, pressing it between her hand and her left breast. She is asleep, or seems to be. For fifteen seconds at least, possibly fifteen minutes, I observe my hand cupping her breast through her clothes. Then close my eyes and feel its warm contour in my palm. Can I feel her heartbeat? There it is. My hand is trembling with its miraculous and paralyzing contents. I have to cough, but there is no way I am going to remove my hand to muffle my mouth. My attempt to swallow the cough jars both our bodies. Ann half wakes up and says, "Hello, what time is it anyway?" She squeezes my hand with hers, gently pressing it against her breast. Now she knows for sure, and I have no idea what to do. I feel my palm sweating and my fingers cramping; my hand is trapped.

Oh man. This is the moment of truth. It's time to make my move, the longer I wait the harder it will be. Distracting Ann with a question about how many acres of orange trees are planted on her ranch, I stealthily raise my right hand and casually float it over to the safety of the back of the couch.

We both act as if we don't notice. A close call. Good night, see you in the morning, an awkward peck of a kiss, then the safety of my bedroom, listening to the chant of Rob snoring. My imagination is full of newfound images and my hand full of newfound sensations that finally let me sleep for an hour before the alarm sounds.

The ranch life: We really do get up at five a.m., eat a giant breakfast of scrambled eggs and flimsy bacon, Hormel canned hash browns slurped in ketchup, white toast smeared with grape jelly, two glasses of OJ. Rob offers me a cup of coffee, I start to say no thanks, then nod sure, why not, as if I drink coffee all the time. A true ranch hand. I flood the cup with milk and let the steam wake me a little more, then slowly sip.

All morning Ann and I work the rows of the orange seedlings together, hoeing the weeds from the irrigation ditches, shoveling dikes to channel the water from the aqueduct at the edge of the orchard. The adolescent trees are no more than five feet tall, with shiny leathery evergreen leaves. Ann tells me they won't have any fruit until they're five or six years old. By ten o'clock it is eighty-five degrees, a good thing we started early. The leaves and oranges and straw laid around the trunks of the saplings slowly bake in the sun, an Indian summer marmalade. The hard work and the sun have eased the awkwardness of last night, so Ann and I are able to joke with a new unspoken intimacy. We race to see who can weed a row first, then suck sweet oranges picked from the old tree by the house, then agree to do one more row before lunch. The Mexican who calls himself Juan Antonio scuttles down the hill toward us and stops on top of the newly shoveled dike, using the heels of his boots for brakes.

"*¿Listos pa' el agua?*" he says, as if we will understand.

Ann and I look at each other, as if expecting the other to translate. We look at Juan Antonio and shrug our shoulders.

He tries again: "*Irrigación. Agua pa' las naranjas.*"

Ann recognizes an important word: *irrigation.*

"I think he wants to irrigate the trees, that must be it."

"*Bueno*," she says to Juan Antonio.

"*Vengan*," says Juan Antonio, motioning with his huge brown cracked hands for us to follow him. We're getting the hang of this Spanish. Real ranch hands. We follow Juan Antonio through the rows of seedlings and up the gradual slope to the edge of the grove, then turn up the hill for two hundred yards. Juan Antonio reaches inside a three-foot-diameter cracked cement pipe planted on end in the ground and turns a steel valve that looks like a steering wheel. A hollow distant metallic gurgling sound from deep in the earth comes closer and closer, like an approaching train. With a wet explosion muddy water gushes from the base of the pipe and floods our feet. The cold water turns ice clear, seeps into the cracks of the dry irrigation ditch like an animal tongue, slowly rises, then suddenly breaks downhill. Juan Antonio jumps into action, running ahead of the river of water with his shovel, filling chinks in the dike, directing the water to the left then down to the right again, until it has reached the rows that Ann and I have just weeded. He frantically shovels dirt to dam the downhill flow of the stream and direct it at a right angle down our rows. Ann and I run along with the stream as it's welcomed by our orange saplings, one tree at a time. In three or four minutes the row is almost flooded. Juan Antonio hands me a shovel and makes an underhanded shoveling movement with his arms, motioning me to un-dam the barrier he has made. In two shovelfuls I have unleashed the dam, sending the water gushing downhill once again. He backs downhill to the next row of saplings, and makes a sweeping motion with his hand pointed at the ground, time for me to direct the water to the next row. I plant my foot on top of the shovel and pry out a giant clod of dry dirt and toss it in front of the flow. Two more shovels and the dam is complete. The water suddenly takes a left turn and heads to a new dry row of thirsty trees. I can almost hear them drinking the water. For twenty rows we repeat this process, Ann and I taking turns at being Master Irrigator, First Class, passing each other the shovel to construct, then destroy, our temporary dams. All under the command of General Juan Antonio. The Wetback Corps of Engineers.

As the last row is irrigated, Juan Antonio gets my attention and points up the hill to the cement pipe, bends slightly at the waist and makes a clockwise turning motion with both hands, like a trucker backing his rig up. I race up the hill, reach down into the pipe, and turn the steel wheel. The wet gurgling sounds retreat into the earth, it is very quiet. Juan trudges up to join us, inspecting the base of the pipe to make sure that the water is completely shut off.

"*Bueno*," says Juan Antonio, approvingly. He taps his watch. "*Pues, debemos almorzar.*"

Ann and I try to look like we know what he is talking about. He holds his hand up to his mouth and makes munching sounds.

"Oh, right, it's lunchtime," says Ann, repeating Juan Antonio's hand-to-mouth motions.

The three of us march single-file through the rows of trees and out onto the main dirt road, our shovels on our shoulders like rifles. At the point where the road heads up the hill toward the stucco house, Juan Antonio peels off to the right.

"*Pues, nos vemos.*"

"See you after lunch, Juan Antonio. *Adiós.*" Ann seems to understand these rituals.

I look back over my shoulder as we reach the porch of the ranch house, and watch Juan Antonio pull back a branch of the old avocado tree and disappear. On the edge of the tree a fine line of smoke, like from a cigarette, curls up from a campfire. Spanish voices mumble in the shadows, men. Sounds like maybe five or six in all.

A meal tastes different after a morning of sweaty work in the sun, like eating in slow motion. Spooning in potato salad, sucking on dill pickles, finishing my second hamburger plastered with mustard, I listen to Mr. Hegardt and Rob talk about pesticides and new irrigation systems. It's clear that our day's work is done, that we are all going to relax before heading home tonight. I'm a little disappointed, wanting to finish twenty more rows before hanging up my hoe. Who knows if I will ever be back here?

"Hey, Mark, have you ever hunted?" Rob brings two rifles from the back porch, sits down at the kitchen table, and straddles them across his knees.

"Nothing alive." I realize that's a pretty dumb answer.

"Why don't we see if we can get a rabbit this afternoon? They're all over the damn place. We'd almost have to shoot up in the air to miss one." Rob puts a bead of polishing oil on the dark wooden stock and rubs it in with his hands.

"I've never shot that kind of gun." I don't admit that I've never shot any gun.

"Not much to it. This one's a .22, single-load bolt-action. This here's a single-barrel shotgun pump-action, 16-gauge. Lightweight." He expertly reams out the barrels with a cloth threaded through a ramrod. "Let's go out back, we'll do a little target practice."

Boot camp, first day of weapons training. Rob has lined up three empty spaghetti sauce and vegetable cans on a decaying log, backed by an embankment of roots and eroded soil. He explains how to sight down the barrel, keep your right elbow tucked into the side of your ribs, your left elbow bent at ninety degrees, exhale before you fire, tuck the butt of the stock tightly into your shoulder especially with the shotgun, pull the trigger back steady, not with a jerk. There. *Ping!* One Chef Boyardee Spaghetti and Meat Balls can bites the dust. It looks easy.

Now it's my turn. Rob talks me through the process, using the .22: pull back the bolt, slide in the shell, snap the bolt shut, take off the lock, raise the rifle, sight, watch the angles of the elbows, a steady pull now. A sharp *crack*, the first time I have fired a real gun. The Jolly Green Giant stares at me in defiance.

"OK, that was a good first try. Let's see what went wrong here. See where the bullet hit behind the can? A little to the right and high. I think you aren't holding your cheek along the stock, messes up the sighting. Don't worry, there's really no kick to these rifles, tuck your face against the wood. Like this . . ."

Rob demonstrates the proper positioning of the rifle, then hands it to me. I hold the weapon up to my face, point it at the cans, and pull the uncocked trigger. Rob stands behind me and sights the shot over my shoulder.

"That's it. Just keep it there, and you'll be right on target. Remember to breathe out and pull steady. A lot goes into making a good shot. Let's try it again."

Rob hands me another shell. I pull the bolt toward me and down, slide in the casing, snap the bolt up and forward, a smooth metallic sliding sound. Unlock the safety with a quick click. Raise the rifle, aim, and fire. The Jolly Green Giant kicks backward against the embankment and rolls down against the log, then is motionless. My body feels like it's pumped with an extra quart of blood, flushed and proud, like the first time I held hands with Ann at dance lessons or read my name on the junior high baseball roster.

"That's it, you've got it, I could tell by the way you held the gun that you're a natural." Rob's not jumping up and down, he's sort of matter-of-fact about this major accomplishment of mine. He shakes my hand formally, like bestowing my marksmanship medal. I'm thinking I'd like this guy to be my big brother.

"Let's go find some rabbits." Ann and her father are off doing something. It's just me and Rob.

We load the rifles, shells, and a jug of water into the back of their ranch vehicle: a WWII camouflaged green jeep, four cylinders, with the floppy clutch pedal, long-handled shift on the floor, and front windshield folded down, brought back from the Pacific Theater and auctioned off at the Navy Surplus Depot in San Diego. Rob instructs me to ride shotgun in the seat next to him, and as we spin out in the dust I hang on to the windshield casing and plant my foot on the bottom of the frame where there would be a door. We grind straight up the equipment road, above the rows of citrus groves where the green disappears, reach the peak behind the stucco house, and drop down on the barren back side of the property, the badlands. Suddenly the jeep pulls to a halt, *chugchugchug* of the idling cylinders, then a tiny backfire as the ignition seizes. Like a tight-assed fart.

"There's one—down where the trail dips to the left, next to the boulder." Rob has spotted our first rabbit, sixty yards away. A clear shot. He hands me the .22 as he points to make sure I see our prey. I acknowledge the enemy with a silent half-nod.

"OK, just remember how we shot the cans, take your time aiming, then steady moves when you fire." I swing down from the Jeep as if it is an old habit and load the shell into the rifle, set it in place with the bolt. Rob moves behind me and watches intently as I raise the rifle to my cheek and sight down the barrel. Neither of us moves, nor the air. My heart is pumping in my right jugular tucked next to the stock, imperceptible movements transferred to the rifle. As I slowly pull back on the trigger the rabbit looks up, smelling a change in the air. I wince as my trigger finger contracts.

Nothing.

"The safety. Don't forget the lock's still on." Rob smiles with the corners of his mouth.

I nod to him as if I knew that, I was just doing one more practice maneuver. I unlock the safety, assume my firing position once again, take aim, and fire the rifle. A clear crack echoes in the clean air. The prey turns and gazes ten feet behind it and to the right, trying to ascertain the cause of the flying dust, then resumes eating whatever plant is the focus of its attention.

The truth: I'm not disappointed by my miss.

"Pretty close, you've got the idea, just keep your cheek tucked in and line up the tip of the sight in the middle of the rabbit."

I fire four more times, all clean misses. The only time the rabbit startles is when the bullet ricochets off the boulder, an echoing *ping*. The arrogant little bastard still holds its ground.

"Let me take a shot, make sure that rabbit's not a mirage." I hand Rob a .22 shell and stand back as he takes aim. He misses two times.

"Must be something wrong with the sight, we'll have to get it aligned." It occurs to me that Rob is missing his shots on purpose.

The rabbits aren't as plentiful as predicted, or perhaps they've gone underground until the shelling ceases. For the next hour our jeep revs up and down the ravines and ridges, spotting three more prey, and each time we repeat the ritual of climbing out of the Jeep, methodically and expertly loading and taking aim, trying to bring a rabbit down, dust flying, the defiant animal nonchalantly chewing at the few stubbly plants that populate the east side of the mountain. After our fourth rabbit leaves the field of battle, a casualty of boredom, Rob looks at his watch and announces that it's time to head back and pack for the return to civilization. A failed expedition.

The jeep heads west, tops the ridge, and heads down into the valley of green orchards in perfect formation, like soldiers at attention. We are met by smells of sweet-sour citrus leaves and damp earth, blown up the valley by the breeze coming over from the coast. As we pass through the avocado grove, a flock of birds runs across the road fifty yards in front of us, then stops in the shaded safety under a scrub oak. Rob slams on the brakes of the jeep and turns off the ignition. Dust and silence.

"Quail." Rob speaks with a mixture of authority and alarm, muffling his voice with his hand cupped over his upper lip, like a platoon leader announcing the discovery of the enemy on a night patrol. "Hand me the gun."

I reach into the back seat and heft the .22.

"No. The shotgun. And the shells, there by the wheel well." The air feels tense and serious, like between lightning flashes during an electrical storm.

I hand Rob the 16-gauge and the shells. He quickly cracks the barrel, plunks in a cartridge, and snaps the barrel back into place, the blue hollow sound of forged steel. He holds the side of his finger to his mouth, ordering silence, and we stealthily dismount from the Jeep, bend at the knees and waist and creep along the side of the road, downwind from the birds. Now we are forty yards from the oblivious quail, a dozen of them in a clump scratching for seeds and grubs, pecking the earth with sideways motions of their beaks. The breeze shifts for a moment and the quails freeze. A male, with its topknot curled over its head, stands on a rotting stump and swivels its head a hundred eighty degrees to the left, a hundred eighty degrees to the right. The lookout.

I've never seen a quail, but I've read about them in *Birds of America*. They are in the chicken family, ground-feeding birds. After their chicks are hatched, different families come together to move in bevies, sometimes as many as twenty birds, mostly running through the safety of thickets, occasionally venturing into open areas to forage. My book describes a scene I must see some day: When the chicks are in danger the mother feigns a broken wing, flopping over and over in the dust and squawking as if having suffered a near-mortal wound, until she has the enemy's attention. Having distracted the fox or raccoon or dog or other predator, she runs another twenty yards away from the clutch, flops on the ground with one wing bent at a terrible angle behind her back, and cries out another death rattle. This theater is repeated over and over until the intruder has been pulled a sufficiently safe distance from the threatened clutch. Assured that the enemy is confused and distracted, the hen's wing miraculously heals and it bursts to the air sounding the *all clear* call, to which the chicks respond by scattering in every direction.

The wind again blows toward us, betraying the birds, and we inch closer. Their constant banter of *kuk-kuk-ka kuk-kuk-ka kuk-kuk-ka* tells us they are unaware of our presence.

Twenty-five yards now. Rob raises the shotgun to his shoulder and sights down the barrel. I try to close my ears to the sound I antici-pate. I have never heard a shotgun blast. I am not looking at the birds.

"Here." Rob whispers in a tone as if our lives depend upon not being heard, holding the gun out to me. "They're yours."

I hesitate.

"Don't worry, it's just got a little kick. Tuck the butt tightly into your shoulder and press it firmly against your cheek, you barely feel it."

I had not considered the recoil of the weapon. Rather I am try-ing to get ready for this moment. I keep taking deep breaths, slowly relaxing. I hear my breathing, clear and steady, without a wheeze. I realize that I have not used my asthma pump all weekend.

I do not remember firing the gun, or the explosion and its echo, or the smell of powder. I do remember the whistling sound of a few birds taking to the air and Rob shouting, "You got some!" I lean the rifle against the front tire of the Jeep, gulp the burnt powder still in the air, and dash to the shady spot where Rob is already bent down under the oak. I kneel beside him and see my prey: seven quail, scat-tered in a ten-foot circle, some chest down, some on their backs star-ing at the sky. Like WWII photos of a foxhole hit by a mortar shell. Nothing moves, no bird feigns a broken wing.

Something I am not prepared for: birdshot from a distance doesn't maim the birds. No bullet holes, no flesh, no shattered wings, no blood. Peppered with invisible BBs. Perfectly unblemished, yet life-less. I pick up a male and its head flops backward on its flimsy neck, dark brown glassy eyes. The bird has a pure black face mask outlined with a white necklace, and a white stripe over its eye, a painted brow. Chestnut and white tweed feathers streak its flanks; its breast is dec-orated with a black round patch, forming a bull's-eye. One perfect feather is inserted in the crown, a black teardrop topknot with a slight comma bend, which I stroke. I stretch its right wing out and run the primary feathers through my fingers three times, preening. No splintered bones. A search of the breast, back, and side reveals no holes where the buckshot entered. Invisible wounds. The entire quail fits in my left hand, still warm. Now I cup the bird between both hands, pressing my right palm to its breast, feeling for a heartbeat. There is none.

"Seven! Not bad for one shot. Read all about it in the *San Diego Union*: 'Mark Lyons today got seven quail the first time he fired a shotgun!'" Rob slaps me on the back with his enthusiasm.

Hunched down, sitting on my ankles, all I can think of is *How can I get out of here?* I roll the bird off my hand into the dirt and rake brown prickly dry oak leaves over it, using my fingers. I blanket the other fallen birds with leaves, stand up, and walk to the jeep as if everything is OK. I want to tell Rob, or Ann—anyone—how bad I feel, how I know I'll never shoot a gun again.

Rob looks at me with his head tilted a bit.

I think he knows.

DUSK NOW, purple and pink washes in the sky. The dusty green pocked pickup rumbles through its last sandy ravine and rolls up on the blacktop—State Route 94, headed west. Ann and I occupy the flatbed padded with two blankets, our heads propped up against a pile of scratchy gunnysacks. We don't talk much, just a few words about the dust in our eyes or how fast Juan Antonio worked or the best meal was the spaghetti and meatballs. We don't find an excuse for our bodies to touch, just huddle up in our own blankets. We go up the on-ramp to Highway 101 and pass a green road sign with reflector letters.

LOS ANGELES 96 MILES

Juan Antonio

The images of Juan Antonio and his Mexican *compañeros* skittering under the avocado tree and cooking tortillas over an open fire, the citrus orchards, the dikes and irrigation systems—all these settled into the nerves of my memory. Wetbacks—*mojados*—supposedly from crossing some river from Mexico. Four years later, when I drove up the Central Valley then headed over to the coastal plains on my way to college in Northern California, I saw farmworkers by the thousands, hoeing lettuce fields, picking strawberries, harvesting Brussels sprouts and artichokes, running irrigation systems. Alongside the fields were trailers and camps, old pickups, barefoot kids. Maybe Juan Antonio and his friends had followed the migrant stream north from San Diego, were working in Keane or Solvang or Castroville or Gilroy, and would continue north to pick apples in Washington. Then return to spend the winter in the nurseries east of San Diego and start the cycle all over again. Following the same route as the birds I had watched massing in the orange groves surrounding my home, on their way to points north in the spring, south in the winter.

In the sixties, when I was in my early twenties, I heard César Chávez speak at United Farm Workers of America rallies and participated in the grape boycott. Like many, I was moved by the stories of the farmworkers, and I had my own private image of learning how to dig irrigation levees from one of them. But I moved on—to work in civil rights in Georgia, then up north to join the peace movement, where I was arrested several times, turned in my draft card, and refused induction into an army that was sowing death halfway across the world. I was trying to figure it all out, while facing a series of failed relationships which convinced me that I was going to do it all alone.

Then I was forty-two, with a wife and two children who reminded me daily that I was not alone, and never would be. I had become a physician assistant and health planner, and one day was ingloriously fired. I got a temp job organizing a conference of community health workers from South America and the United States. I invited The Farmworker Support Committee—*El Comité de Apoyo a los Trabajadores Agrícolas*—which was organizing in the truck farms of New Jersey and the mushroom barns of Pennsylvania. They offered me a job, and for the next eight years I was the director of the Farmworker Health and Safety Institute, a consortium of grassroots farmworker organizations in New Jersey, Pennsylvania, Texas, Florida, North Carolina, Puerto Rico, and the Dominican Republic. We trained farmworkers to be educators and organizers around farmworker rights, AIDS, housing, field sanitation, pesticides, and work-place safety. I spent hours in camps and fields, where farmworkers taught me about their living conditions, work practices, the hazards they faced, what it was like to be separated from their families, the dreams that brought them to America. We confronted the Environ-mental Protection Agency, OSHA, state labor boards, farm bureaus. Sometimes we won, sometimes we lost.

After working with farmworkers for eight years, I dreamed in Spanish and learned to tell jokes in Spanish. In a sense I had crossed my own Rio Grande, emotionally going south where I felt most at home. Feeling compelled to share the stories I had heard working in the fields and camps, I wrote a book of oral histories of migrant farmworkers, *Espejos y Ventanas/Mirrors and Windows.* I founded the Philadelphia Storytelling Project, which works with undocumented immigrants to teach them to record and edit their own stories, to give them a voice, a face. My favorite project: working with a group of Latino kids, ages five to fifteen, who made dolls. They then recorded a message about what would happen to their families if their undoc-umented parents were deported, asking President Obama not to sep-arate them. We implanted the kids' voices inside the dolls, ran a wire to a felt heart on each doll's chest. Push on the heart and the dolls—the kids—tell their stories. Heartfelt. I met Liliana Velásquez, who suffered horrendous poverty and violence at the hands of her family and two men who tried to rape her. At fourteen, she walked out of her village in Guatemala alone and headed north to the United States, where she'd heard women were treated with more respect. She was robbed by *narcos* and rode the boxcars in Mexico, encountered death in the Arizona desert, was captured by the U.S. Border Patrol, spent months in detention, and finally convinced the immigration court that her life was in danger if she were sent back home. With her new-found asylum status, she dedicated herself to her studies and find-ing a way to help her community back home. One day she asked me to help her write a book about her story, so we set to work. She pub-lished her bilingual memoir, *Dreams and Nightmares/Sueños y Pesadil-las* and continues to share her story in schools, universities, churches, and teacher workshops. We have been a great gift to each other.

At fourteen, what I remembered most about my trip to Ann

Hegardt's ranch on the Mexican border was her right breast and a dead quail—both of which I had held in my hand. But it was Juan Antonio whom I carried with me.

An Increased Sense of Well-Being

Except for the brief glimpse of her in the window at Edgemont when I tried to visit, I haven't seen my mother since June. Five months. She's coming home just in time for Thanksgiving. I hear the car roll up our asphalt driveway and run outside to greet her. I open the door of our cream and green '57 Chevy, reach in and give her a silent hug. She looks puzzled, gives me a half-hug back, doesn't say anything. I give her one more squeeze, and Dad and I walk her to her chair in the living room.

"So, Mom, you look pretty good. How you feeling?"

She looks into the fireplace, glances at my father, looks at me. Her eyes are squinty and unfocused.

I try again. "Want some coffee? I'll put a new pot on . . ." She turns away as if she doesn't hear, head tilted to the side. She finally looks at my father. She seems frightened.

"Who's he, Bill?"

"Mom . . . Mom, it's me. Mark." I try to hide a scowl growing in my jaw.

"I'm sorry. Of course . . . *Mark*."

After my mother is settled in her chair, Dad stops me in the kitchen as I gulp some milk and a mustard sandwich. "Mark, listen, they gave your mother some treatments at the hospital which will affect her memory for a little while. It'll just last a few days, then she'll be just like always. Please try to be understanding. She'll be like new soon."

I hold up my sandwich. "So, what'd they do?"

"Do what?"

"You know, what happened at the hospital to make it so Mom can't recognize me?"

"Oh, it's this new thing. They say it's supposed to really work for people who are depressed, though it may take a few times. They call it ECT. The doctor who does it is the top of the line, really well respected. I'm sure that it will really make a difference for your mother." I have learned that when my father tries to make things all right, he punctuates his sentences with *really*.

"You mean shock therapy." I'm impatient that my father tries to cover up what they did to mother. *ECT,* my ass. As if I don't know what that means, what they did to her.

"Well, I wouldn't go as far as to say *shock*," my father says.

I'm thinking to myself, *Come on, you're an electrical engineer.*

THE FIRST TIME I ever heard about shock therapy was last year, eighth grade. The year before my mother's first trip to the hospital. Mrs. Cox, my social studies teacher, told us we should be thinking about our future, because next year when we started ninth grade our grades would count toward college. So, because we needed to start thinking about what we wanted to be when we grew up, we were assigned to write a report about a profession we might pursue. One evening I picked up the *Saturday Evening Post* sitting on our coffee table, and read an article that made me think I might want to be a psychiatrist. It was about Bellevue Hospital in New York, and all the hopeful progress they were making toward helping depressed people. People who were afraid to talk to people or couldn't keep their jobs or just withdrew from the world or were so sad that they had to stay in a mental hospital. I didn't know anybody who was depressed or who had even seen a psychiatrist, but I imagined how terrifying it must be to be locked away from your family in a hospital where nobody knew you.

The most interesting part of the article was about ECT: electroconvulsive therapy. I could not imagine saying it without a deep voice: *E-LEC-TRO-CON-VUL-SIVE THER-A-PY.* On the second page was a huge black-and-white photograph of a patient lying on a hospital bed. She was covered with a white sheet, leather straps around her ankles and arms, a huge elastic strap over her chest, with wires coming out from under the sheet and stuck into her head. People in white coats and what looked like French chef's hats stood around the bed, and there were meters and switches and dials on the wall. The patient's eyes were open, she was still awake. The caption described how the doctors were preparing a severely depressed patient for electroshock therapy, strapping her down to prevent her from injuring herself when she convulsed. I thought of the first time I saw a man having a seizure, in the May Company department store when shopping with my mother. He thrashed around on the floor, bleeding from his mouth, kicking over furniture, while people screamed and jumped out of the way. He finally let out a terrible gasp as his body arched then went limp, and the smell of shit oozed across the marble.

Under the heading "The Miracle of Electricity," the author described how doctors had known for a long time that epilepsy patients often had an increased sense of well-being for a few days after having a seizure. Then by chance they discovered that depressed diabetics who took too much insulin and had convulsions because their sugar fell too low seemed to feel much less depressed for a few weeks after their seizures. They tried giving depressed people who weren't diabetics enough insulin to make them have low-sugar seizures—insulin shock—and found that it worked: the patients were less depressed, at least for a while. But occasionally they gave too much insulin and the patient went into a coma or even died. Then some famous doctor remembered reading about how sometimes linemen working on telephone poles got shocked by thousands of volts and went into convulsions. Why not create the convulsions by shocking depressed people with electricity? It would be much safer than insulin because you could turn the amount of current up and down, and even stop it if you wanted to stop the seizure.

The *Post* quoted the man in white at the instruments in the photograph as saying it was the greatest breakthrough in the treatment of depression in the history of psychiatry, that it would provide relief to thousands of hopeless people who had suffered too long.

So now I imagine Mom strapped down in the black-and-white photo at Bellevue, all the people around her bed standing back to be clear of the shock. Her eyes are still open. A man in a white jacket is reaching for some dials.

"Your mother will be really fine in a week or so," says my father. "It's been a long day. Why don't you let her rest for a while, maybe clean your pigeon pen, maybe go over to Richie Cary's? By then it'll be dinnertime."

"Good-bye, Mom, I'll be outside." No answer. She searches for her memory in the fireplace.

The colors in the sky are fading, the temperature has begun to drop. My birds return to their coop, poke their heads through the trapdoor. Wires and leather straps and levers and gauges. Did the *Saturday Evening Post* mention how the miracle of electroshock takes away memory along with the depression? I don't remember. Is that the secret of sadness—memories?

I easily corral James in the corner of the coop, he knows the routine. Tuck him into the basket strapped to the back of my bike, head for the orchard over by the junior high school. The orchard is cool, sweet with the smell of the fall orange crop. I open the top of the basket, James cocks his head and peeks out. Two flaps and he is airborne. It takes him only three circles to become oriented—he's really good at this—and he turns for home. I push my bike out of the orchard and head along Raines Street. James will be waiting for me in the coop when I get home. I'll latch the doors to keep my birds safe from predators, then go inside for a silent dinner.

A Conversation with My Mother I

"Mark, come look at this photograph of Sir Winston Churchill."

My mother has been home about three weeks, seems to be out of her haze this morning. She's staring at this photograph of an old fat guy with a cigar in his mouth. Big deal.

"You know who took this photo? Yousuf Karsh."

I shrug.

"Karsh of Ottawa, that's what he calls himself. Best portrait photographer in the business. The very best. Just look at that, will you? All his photos are in black and white. Mood and light."

Mom sips from her coffee, frowns. It must be cold. She's looking right at me. She looks back at the photo and shakes her head.

"His photographs are like poems, intense and revealing. You look into those eyes and you feel you've learned something about someone. This one of Churchill is his most famous photo, taken early in the War—I'm sure you've seen it. It was on the cover of *Life*, around the year you were born. He looks like a bulldog, gruff and growling, dangerous. *This is what you're up against, Hitler.*"

She chuckles at that. I like seeing my mother revved up; it's been a while.

"Know how Karsh got that photo? Churchill was in a hurry, so he said, 'You've got two minutes to shoot.' Sir Winston sat down with a cigar sticking out of his mouth: *Let's get to it, I haven't got all day.* Karsh didn't like that cigar, so he went over to Churchill as if to brush some lint off his suit, then quietly snatched the cigar out of his mouth and turned around to return to his camera. With his back to the Old Man, Karsh pushed the remote button on the camera cord and caught that famous scowl: Churchill outraged that an upstart photographer would dare yank a cigar out of his mouth."

(To be honest, I'm not sure who Churchill is. But no matter.)

"He's done the greats: Hemingway. Grace Kelly before she got married. Einstein. Bogart. Hepburn. Albert Schweitzer. Popes and kings."

There she goes again—my mother, this small-town girl from Wisconsin, giving me a lecture about some photographer from Canada. How many people in this town know about Yousuf Karsh? One: Mom. Now two: Mom and me. Three weeks ago, she couldn't remember who I was. Now she's telling me about a photograph she first saw in a magazine fifteen years ago.

Thanks to Karsh—or Churchill—my mother has her voice back. May it still be here tomorrow.

What There Is to Tell I

More night sounds. Mom in her drugged three a.m. hysteria, begging Dad for more medicine. As always, he starts off firm, as if this is the night he's not going to give in. She has gone through her dramatic repertoire of reasoning, then begging, then demanding, then shrieking. Now she goes for hysteria, her ultimate theatrical ploy. He still holds his ground. Silence. Maybe my father has won this time. I'm rooting for him to not give in. Her voice shifts, a new tone, lower, guttural, controlled. *Oh yes. You know, Bill. You damn well know.* Her voice grows intense, menacing, almost a growl. *Don't think I won't tell the children about Jimmy MacFarland. What will they think when they learn he's Michele's father? Not you! And believe me: I will tell the children if you don't give me the Thorazine. I will. I'll tell them. Don't try me. Give me the Thorazine!*

My father tries to calm her. *Please, Phyllis. Please.* But she keeps screaming the same thing over and over. *Tomorrow morning I'm telling the children!* That's it. She's won. Two bodies scuffle down the hall to the bathroom. Unlocking of the medicine cabinet, rattling of pills from plastic containers. Running of tap water as a glass is filled. Gulping. He will give her whatever she demands tonight. To shut her up.

Silence.

The next morning at breakfast, Mom's still in bed, will sleep until noon. Dad knows that last night I heard, in my bedroom next to the bathroom. He sips his coffee and folds the front page of the *Times* over.

"Whatever you may have heard last night—it's just the drugs," he says. "I hate these drugs. She was hallucinating, she'll get better. Really. Don't worry about what she said. Tomorrow I'm calling the doctor to see if we can change the medicines. OK?"

I nod.

"Want the sports page?"

"Sure."

A part of the picture that I cannot bear to bring into focus. Something under my parents' bed: the ghost of Jimmy MacFarland, best friend of the family, whom we haven't seen for six months. Whose blond hair and blue eyes match my sister's.

Sister Michele

Until she was fifteen, Michele was frequently and unofficially fostered to Jeannie B's home. Jeannie was gargantuan, loud, diabetic, overwhelming, generous, big-hearted. She had worked at Boys Town, in Nebraska, then migrated west to California with all of the other pioneers. My father hired her to take care of Mother when he was at work or had to go away for business. Jeannie would show up at 7:30 in the morning, send Dad off to work, then *Toodle-Do!* when he came home in the evening. Michele and I both hated being in the same room with Jeannie—her loudness, how she consumed all of the air, how she reminded us that our mother needed someone with her twenty-four hours a day. And always would. When Mother went to the hospital, Michele packed up her clothes and school books and moved in with Jeannie's family. I would see her two or three times a week. Years later Michele told me that Jeannie's husband beat their kids with unpredictable regularity, that their house was filled with land mines waiting for someone to trip them. She hated Jeannie. She hated my parents for sentencing her to live with Jeannie's crazy family from the time she was two. For abandoning her.

For many years Michele and I were too wounded to talk about all of this. We had to find some other way to bridge our twelve-year age difference and be there for each other. It began with baseball before she was three and I was fifteen. Then Frisbee. I left for college when she was five. Every time I returned home, for holidays, summers, we would grab a Frisbee or softball and head for the front lawn, our sanctuary.

Variation on a theme #1: Frisbee. We would march fifty feet apart on our front lawn, then toss the Frisbee for an hour. At first our goal was to make twenty-five tosses without a miss; then fifty; a hundred. Our record was three hundred twenty tosses without a drop. Spectacular leaps, sliding saves, holding the red disk up to show it was a clean catch, back slaps for saving the day.

Variation on a theme #2: Softball. Start off with grounders. Now to the left, then the right. Two steps, three steps, then five, stretching her range. Now put some speed on them, a little pop. How about some tough bouncers, one-hoppers, five feet in front of her? She developed a strong and accurate arm, stretching to get a grounder, pivoting, firing to me, the first baseman. At least a hundred ground balls per session. Fly ball practice: twenty feet up, then forty; above the top of the evergreen tree, at least sixty. Over a hundred feet up, as far as I could throw it. Over her head, making her run backward, an over-the-shoulder catch, à la Willie Mays. Oh yeah! This kid is *good*!

In the early seventies, organized girls' sports were just catching on. Michele became a star on her junior high softball team. She stayed after school for practice, filled her summers with sports. The baseball diamond instead of Jeannie's or home: her salvation. Whenever I was home, we did warm-ups in the front yard. I went to her games and umpired. She once told me she thought sports saved her life. At fifty-five, she still played first base on men-women softball teams.

Michele's childhood was a perfect setup for depression, self-destruction, addiction, choosing bad relationships. But no: she became a decorated policewoman, one of the first on the Long Beach Police force, and she's been married for over thirty years to another cop, a complicated guy who loves her. They raised a happy daughter—an athlete—who became a lawyer. Michele still picks up a bat or racquet or golf club. She has not been into drugs or abusive relationships, has never seen a therapist. Of all three children, without a doubt she has been happiest. Go figure.

Sometime when she was around twelve, in the middle of the night, she heard my mother shouting at my father something about Jimmy MacFarland—this man whom she could not remember—being her father. For many years she carried by herself that auditory image of a scream in the dark. She and I never talked about it until she was much older, probably in her thirties. She asked me, "Do you think the reason Dad put so little energy into caring for me and farmed me out to Jeannie was because he knew that my real father was Jimmy Mac-Farland?" At first, I tried to disabuse her of that notion. "I think Dad was just too overwhelmed by Mom's illness to care for anyone else—including himself."

Over the years Michele kept returning to the Jimmy MacFarland question, and I said that there was no way to know, that the secret died with our father. When genetic testing became easily available and Michele's questions persisted, I suggested she consider it. She sat on the matter for several months, then decided no. Better to live with not knowing—neither answer was less painful than the other.

This is what Michele and I came to understand when she was three and I was fifteen, that summer when we began our baseball and Frisbee marathons: we needed each other. We were each other's sane connection in a family where all other connections were disintegrating beyond repair. We would not abandon each other. We were a gift to each other.

For many years Michele was the reason I came home.

My Cool Day with Johnny Otis

It's a Saturday morning, the October leaves of our apricot trees are red-orange. Dad has gone to the hospital, dropped Michele off at Jeannie's for the day. He'll call from the hospital to tell me if he'll be home for dinner and pick up my sister on the way.

The phone rings. It's eight o'clock, and I'm not awake. Might be Dad. I trip on my PJ's as I straggle to the phone.

"Hello, is this Mark Lyons?"

"Yeah."

"Do you raise pigeons?"

"Yeah—who is this?" I feel a prank coming on.

"Johnny Otis. You know, from *The Johnny Otis Show*? I'm looking for some pigeons, and heard you might be able to help me out."

"Fuck you!" I slam down the receiver. Right. Johnny Otis, L.A.'s Godfather of Rhythm and Blues, on the phone. Johnny Otis, the KFOX DJ who now has his own TV show. Black music that I listen to all the time holding my black transistor radio up to my ear, walking up Downey Avenue. Johnny Otis, who wrote *Roll with Me, Henry* and *So Fine*.

Five minutes later the phone rings again. I pick it up. "Say, man, I'm sorry if I called you too early and all. I put out a call on my show last night that I'm looking for some fancy pigeons for my coop. Someone called and said you're the man." Some asshole trying to talk cool jive, sound like Johnny O. *You're the man*. Right.

I hang up. Who's fucking with me? Someone from school who thinks raising pigeons is for wimps? I need some sleep.

About eleven, still in bed, a knock at the door.

"Sorry for being so persistent, but I hear you got some good birds that you might be willing to sell."

Johnny Otis stands at my front door, with his cool trimmed mustache and his Brylcreemed hair slicked back. That voice, definitely him—I wasn't paying attention when he called me on the phone. Deep and silky smooth, the kind of voice that could sell anything. This voice just happens to sell rhythm and blues to white kids like me.

Damn! Johnny Otis is standing at my door.

The truth is, most of my birds are runts or mixes, except for

Pinky, my muff, and Arnie, my Jacobin with the reddish feathers on his head like a hat from a French court, and Peter my pygmy pouter, or James whom I've trained to home. And they aren't for sale.

"Any idea, then, where I can get some fancy pigeons?" Somehow *fancy* doesn't fit Johnny Otis. Maybe *fine*, but not *fancy*.

Johnny Otis and I spend the rest of the day driving all over Southern California, visiting pigeon coops filled with English Trumpeters, Danish Suabians, Turbits, Carriers, Archangels, Croppers, Rollers, Danzig Highflyers. Only place I've seen these birds before is at the L.A. County Fair. Everywhere we stop we ask the breeder to tell us of other breeders he knows, and we follow the trail from Anaheim to Altadena to Pico Rivera to Fullerton. Together we discover the underworld of pigeon crazies, who tell us the stories of their birds—what line they came from, what competitions they won in races or county fairs, how the breeders got hooked raising them when they were kids, how they train their tumblers and homers. Johnny Otis tells me he's new to pigeons; but he's discerning, not just gobbling up birds because they're pretty. He asks the breeders lots of questions, scopes them out to see if he trusts them, then buys one or two birds and moves on.

About two hours into our trip, I realize something: Johnny Otis is white—he's got a nice tan, but this guy is definitely white. Listening to him on the radio, with his disc jockey jive and playing all this rhythm and blues, writing *So Fine*, I assumed he was black. I mean he talks like a black guy, he's doing black music. I really want to ask him about all of this, but have no idea about how to talk about it. I've never talked to a black person, much less a white person who I thought was black. A white person who acts black.

By four o'clock. Johnny's got ten birds in wire crates and cardboard boxes in the back of his station wagon. Our last stop is the grungiest leg of our trip—Bell Gardens. Behind a tile warehouse and next to a lumberyard we find this bunch of coops, like a Brazilian shanty town I saw pictures of in *National Geographic*. But inside, the coops are immaculate, no shit on the ground, water feeders clean, nest boxes like perfect little apartments. We find the owner, a Mexican who talks about his birds like they're his children. He doesn't give them names, though, just calls them by their band numbers—

"Number 29 there, see how *elegante* she is, she's *mi reina, la* queen of the coop."

Johnny finishes negotiating with the guy and turns to me.

"Pick one."

I assume he's asking me to pick out a bird I think he should buy.

"No, man, I mean it. Pick one out for your coop. My payment for being my guide today."

I feel like the time when I was eleven and Mr. Jamison brought the baseball shoes over to my house to try on. Cinderella and the glass slipper. I put my hands up on the mesh wire of the coop and watch the birds. A beautiful pure white fantail is strutting his stuff, trying to drive his lady-love into a nest box. Seriously courting, his tail spreads in a perfect white fan, catching the sun.

"That one."

Johnny Otis and I pull up to the curb of my house about five o'clock. Dad's car's not in the driveway. Johnny hands me the cardboard box with my fantail, puts down the hatch, extends his hand. "Thanks, man. Really. No way I'd have found these birds without you. Today was far-out. I might be looking you up again."

"Sure, anytime. You know where to find me." I'm thinking nobody would believe I'm telling Johnny Otis *You know where to find me.*

"Stay cool."

Oh, yeah.

A half hour later my father comes home from picking up Michele. "How'd your day go?"

"OK. Do you know Johnny Otis?"

"Never heard of him."

My father has never heard of Johnny Otis. Amazing.

"I got a new pigeon today. A fantail."

My father nods. "You hungry?"

He doesn't want to know about my fantail. Tomorrow I'll call Richie Cary and tell him.

JOHNNY O. POSTSCRIPT: In my seventies, more than fifty years after my first and only encounter with Johnny Otis, I decided it was time to learn blues harmonica. After studying with a teacher for a year, I headed south to Clarksdale, Mississippi, where Robert Johnson sold his soul to the devil at the crossroads of Routes 61 and 49. Twelve hours a day for five days at a blues harmonica camp learning riffs and scales, cross-harping, practicing with a house band, finally playing at Ground Zero, a famous blues club. Pure heaven. On the way home, I stopped at the Blues Museum in Memphis, learned about the greats, bought some CDs, and strolled the Blues Hall of Fame. There was my man: Johnny O., named to the Hall in 2000, along with Stevie Ray Vaughn. I started to tap the shoulder of the guy standing next to me: *Hey, I knew Johnny Otis way back when. We spent the day together buying pigeons!* Then realized he'd probably be thinking to himself, *Who the hell is this crazy old white head?* So I decided I'd keep secret my one degree of separation from greatness.

The Snow Goose

1997: My mother had been dead for seven years and my father had a few months or a few weeks to live. On my monthly visits from the East Coast to be with Dad, I began to pack the belongings of our household, bringing an extra piece of luggage to fill with papers, books, photos. On a steamy August night after Dad had finally fallen asleep, I visited the mantel. My fingers ran the backs of my mother's books like keys on a piano. The same books that had been in the same place since my childhood. I picked up Paul Gallico's *The Snow Goose*, half an inch thick with a ripped gold and white cover, and put it in my backpack. On the plane home to Philadelphia, forty years after my mother had insisted that this was the one book I must read, I pulled out *The Snow Goose* and began.

The story is about a hunchbacked old bearded man, Philip Rhayader, who has a crippled left arm "like the claw of a bird," and lives in an abandoned lighthouse hidden in the salt marshes of the English Channel. Rhayader is a hermit and a fisherman who shares his sanctuary with birds who have been shot for sport by avid English hunters. At the end of each smoke-filled autumn day when the hunters have gone home, Rhayader skiffs into the marshes and gathers the injured ducks and geese hiding in the reeds, gently placing the shocked creatures in gunnysacks. During the quiet winter he nurses the birds back to health and, in the spring, sets them free to head north. On page fifteen, Fritha, the twelve-year-old daughter of a village fisherman, brings the old man a snow goose, blown seventeen hundred miles off course by a Canadian storm and shot in the marshes of England. The girl has heard the stories of the ogre in the lighthouse who has the power to heal injured things. She and the hunchback nurse the snow goose back to health, and every fall for the next five years they are reunited when the goose returns to spend the winter. It is a secret friendship unknown to the villagers, the only friendship the cripple has. But Fritha turns seventeen and sees her growing body reflected in the old man's intense eyes. She is frightened, and stops returning to the lighthouse with the fall migration. It is 1940 now, and the English are at war with the Germans. The BBC flashes a call for all able-bodied seamen to sail across the Channel to Dunkirk to rescue the beached soldiers from the merciless slaughter of the enemy hunters. Rhayader sets sail in his sixteen-foot boat, followed by the snow goose. After three days on the water the great white bird returns to the lighthouse, alone.

As I thumbed through the pages wondering about the fate of Fritha and the goose and the old man, I noticed that certain paragraphs were bracketed with notes that said *start* and *end*, in my mother's proud angular handwriting—at one time she had used the book for a public reading. On the cover page the book was dated December 1942, the month and year that I was born.

WINTER 1958

A Conversation with My Mother II

Home from school, a drizzly winter afternoon. I drop my book bag by the door, fix myself a PB&J, pour a glass of milk, and sit on the couch across from my mother.

"How did your day go?" she says. Her day must be going OK—it's unusual when she asks about mine.

"OK. Leota Haas really kicks butt in English, but I think I'm learning a lot." I got the luck of the draw and ended up in Leota Haas's tenth-grade English class. Miss Haas (that's what I call her in school) and I have this history—The Little Theater and all—but she never mentions it. I think she has a secret fondness for me, and I try to reward her by working really hard on my paper about Arthur Miller's *The Crucible*. Once she asked how Mom was doing. "She's OK," I said. What else was there to say?

Mother doesn't want to talk about Leota Haas. Out of the blue she says, "I've been thinking . . . I know you're concerned about being so short. But don't worry—boys mature later than girls. You've got plenty of time to grow."

(I don't really need to talk about being short.)

"You'll hit your growth spurt, you'll see. Within the next year, I bet. Then you'll just shoot up like a weed."

(OK. OK. I got it: I'll be the shortest kid in the class just a bit longer. By this time next year, I'll be six feet tall.)

"There's really no need to see a doctor. He'll just tell you to be patient."

(Who said anything about seeing a doctor?)

"A year ago, there wasn't any girl your age shorter than you, except for Ann Hegardt. Now that you're growing, there'll be lots of girls shorter than you."

(Right. Lots of girls . . . Lots. I'm holding my breath.)
"You know, it's a proven fact: small men have big penises."
(???????)
"Napoleon was only five-foot-two. And look what he was able to accomplish. And I read somewhere he had a very large penis."
(What just happened here?)
"So don't worry, you'll be fine."
"Can I go now? I have to check on my birds."

Handwriting on the Wall

After school, I walk over to Ann Hegardt's house. She's been acting a little weird lately, maybe because her mother died over the winter. We never really talked about it. I realize I don't know how to talk about such things. I know I should say *something*. Maybe that's what being an adult is—knowing what to say when somebody dies. She doesn't act like she expects me to say something deep or important—maybe she doesn't know how to talk about it either. But I know she must *feel* something. But feeling is different from saying.

Mostly with her I feel like I'm fumbling. I have no idea how to do this boy-girl thing.

I knock on Ann's door. She lets me in and walks to the small empty closet by the living room. She has a pen in her hand, and starts to write something on the back wall of the closet.

"What are you writing?"
"Oh nothing, just scribbling."
"Can I see?"
"Not really."
"Not really? Come on, let me see."
"OK."

She backs out of the closet, and I enter to inspect the writing. It's very small, and I have to get close to see what it says.

Chris Chris Chris Chris Chris

I know this guy. Tall Chris. Cute Chris with the wavy hair. Cute, the way girls like cute. But kind of dumb, I have always thought. I back out of the closet.

Ann looks at me. *Chris?* I am waiting for her to tell me something, some kind of break-up message.

She enters the closet, pen in hand, and writes *Chris* on the wall one more time.

That's it? I'm thinking to myself.

I have the feeling that something cruel is happening, that I should be hurt.

"Want some potato chips?" she says.

"No, I think I'll just go home."

"OK."

She closes the door behind me.

That's it. Is this the way people break up? Shouldn't I feel sad, or angry, or surprised, or jealous—*something?*—about my first girlfriend breaking up with me? Where's the heartbreak? I want to feel something, but nothing's there.

Now *that's* sad.

Studee

Richie Cary's not excitable, but today he's excited. "Something I gotta show you . . . " He leads me out back, I figure he's got some new animal, maybe a turkey or a goat. He opens the garage door instead, walks to the middle of the garage, and grabs the edges of a canvas tarp laid over this giant hump. He snaps the tarp off like a magician revealing a rabbit in a hat, and there it is, his pride and joy: his '49 Studebaker. His *Studee.* He's replaced the smashed-in right fender, knocked out and filled the dents on the top and side panels, replaced the cracked glass panel in the right rear window, sanded it all down, and primed the body with reddish paint. Ready for a paint job.

How does he do that?

"Damn, my man. She's a beaut." I know Richie wants me to say that; but I mean it, too.

"Now I just got to finish up the engine, set the clutch, and put in a new drive shaft. Then she's ready to roll."

Over the next couple of months, Richie lets me help him rebuild the engine, cleaning carburetor parts in the kerosene bucket, slipping on new piston rings, bolting down the new block. I am completely ignorant when it comes to fixing cars, but Richie just calls me the virgin mechanic, he'll show me the way. After we work for a couple of hours on his car, we wash our hands in kerosene, grease dripping like black blood, then slide into the front seat and turn on the radio. Richie pops the top of a Coke bottle, takes a swig, and passes it to me. I tip my head back and gurgle the Coke down. My friend Johnny Otis, spinning his 45's on KFOX, announces *This one's for all the young ladies over in Compton lookin' for their Sugar Man—sweet and slow, my friends, sweet and slow*. The voice of Jimmy Reed singing *Honest I Do* oozes out of the speaker on the dash.

As we clean and polish and reassemble the pieces of Richie's Studee, we begin to imagine its shiny pointed nose cruising down the highway, climbing mountains in second gear, zipping through desert mirages. *Adios L.A.*, the corrals of this cow town can't keep us home anymore. In the front seat of his not-quite-ready-for-the-highway Studee, we begin to plan our first road trip. For next summer, when we're sixteen and have our licenses.

"Let's go to Tijuana."

"No, man, women shoot ping-pong balls out of their snatches down there. How about up the coast to San Francisco?"

"If we really had balls, we'd head for New York City."

"New York City, then."

"Maybe we'll never come back."

"May-be . . ."

Record

One late night or very early morning, after I had soothed my dying father to sleep, I went to the bookshelf in the bedroom where I had slept as a boy, searching for familiar titles. I came upon a simple, thin, red and black bound book: *Record*.

On the inside cover written in primitive cursive:

Mark Lyons
Pigeon Raiser
My Accounts on My Pigeons

The first entry was dated December 12, 1953, when I was eleven:

Bought 2 pigeons from Richard Cary.
Spent 63 cents for food grit and supplies.

Over the next three and one-half years there were many entries: describing my trips to Thompson's Feed to buy food and supplies and delousing powder; enlarging my pen; being told by the health department that my pen was too close to the neighbor's house (minimum 35 feet); the process and progress of building my new pen, which I now called a *coop* (digging postholes and sinking the posts in cement, framing, covering with redwood clapboard, stretching wire over the fly pen, building a one-way trapdoor for my birds to return home); the litany of pigeon disappearances and deaths (primarily in the jaws of cats and rats, maybe a gopher); my coop becoming overcrowded (up to 36 birds) and selling off some to keep the population down to "around 25"; matings and new pairings; adoption of pigeons from other coops that came around looking for food; inspection of droppings to detect disease; natural disasters resulting in leaks and drownings of babies; dates eggs laid and hatched; books on pigeon husbandry purchased from General Mills; training my birds to fly and return to the coop; training James to long-distance home; descriptions of the breeds of my pigeons (homer, racer, trumpeter, tumbler, pygmy pouter, muff, fantail); photographing my birds; cat-proofing with smaller mesh wires (the cats would reach through the wire and pull the pigeons' heads off); expenditures for purchasing pigeons, food, supplies, coop construction, and repair.

Some of the names I gave my pigeons, according to the *Record*: Elmer, Oscar, Jessey, James, Knip, Tuck, Roger, Ralph, Bonita, Bonito, Pronto (a racer), Tuffy, Rainy (found near-drowned in a storm), Pinky, Blackie, Happy, Tommy, Wimpy (?), Brownie.

My pigeons are coming along fine. They are producing some good babies, but I hope they don't have too many. I am having a little trouble with twins (brother and sister) mating, but I think I have the problem solved. I replace their eggs with a good pair's eggs.
Mating: Most pigeons mate with other birds that they like.

Sleeping: They usually sleep on their stomach in the nest.
Rusting [sic]—they usually sleep on one leg, with the other pulled up
under their feathers.

And more observations on Diseases, Seeing (theory), Bathing, Drinking, Eating.

In the back of the book was a page entitled *My Favorite Pigeons*:

Elmer—my first; Tuffy (trumpeter)—playful; Pinky—most personality;
Jessey—who died while trying to save his babies; Brownie—Elmer's
great niece.

Between the pages of the *Record* was a 3" × 5" card, with the name *Pinky* on the top left corner and the following information: breed (muff); color (white); date of purchase (August 22, 1954); first eggs laid; offspring. She had pink feet, covered with feathers, hence her name and description. She was my favorite bird. I kept similar cards for all of my pigeons.

The last entry in the *Record* was April 15, 1957:

I banded my birds today.

Two weeks before this last note was written, my mother made her first trip to the mental hospital.

How to Delouse a Pigeon

Pigeons have at least 4,000 feathers, counting primaries, secondaries, and down. A lot of territory for lice to hide out in. Lice are the scourge of the coop: they suck so much blood that the birds grow weak and anemic and infected with diseases that attack the brain. Miniature vampires. Bird lice are so small that if there is just one you won't notice it. But they like to hang out together, socializing and sucking blood, and a pack is easier to spot than a loner.

I do a louse check on my pigeons every month. The best way to find the predators is to raise up the wing and inspect the white armpit, which shows tiny red spots if the lice have come. If they are there, you can be sure that they are everywhere, tucked in the barbs, hiding at the base of the feathers, crawling around the eyes. If you find them on one bird, you know every bird's got them; no sense in even looking, the whole coop's infested.

There is a trick to delousing pigeons. First you need to know something about how birds preen themselves. To begin, a bird tips its head back and dips its beak into a small gland hidden on its rump, at the base of the tail feathers. The gland is a fountain of oil, the bird's Brylcreem. After dousing its beak with the heavy oil, the bird takes one single feather at its base and runs it through the beak, all the way to the end of the feather. The motion spreads a thin film of oil over the feather for conditioning and waterproofing and reconnects all the barbs so it is solid again. Like closing a zipper, like Velcro. Or combing your hair. Birds spend hours each day preening, dipping their beaks in their oil glands, returning to the next feather on the wing or breast or back or wherever. Thousands of trips to the well, thousands of feathers combed perfectly and coated with sealant.

So, here's the trick: Sodium fluoride powder kills lice. It comes in a round cardboard container with holes punched at the top, like Parmesan cheese. Sixty cents at the feed store. First you have to dust behind the head and neck, the only places the bird can't reach with its beak. Careful to avoid the eyes. Then dust under each wing, the favorite louse hideout. Finally, take the powder and rub it into the oil gland at the base of the tail. Let the pigeon do all the rest of the work, it won't miss a feather.

A little dab'll do ya.

After the Storm I

When Bill left to live in his own apartment, I moved into the den. I like it here—it has one-inch-thick sandblasted oak paneling Dad put in, and it's bigger than my old bedroom, with bay windows overlooking the side yard. And it's down the hall from my parents' bedroom, rather than right next door—easier to shut out all the night stuff. The TV is along a large wall that is graced with a Monet print in a Woolworth's frame—*Rouen Cathedral at Dusk*—a gift from my Aunt. *Tant*, as we call her, has only lived in Wisconsin and Southern California and has never traveled—but she knows the nineteenth-century streets of Impressionist Paris better than she knows the streets of Downey.

All from reading art books. She lives in the wrong country and the wrong century, speaks the wrong language. Her entire house is covered with cheap framed posters of Impressionist paintings, from floor to ceiling, every room. Her own museum, which donated a Monet painting to our den when it was constructed two years ago.

However, the great paneled wall of the den, the west wall with no windows where my bed is, has had no hanging ornament. Until last month, when my mother returned from her most recent winter stint at Edgemont—her third visit—carrying a simple pine-framed 24" × 30" painting: *After the Storm*. Signed, *Phyllis Teague Lyons*. My father carefully hung her painting on the empty wall space overlooking my bed.

My mother has never painted anything in her life. She knows nothing about painting, nor cares, always sneaking out on the inevitable conversations begun by Tant, who wants to debate the worth of Manet vs. Monet or whether pointillism is post-Impressionist or pre-Expressionist.

After the Storm, by Phyllis Teague Lyons, is a paint-by-numbers winter seascape, with the sun breaking through giant translucent waves just before they crash on the rocky shore as dark clouds disappear on the horizon. Blue and white and green foam menaces in the foreground, the storm passes in the background. One night after Dad and Michele had gone to sleep, I looked at the painting for a long time, trying to imagine my mother seated alone in the corner of the green-tiled sun room of Edgemont, windows overlooking a courtyard with silent people stumbling toward cement benches, no conversation. I imagined music, too—mother proudly brags that the famous actor and pianist Oscar Levant (he of *An American in Paris* and other movies and his own TV show) is also an inmate at Edgemont, and often sits at the piano and entertains the silent and drugged troops. Unable to read, "because I was too nervous," mother took up painting. I imagine how she squints at the tiny numbers printed on the canvas, runs her pointed brush along the plastic vials of paint until she finds the matching number, dips the brush and wipes off the excess paint, then turns her whole body at the waist to the painting, leans forward, eyes six inches from the canvas, and mechanically applies #6 here, #6 under the breaking wave, #6 for the shadow as the foam flattens out on the sand, #6 to contrast the pointed rock against the big boulder in the left-hand corner, making sure she has all the #6's done before she cleans the brush with thinner and begins with #4.

MOM HAS RETURNED to Edgemont, after just a month at home. Maybe she wants to paint some more. Maybe she loves Oscar Levant's music and jokes. Maybe Edgemont has become her home. It's just Dad and me, Michele was dropped off last night at Jeannie's again for the weekend.

Dad and I have not solved the mystery of what happened last night as I slept under my mother's painting. He thinks it might have been a mild earthquake, or maybe I pulled the painting off the wall in the middle of a dream, or the picture hook just gave out. This is what I do remember: I am awakened in the dark by a searing blow between my eyes, thinking I have been struck in the head by a hammer or some other weapon, and I swing my fists frantically to defend myself against an intruder. In the dark I find no shadows of another being, just the sound of the giant framed picture tumbling over the oak coffee table and smacking the floor. As I rub away the pain between my eyes with the palm of my hand, I feel something seeping between my fingers, viscous like slightly warmed oil. Almost awake, I begin to figure out what has happened. The warm fluid oozes down my forearm and begins to drip off my elbow onto the sheet. Suddenly I am very rational.

"Dad," I call down the hall to him asleep in the bed vacated by my mother. "Dad, wake up."

"What's happening?" The deep-voiced rumble of the half-awake.

"There's been an accident. I need your help, I can't get up. Can you bring a cold washcloth?"

My father shuffles to the bathroom, I hear the water running, the wrung washcloth dripping on porcelain. The den door opens.

"Can you turn on the light? I think there's going to be some blood. I'm OK—I think."

"Lie still," Dad says, as he carefully washes the blood from my face and arm, between the webs of my fingers, running to the bathroom and returning with a fresh rinsed cloth, giving me one of his white handkerchiefs to put pressure on the wound. I think to myself how only old people use handkerchiefs, how they fold them over and over to cover the snot until there are no folds left. I close my eyes and feel his gentle attention. Lying there in the wet sheets, I am almost glad for the injury. A gift from my mother.

Dad calls Dr. Steere and asks him if I should go to the emergency room. "Are you crazy?" says Dr. Steere, "They're butchers down there. Bring him down to my office and we'll sew him up. I open at 8:30."

"Pretty deep," says Dr. Steere a few hours later. "We'll have to do two layers of sutures. Ever seen anyone stitched up?"

"Just a cat, these are my first stitches ever."

"Well, it's about time. Now you've got your badge of honor. You'll have to make up a good story about defending your family against robbers with just your bare hands. Want me to leave the bandage off so everyone can see the stitches?"

"Will the scar ever go away?"

"Depends. Some deep scars stay forever, become another line in your face. Some wash out with the next summer's sun. This one looks like it might be here to stay. Actually, it makes your face look kind of interesting, gives you some character. Like you've seen something of life."

On the way home Dad says, "Don't tell your mother what happened, hear? No need to upset her." I think about reminding him that Mother is back in the hospital; but, no.

Father stops the car in the driveway and goes directly to the garage, sorting through tin cans until he finds an extra-large picture hook. He then heads for the den, drives the hook into the great wall with a hammer, and puts *After the Storm* back where it belongs. Then he peels the white bloodstained sheets off the bed and carries them, arms outstretched, to the clothes washer, switches the button to *Cold*, pours in an exact cup of Clorox, adds Tide, and turns the switch to *On*.

"You should get some sleep," he says.

I wake up after a long nap, afternoon now, finally no headache, and look out the bay window of the den. In the side yard the sheets gently bellow on the clothesline, loose sails of a boat coming about, scarred with brown stains.

After the Storm II

In 1993, three years after my mother died at seventy-nine, my wife Jeane Ann and I were taking a ferry to a Maine Island. As I bought my tickets at the ferry house, I glanced over the shoulder of the ticket master, and there on the wall in all of its paint-by-numbers glory: *After the Storm*. I would recognize that painting anywhere. I stared until the ticket-master said "Next." I stepped aside for the next passenger and continued to look at the painting, sucked into the waves as if in an undertow. The ferry horn sounded. Last call.

Jeane Ann took my hand, "Time to go." On the ferry, crossing over another ocean, amid wind, waves, sun, I was somewhere else. Jeane Ann, ever watchful of my moods, asked me if I was OK. "I will be," I said. And by the time we landed on the island, I was.

Crash and Burn

Home from school, an empty house. I open the trapdoor to my pigeon coop and lie on my back in the sun, a lizard on a rock. Pure white clouds moving above the naked limbs of the dead pepper tree overhead give me a reading on the wind speed: about fifteen miles per hour, from the east.

Six of my birds immediately fly to their gnarled pepper tree perches forty feet above, shaking their feathers, preening, stretching, pre-flight preparation. Anthony is the first to leave the branch, two flaps and a glide. Instead of circling in ever-widening rings, the usual practice of pigeons, Anthony flies three tight laps to loosen his muscles, then climbs vertically, higher and higher, almost straight up. At least four hundred feet, an insect against the cool blue sky. Suddenly he stops flying as if shot, rolls, tucks his wings and feet, tumbles over and over. Straight down. A faint whistle as he picks up speed, rush of air through barbed feathers. Flashes of sun reflected in orange eyes. Somersaulting over and over, at least four seconds, now sixty feet above the ground. Wings open to break his fall, swoop out of the dive.

But today, a sound I have never heard before: the collision of bird falling seventy miles per hour and dead tree branch. Anthony crashes

at my feet, tries to upright himself with outstretched wing tips, stag-
gers sideways, collapses with open unblinking eyes. I hold his chest to
my ear. No heartbeat.

I bought Anthony two years ago from Douglas Donner, this older
kid Richie introduced me to. "Let me warn you," Donner said, "he's
a tumbler. It's in their blood—they ain't happy if they ain't tumbling,
that's all they want to do. Bred that way. In England they have contests to see whose bird can tumble the longest, use binoculars and
stopwatches, count how many rolls they do, how long they fall. Big
money, serious shit. Of course, the bird can't hit the ground or it's
disqualified. Eventually they all die, get careless or maybe their gyro-
scope gets all fucked up on accounta all that spinning. No way around
it—they're gonna crash and burn."

"Maybe I should just keep him in the cage." I didn't like the idea
of raising a bird to send to its certain death. Like breeding bulls in
Mexico.

"Nah, why would you want to do that? You'd have a miserable
bird on your hands, pacing, fighting the other birds, plucking its own
feathers out. It'd never mate. It's kind of neat when you think about
it, dying doing what they like best. Like I want to have a heart attack
when I'm on top of some woman."

"How much?"

"Eight bucks, he's not a pure-breed, I wasn't watching the coop
too carefully. Remember, don't count on this bird being part of your
flock too long. But look at it this way: while all them other birds are
doing their circle thing, living the dull life for six or eight years, this
little guy will know the rush of tempting fate every day. Even if it's
for a lousy year or two. He'll pull up from enough dives to fill a lifetime, then go down in a blaze of glory. What would you rather do?"

"I only got six bucks."

"Deal."

For two years Anthony dipped and rolled, a sight to behold. Then
a blaze of glory. I run my fingers along the edges of Anthony's wings:
one jagged bone juts out, first contact with the tree branch. Otherwise
no blood or cuts. Hidden injuries. I scrape away the brown prickly
leaves under the olive tree, dig a hole, two shovelfuls. Tuck Anthony's
wings along his body, lay him sideways in the hole, push back the dirt

with the side of my shoe, tamp it, rake back the leaves. Usually, when my birds are killed by cats or don't return from a training flight, I'm up all night and don't want to go to school, embarrassed by my red eyes. With Anthony I don't feel sad. Maybe Donner's right. *Crash and burn. Enough dives to fill a lifetime.*

Dusk now, wind and color seep from the sky. The other birds circle twice more, glide down to the trapdoor of the coop, hover around the food troughs. Out front Dad's car rolls into the driveway, a door slams. I walk around the side of the house. My father and I go through our ritual greeting.

"Hey, how was school?"

"OK. How's Mom?"

"'Bout the same, not any worse."

"When's she coming home?"

"Doctors didn't say. They can't quite figure out why she isn't getting better quicker. She's pretty exhausted, maybe we're pushing her too much."

More of Dad's codes: my mother isn't coming home soon, they don't know what's wrong. Hidden injuries. Maybe sometime she'll fly again. Maybe not.

Reunion

July 1978: My mother—a hermit who had cut all friends and extended family out of her life for two decades, who had never been back to her home in Wisconsin since we moved to California in 1945—decided that she would return to her hometown of Mineral Point for her fiftieth high school reunion. She was terrified of flying and had never seen the inside of an airplane, even though her husband designed them for a living. So, she and my father would make the fifty-five-hour train trip from Los Angeles to Milwaukee, rent a car, and drive north to see relatives where she grew up, visit her best friend Bets from college, and reunite with seventeen sixty-eight-year-old surviving high school classmates whom she had not spoken to in fifty years.

Before her breakdown, my mother regaled my brother and me with stories of living in rural Wisconsin: about her father the beloved postmaster of Mineral Point; about her mother and love of her life,

Birdie, who died of breast cancer at thirty-nine, and how Birdie
threw her out of the church window for making too much noise during services. About how Birdie's sister, my Aunt Gladys—Tant—got
lost in a snowstorm walking home from the school where she taught,
almost died, and was rescued—but not before frostbite had destroyed
her right hand and turned her into a lefty. And then there was her
best friend ever, Bets, "the only person in the world who was smart
enough to keep up with me." As much as she loved the place where
she grew up, after her parents died, my mother could not bear to go
back. Yet suddenly, after living in a cocoon for twenty-one years, and
away from her Wisconsin for over forty, she decided to return home.

Somehow this decision inspired me: I would join my parents in
Milwaukee, and we would hit the road together. We'd ride through
my mother's old haunts: first Warwick, where she was born, then on
to Mineral Point, where she grew up. Then we would head up to my
father's home in Appleton, where his father grew up being the best
friend of Ehrich Weiss, a.k.a. Harry Houdini. There on the road I
would find a way to connect to my mother, to find her as she used
to be before it all fell apart. I would sit in the back seat, the mic of
my battery-powered cassette tape recorder held between the two of
them, and ask questions about family and rural Wisconsin and how
a Jew and a Gentile found true love at the University of Wisconsin. I
wrote them a long, enthusiastic letter outlining my plans for them to
be my tour guides.

My hopes: we would forget the sad and awful present by sharing
their past. This would be a new start, away from our home in California that had become a prison for us all. And it was, but not in the way
that I had expected. Here are some of the notes I made on that trip:

> Watching the rituals Mom and Dad share daily, especially
> the complicated rituals around her medicine. She has separate
> matching luggage for her medicine. Filled with twenty-two bot-
> tles (I counted them) used daily. Varying doses of Thorazine and
> Valium and Phenergan to put her to sleep; more Thorazine and
> Ritalin to get her going in the morning; medicines for her arthri-
> tis and reflux. She very deliberately places her medicine at the
> back of her mouth with thumb and first finger, tilts head back,

puts the water glass to her mouth and swallows with great difficulty. In her nightgown, she sits in her chair while Dad, fully dressed and ready to go, dutifully brings her coffee, then Thorazine, then Ritalin. Dad helps Mom rise to go to the bathroom; an hour later she appears, and our day has begun. Sucked into this ritual vortex still, at thirty-five, I have to flee and go to my hotel room next door. I am crazed, out of control. I throw things. I scream. If I become a participant I will drown.

So, I become the observer, and this is what I see: a sad, pathetic slow-motion couple, life filled with tragic rituals repeated daily. Can they feel me just watching? I begin to see Dad differently, a new perspective. He is not a victim, he has chosen to participate in these rituals, in some way has helped perpetuate them, encouraged them. He chooses this, just as Mom does, recommits to his choices every day. Years ago, they both passed the point of no return, passed the place where it was thinkable to get up in the morning and make a different choice. Did new choices demand too much bravery? I feel impatient with him for having made the same limited, painful, yet safe and rewarding choice for so many years.

On my visits home, one way I have found to connect to my father is through listening to him tell of his bitterness and frustration and loneliness of the last twenty years. I am sympathetic, hug him, commiserate, participate in the scenario that he is victim and martyr. But somehow, in the middle of Wisconsin where their relationship began forty-six years ago, I don't want to be part of an alliance that says we can't be free of her, that we are victims with no choices. I don't want to believe that my life will inevitably be filled with endless daily lonely rituals.

I feel a shift in me as I watch my parents prepare for another day that neither will find joy in. Over the next four days there are moments when I begin to understand the shift, to name it.

Moment # 1: Sunday afternoon, we are having a Sunday picnic at cousin Eunice's house in Warwick, a one-intersection village, where my mother spent the first six years of her life. On one corner is the Grange Hall, another the church, another a cemetery where her parents are buried. The remaining corner is empty, the location of her father's long-gone general store. The place where she was born has not changed at all, and she sits at a table eating, surrounded by four generations of family. Stories fly back and forth between twenty-three cousins and aunts and uncles, stories of farms and children gone to the big city, of snowstorms and long-dead, a kind of joy in the place. My mother sits at the table, white head slightly bent over her food, obese and puff-faced, agitated, Thorazine-tongued, intently looking at her cigarette. Not participating, not taking it in nor observing; there but not present. Alone. She came all this way from California and has nothing to say. I wonder if she notices, if she imagines what her role in the conversation would have been twenty-five years ago. I excuse myself from a conversation with Aunt Judy, walk around the table, give Mom a hug and say, "All of this must be overwhelming at times." She says, "Yes, I am tired." I ache for her, do not want to expose her aloneness. I am not furious nor frustrated nor embarrassed, I don't wish I could disappear. This is all new to me: to feel a spontaneous sadness for my mother, for what her life has become. Is this the first time I have cared about her, for her, in twenty-one years? I feel free of what? Being a victim?

Moment # 2: The Teague home. Before the Teague General Store went bankrupt and they moved to Mineral Point, my mother's father built a house for his wife, a work of craftsmanship "befitting such a fine woman." In an abandoned weed-covered corn field we find the house where Mother lived until she was six, splintered peeling clapboards, porch collapsed, shingles missing. My mother refuses to get out of the car, cannot move herself to those memories. She waits as I find an open door and explore the house in wonder, taking photos. Even in its decomposition, the house is beautiful, oak woodwork, a handmade porch swing, wide pine floors, ornate grillwork over the heating registers. A lone rocking chair sits in the living room. After ten minutes she orders my father to tell me we have to leave. Now. I climb into the back seat excited, describing how beautiful the house is inside. I turn on the recorder and ask her to tell me stories of living in that house, of her childhood, of her life before. She says nothing except, "Can we go now, Bill." An old script, the point where I usually feel rage when she shuts us down. But today I understand: old memories of times that were good, of a six-year-old girl who would grow up to found a community theater and love good books, who could not envision life inside a mental hospital—memories that force comparisons of what might have been and what has come to be—are unbearable for her.

Moment # 3: My mother wants me to meet Bets, her best friend from college. After getting off the phone with Bets, my mother is animated—her friend's deep voice and gruff laugh had not changed in thirty-five years. Bets meets us at her front door leaning on the crutches she's used since contracting polio in her thirties. She is like my mother had described her when she entertained Bill and me about their college days together. Her hands go in different directions as she talks with irony about the fate of crippled widows and how crutches are great martial arts weapons. She tells of her plans to visit her children, classes she is enrolled in, the next thing she wants to learn, how her husband met Frank Lloyd Wright on a plane from Chicago to Milwaukee and became his portrait photographer. She jokes, makes *double entendres*, asks my mother if she remembers the time that . . . or the time that. . . . She wants to know how my mother is, what she's been up to, what she thinks about President Carter, about her kids. What the hell is Southern California like, anyway? Tell me. Tell me.

I really like Bets, want to join in on the conversation, ride along on her energy. But, no, this is their conversation; so, I watch and listen. Bets begins to notice: how my mother doesn't know when her friend is joking or being ironic, how she seems puzzled and nods when she really isn't following the conversation. Bets realizes that my mother—who was so quick and irreverent and playful with words and ideas way back when— isn't keeping up. There is an imperceptible pause when all of us understand what's happening. I can feel Bets shift gears, slowing down her rapid-fire speech, eliminating innuendo and double meaning and irony, her words becoming concrete and direct

133

as the conversation slows down to a pace my mother can sustain. Nothing said in this recognition that we all share, too painful to acknowledge.

Trying to fall asleep back at our hotel, I remember the theater parties that ended twenty years ago, my mother entertaining the troops with her raucous readings of poetry, twisting her body into metaphors in charades, cornering Harry Francisco to play a part in *The Monkey's Paw*, waxing poetic about how Adlai Stevenson was the last great statesman. Bets would have loved it.

I have not recorded one conversation with my parents. Nor will I.

Moment #4: On their way to Milwaukee to take the train back to California, my parents drop me off at the airport. They say good-bye and head for the parking lot. I watch them through the floor-to-ceiling plate glass, like seeing a movie on a theater screen. She moves with a painful snail-pace hobble, held up by my father on her right side, a gold-headed ebony cane on her left—the cane that belonged to my great-grandfather Mark Lyons—hence my name—who co-founded the synagogue in Appleton with the father of Harry Houdini. A bent-over snail-motion couple inching toward the horizon, shuffling in their sad tragedy. They turn a corner and are gone, as if the movie is over and the credits will begin to roll. I am crying.

My trips home have always been dangerous endeavors, sucking me back into a world that I am sure I will recapitulate. When my father would drop me off at LAX at the end of a visit, I felt out of control, desperate to escape to my home in Philadelphia, where I could begin to re-convince myself that my parents' life was not mine. But this time, in this Wisconsin airport, I do not need to run, do not feel netted by the drag lines of their story.

I am crying for them, not for me.

What There Is to Tell II

Hunched in her chair, sucking on a Pall Mall, my mother stares at the fireplace with no fire. Dad sits across the room on his couch, his stocking feet resting on the coffee table, outlined by the light cast through the small side window. I sip some hot instant Nestlé's chocolate, cross my legs on the comforting carpet, and open the sports page to read about how they're rebuilding the Coliseum to be the temporary home field for the Dodgers when they finally come this spring.

There's something in the room, a silent kind of tension, the way things are absolutely still before an earthquake. Like when I was ten and woke up in my bunk bed before dawn on our vacation in Sunset Beach. Something in the air was not right: no breeze, no crickets, no waves. Nothing. Then, boom! The Tehachapi earthquake knocked me to the floor.

I look up. My mother looks at my father, wild-eyed, a signal. My father obeys.

"Mark, your mother needs you to leave the room."

"But I just want to read the sports."

"Please, just go into the den. Or maybe check the door on your pigeon coop—I saw a cat in the backyard earlier." He's on edge, a hint of panic. I can't sit down in my own house?

"*Bill* . . ." My mother finally clears her throat and speaks, her voice a strange quiver. "*Tell him.*"

"Tell me what?"

She's still looking at my father. "Tell him about the Black Dog."

I'm tired of all of this. "What the hell's the black dog? I've never heard of a black dog."

Dad tries to take control, stands. "Mark, don't swear at your mother. I've asked you once. *Please leave.* I'll explain later. "

I hold my hands palms up, like showing I have nothing to hide. And look at my father through the tops of my eyes as if to say *what the fuck?!*

"*Leave!*"

I LIE ON MY BED, pillow propped up against the windowsill, having one of those moments that make no sense, but I know I will never forget. Why is my mother afraid of me? My body feels helplessly sad, no words or images. An hour later my father opens the door and sits on my bed.

"Your mother wants me to tell you about the Black Dog."

I nod. Just get on with it.

"She's afraid she is going to ask you to do something horrible."

"Like what?"

For two or three minutes, just the sound of our breathing. My father can't look at me.

"Like what? *What?*"

"Like take down your pants . . . and let her see you." It takes my father a very long time to say this, like playing a 78 record at 33 rpm, the volume way down. His lips are all thin and stiff, like he's having trouble getting each word out.

"What did you say?"

"You heard me."

I did hear him, but want to make him say it again. "I'm not sure I heard you."

"She is afraid she will ask you to take down your pants."

"What's there to see?"

I stare at the green wall: three unpatched cracks, like a desert road map.

"Or let her touch you." His face is turned away from me; his hand reaches for the bony angle of his chin.

"Touch me?"

"Yes, and ask you to do certain things. And she feels guilty."

"What's there to feel guilty about?" Somehow I know, but don't know, the answer to this question. I close my eyes and hope that my father will not reply.

"Also, you know how when you wake up in the morning your penis is all stiff because you have to pee?" His head turns away more, eyes stare at the hardwood floor.

"Yeah, so what?"

"Well, that happens to Mother sometimes when she thinks about you, and she feels guilty."

I want logic to get me out of this, to end this discussion. I start to argue that Mom doesn't have a penis, but somehow know that isn't the point. My mouth tightens, and I cover my ears with my hands. My father's voice is muffled, but not enough:

"It's the Black Dog."

Our exquisite discomfort leaves my father and me mute. Finally, when he closes the bedroom door behind him, I breathe again.

None of this makes any sense to me. *The Black Dog.* Three hours later, my father taps on my door. Dinner's on the table. I come out of my bedroom and we eat, a haze of awkwardness. *Have a second helping of green beans, the roast beef is just right, dear, pass the mashed potatoes, please.* I choose to read myself to sleep, something I never do. Audubon's *Quadrupeds of North America.* Another night of relentless shuffling sounds and cries and shadows down the hallway from my bedroom, then the merciful morning. I am awakened by determined activity, packing sounds of leather suitcases. By the time I am dressed, Mother is already in the car, staring down the blacktop driveway, waiting for Father to deliver her back to the hospital. Her second visit this winter.

"I tried to call your brother, but no luck. Jeannie's not answering the phone. I need you to watch out for your sister. Mom wants me to tell you she's sorry, she just can't control the Black Dog. She'll be back soon. I'll call as soon as we get settled in." My father, the messenger. The Chevy cautiously creeps down the street.

So: The *Black Dog.* I am the Black Dog, hounding my mother, driving her to the hospital.

The Black Dog

The Black Dog. As a teen who was not yet enamored with metaphors, the Black Dog made no sense to me. We were not a dog family. Where did my mother get this dark vision of a black beast ordering her to her chair, filling her with paralytic sadness, commanding her to ask her son to do things our family could not say out loud? I assumed this vision came from her head, fried by ECT and mashed by Thorazine. The Black Dog? No way.

Come to find out, her Black Dog had a long history.

Winston Churchill, my mother's hero who defiantly smoked cigars, read classical literature, and conquered tyrants, suffered severe paroxysms of depression, which he described as walking around "with a black dog on my shoulder." My mother read a lot about Churchill, she must have known of his melancholia. Perhaps he was her hero because he did not retreat to his bed or chair, and he refused to be defeated—either by Hitler or by the Black Dog.

But Churchill was not the inventor of the Black Dog. In the late 1700s Samuel Johnson wrote to James Boswell, who suffered from depression, "what will you do to keep away the black dog that worries you at home?" In the first century BC, the Roman poet Horace described melancholia as "the black dog [that] follows you, and hangs/Close on your flying skirts with hungry fangs."

So, my mother was part of a long line of black dog owners. Poets, writers, biographers, statesmen. Perhaps that provided her some comfort.

Recapitulation Nightmare #1: It's a Boy

Recapitulation: In biology, a hypothetical pattern in which an organism repeats ancestral evolutionary changes in its own development.

1980. Sherry, my first wife, was pregnant. Something we had not planned, but that brought us great joy: we were ready for this.

Her ultrasound at four months. As the doctor passed the sensor over Sherry's belly the black-and-white image appeared on the screen, and the *lub-lub* rhythm of the baby's heart filled the exam room. There it was: a penis. A penis! I began to sob.

Not the sob of a proud father who is assured that he will have the son he always wanted, that the family line will continue. Not the sob of a father when told that his baby appears completely normal.

No: the relieved sob of a father terrified that he would have a daughter and visit upon her the sins of his mother.

Prophecies

I carried three prophecies with me for almost three decades, assumptions about love I learned in my fourteenth and fifteenth years, assumptions that caused great suffering and loneliness for me and for people I loved, or tried to love.

Prophecy #1. This is the danger in loving someone: they take and suck all from you. An emotional leech lurks behind every profession of love and request for commitment. Loving is a trap—more dangerous the more you want it, the more you are in love. Once trapped, you will spend your life sitting on a couch across from someone who can no longer talk, you will be called away from your friends and children, there will be howling in the night and empty stares in the morning. Your passions will dry, shrink, and become brittle. Loving is slowly dying, giving your life over to someone else. Beware of love.

Prophecy #2. Whatever piece of understanding I was able to absorb at fifteen about the meaning of the Black Dog, of the detailed messages my mother made my father deliver to me of her unfulfilled sexual longing for me, this I knew: the morning after my father's revelations, my mother returned to Edgemont, where they tried to put her back together and failed. There it was: I was the cause of her breakdown; loving me is dangerous business. Beware.

Prophecy #3. I will always be alone. See Prophecies #1 and #2.

UNTIL I WAS in my forties, these prophecies proved to be true. In my desperate fear of being alone I attempted love many times. I had it all together: passion, wanting to share everything, telling my new true loves how remarkable they were, wanting to know everything about them, being present in a way that was irresistible. I meant it. I was easy to fall in love with. I wanted to be in love, to not be alone. Sometimes I succeeded.

At about three months, I began to see it in a kind of fog, a premonition of a seizure. Then I would seize up with horrific visions of the future, of being trapped, of night sounds and silent mornings. And overnight, postictal, I would say *I'm sorry, this is not working, there is no sense in going further, I know I will leave you.* They would often say *No, let's try to work through this,* and sometimes I would try. But inevitably I would leave. *I'm so sorry for causing you such pain.*

Seize and desist.

I loved several people dearly, really. I dreaded being alone. And each time I walked away, guilt-filled, alone.

SPRING 1958

Putting on Her Face

For as long as I can remember, Mother has had a standing appointment with Midge, her hairdresser. Every two weeks, on a Thursday morning. Before she got sick, she used to take a cab, but now she has Jeannie drive her. She gets the works at Midge's: the shampoo; the cut; the tint (strawberry blond seems to be her new spring color); the curl; the perm; the dry (with her head inside one of those space-age-looking machines). *Permanent*—for at least two weeks, until her next date with Midge. Since she jettisoned her friends, Jeannie and Midge are the only people from the outside world with whom Mom has contact. She returns from her hair-dressing trips all animated, full of stories about Midge's divorce, her being a single mother, jokes they tell, gossip they share. She talks about Midge the way she used to talk about her friends in The Little Theater.

In the afternoon after her Midge date, my mother goes to the bathroom and situates herself on the vanity chair in front of the six-foot mirror. She then proceeds to *put on my face*, as she calls it. First, she cleanses her skin with some kind of antiseptic stuff, puts on her cold cream and removes it with Kleenex. Now the artistic part, the makeup: some kind of base, then skin toner, then a soft powder to take away the sheen. Next, she works on her eyelashes and brows. No eyeliner—*eyeliner is for streetwalkers*. Finally, a spray of fragrant cologne on her neck. Just a trace, not too much—again, that streetwalker thing.

Forever, I have watched my mother put on her face as I wander in and out of the bathroom to do my business—to get a Band-Aid for a blister or cut, a drink of water, to check my pimples, brush my teeth. One thing I have noticed when she goes through this routine: she hums to herself, a kind of nonsense tune, not really a melody, nothing recognizable. But she's content.

When she finishes her face, she goes to her closet and puts on a nice pair of pressed pants and a colorful patterned blouse. Her make-over complete, Mom's *all decked out*, as she calls it. She finds her chair, lights up a cigarette, pulls out her latest novel or whodunit, and waits for my father to come home from work.

Tonight, my father is home on time. He greets Mom with a kiss on her perfectly made-up cheek, stands back and admires her perfectly coiffed hair, and tells her how beautiful she looks. He thanks Jeannie for looking after my mother, says he'll see her tomorrow, same time, same station. Then he goes to the kitchen to mix their martinis. Bottles opened, shot glasses filled, the rhythmic sound of liquid and ice shaken, the soothing gurgle of it all being poured through a strainer. Dad returns to the living room and ceremoniously presents the drink to Mom. They sip and chat, sucking on their green olives. Mom tells Dad about the ongoing saga of Midge and the denizens of the beauty shop. They chuckle. Dad talks about the electrical system he's designing for the new Douglas DC-8 passenger plane. He sounds proud, but he's not a bragger.

Three-year-old Michele and I build a Lincoln Logs cabin on the floor, taking it all in.

THE NEXT MORNING. Mom, in her coffee-stained nightgown with a quarter-inch black burnt hole where she had dropped a cigarette, returns to her chair. She lights up and stares into the fireplace. "Good morning, my sweet," says Dad. She half-nods, says nothing. He brings her coffee. Jeannie and Dad do the handoff and he's off to work.

I slurp down a bowl of Sugar Frosted Flakes. Pick up my book bag. "I'm working on an English paper, got to go to the library, so I won't be home 'til 5:00 or so." She doesn't even manage a nod.

Here we go again.

Maybe my mother should go to Midge's every day.

Land of the Gimps II: Forty-Fifteen

Forty-fifteen, second serve. I bounce the ball three times to get my rhythm, toss it overhead, drop my racquet, and arch my back. My arm sweeps in a big arc to put topspin on the ball, and I charge the net. Bobby Jenkins returns my serve, I drop down to meet the ball just above my ankles and angle it over the net, a drop shot with nice touch. Game. Six-four, third set. I have just become the eighth man on the Downey Senior High School varsity tennis team.

Until last fall, when I moved from junior high to tenth grade at the high school, I had never played tennis. As was promised, my asthmatic body was exiled to the Land of the Gimps, to face the humiliation of sharing the same gym class with the pock-faced big-gummed kid who might have a seizure any moment, the skinny paleface whose heart valves leaked blood so loud if you listened carefully you could hear, the menacing crip who would trip you with his crutch and dare you to do anything about it. Mr. Hudson, the football trainer, ran the class. He talked shit like a drill sergeant. *There's no way I'm going to let you kids grow up to be pathetic anemic weenies. Everyone on the floor, twenty push-ups. Roll over: thirty sit-ups.* Hudson was fat and bald, not the perfect specimen of physical fitness. But something began to happen to me, aided by my new inhaler: I liked working out, got so I could do sixty sit-ups in two minutes. My biceps grew under free-weight curls. In the gym mirror after showering, I noticed.

Hudson noticed, too. He felt comfortable enough with two or three of us doing more exercise without risking death, so he began to increase our activity level. One day he watched Fred Wechsung and me play a down-to-the-wire best-of-three badminton match and stopped me before I went into the showers.

"Say, Lyons, you look like you might know what you're doing with a racquet. Ever play tennis?"

"Nope."

Come to find out, Hudson had gotten the short stick of the draw, and was ordered by the Athletic Department to coach the tennis team.

"Why don't you meet me on the courts after school, we'll hit a few. I've got an extra racquet."

So here I am, three months later, shaking the hand of Bobby Jenkins, heading to the gym to tell Mr. Hudson that I've moved one rung up the ladder: varsity.

What does this mean? It means that I will practice tennis five days a week until five o'clock. I will go to weekend tournaments and take on Long Beach Poly and Lynwood and Compton and Norwalk in league play. Instead of going home, I will be hitting cross-courts, down-the-lines, deeps, shorts, drop shots, flat serves, English serves, overheads, slices, topspins. Then I will dry off with a towel and take a shower, and sit on the bench wondering how this all happened.

I will play tennis every day until I leave home.

The Pause That Refreshes

Mom seems to be feeling good today, I can tell because she's dressed before noon. And Dad's outside pushing the lawn mower, making the ratchet sound of spring grass. When she lets him work in the garden, it's a sign she's doing OK. He's *piddling in the yard*, as Mom calls it. *Piddling*: all those things that my father loves to do outside—mowing, raking, weeding, cutting the ivy off the lath house, sawing down the dead palm fronds, edging the grass, watering with the Rain Bird. My father, the long stork bird with lily-white spindly legs, the engineer, piddling in the yard, his little piece of heaven.

Mom lights up her Pall Mall, takes a puff, sips on her cup of coffee, crosses her legs. She doesn't stare into the fireplace, she looks at me.

"So, are you and Richie Cary still working on his Chevrolet? Did you ever get the engine working?" She sorta sounds interested.

"It's a Studebaker. Yesterday we put on the piston rings, we're about ready to put the pistons back into the cylinders. He got the valves ground last week."

"*Piston rings, cylinders, valves.* Listen to you, talking like an engineer. You sound like your father. Where in the hell did you learn all this stuff?"

"Richie: he knows engines." I try to sound nonchalant, like now I know engines too, no big deal. My father is an engineer, my brother wants to be one. But yesterday I did a ring job on a 1949 Studebaker.

"So, when you get it running, are you and Richie going to take me for a ride?"

"As soon as you let me get my license."

"I knew that was coming."

"Think I'll go out to my coop, gotta scrape all of the crap out of the nest boxes. OK?"

"You do that. I'm going to curl up here with my corpulent friend Hercule Poirot and solve another murder." As I leave the living room I turn around and look at my mother, her chair, her cigarette, her cup of coffee, her Agatha Christie whodunit. She looks happy, like an old photograph taken before the ghosts visited. Maybe they're gone, maybe Mom is back. Or on the way.

It's already hot outside, the way late Mays are sometimes; the breeze stops and the heat just sits on you, daring you to move. I get a bottle of Coca-Cola out of the fridge, pop the top, close the back door behind me, and head out to my coop.

I'm not sure how this happened, nobody would believe me anyhow. I've finished raking my pigeon pen and watering it down, already sweating like I've run ten miles, so I sit down for a sip of Coke and lean against the wire of the fly cage. Three gulps, and then I do something that I often do when drinking soda: I suck on the bottle and create a little vacuum, so the bottle sucks my tongue in. Suck a little harder, then *thowck*, the sound as I pull my tongue out and break the seal. One of the pigeons startles at this foreign sound, eyes me, then resumes his pecking at the feeder. If I suck a little harder, let the bottle pull my tongue in a little further and tighter, then the *thowck* sound is even louder: *THOWCK*. I wonder how loud a sound I can make, so I suck even harder, the bottle starts to pull on my tongue, a little painful. I have to use a lot of force to extract my tongue this time: *THOWCK*, a pure-pitched sound. That one hurt.

Why not? I am going to make the loudest *thowck* I have ever made, the *thowck* of all *thowcks*. The *Great Thowck*. I start sucking, and feel the neck of the bottle gradually inch up my tongue. Take little sucks, making a bubbly sound as the bottle squeezes the saliva out of my tongue and tugs at the base. I have never thought about where my tongue is attached inside my mouth, but now I can feel that place, back between my tonsils, stretching taut, starting to hurt a little more

147

each time I take a suck. Now it really hurts, more than a dull ache, but I enjoy the pain in a weird way because I have control of it. All I have to do is curl my tongue a little and pull on the bottle and *THOWCK*, the pain goes away.

I notice a cat sneaking along the wall, eying my pigeon coop, the black one with one white paw from the Burridges'—the cat I suspect has gotten three or four of my birds over the last year. I hold the Coke bottle, now firmly attached to my tongue, with my left hand, reach over and find a rock in the ditch that drains my birds' bath, and fire it at the cat. I almost nail it from twenty feet—an arrogant screech as it leaps on top of the six-foot cement wall and disappears on the other side. I realize that when I threw the rock at the cat, I took a giant gulp on the bottle, and now my tongue's much further inside than it's ever been. It hurts too much, time to extract it. I hold the bottle horizontal between my hands like a clarinet and start to curl my tongue as I pull, anticipating a perfect pear-shaped *Thowck!*

Nothing. No sensation along the base of my tongue that air is starting to leak in and the seal is about to break. Maybe if I twist the bottle a little—but it hurts more, that's not working.

"The vacuum is one of the most powerful forces in nature." That's what old man Pearson said in eighth-grade science. "Think of it, the paradox: *the force of nothingness.*" He said it like it had some deeper meaning that we were supposed to ponder, but he realized that we had no idea where he was going and we didn't care. So he returned to earth and asked John Simpson if he knew why Thermos bottles had vacuums.

The bottle feels like it's some wild animal that has hold of my tongue, we're in a battle to see who gets it, a tug-of-war. The bottle is winning, sucking my tongue in further and further; I can feel the neck of the bottle against the back of my throat, almost gagging me. It feels like my tongue is being pulled out of its roots, taut fibers stretching then finally snapping. I imagine blood trickling down my throat and want to vomit. But how? I try several more maneuvers, combinations of changing the angle and twisting the bottle, tongue curls, trying to get a little more spit to lubricate the surface where the bottle has its jaws clamped on my tongue.

"*O-no-ma-to-po-ei-a*. When a word sounds like what it is, that's onomatopoeia. The *e* before the *i*"—my mother explained to me when I was ten, and I prided myself on being the only fourth grader who knew that word, much less how to spell it. Then she gave me some examples: Bees *buzz*. Boards *clack*. Snakes *hiss*. *Suck* is an onomatopoeia, especially if you hold the *S* a little when you pronounce it. If you mix a little saliva in, you really have onomatopoeia. "The riptide *sssucked* the swimmer under, never to be seen again!"

Tears flood my cheeks, my tongue is being ripped out. I'm about to be mute forever.

He was such a nice boy, then when he was 15, he had this tragic accident with a Coke bottle, lost his tongue, that's why he uses sign language.

Oh, that's terrible. Did he cut himself with the bottle?

No, worse than that. The bottle just sucked on his tongue until it pulled it right out of the socket. They tried to reattach it, but it was mutilated beyond repair.

This image dances on top of the Coke bottle: My tongue does not snap off; rather the bottle mercilessly digests my entire body, like a boa constrictor eating a rabbit. Slowly I am turned inside out, like a sock. Inch by inch the bottle sucks me in, popping my eyes, compressing my guts, breaking my bones. All they find when they come looking for me are unrecognizable fragments of tissue and cloth inside the bottle. They see my bloody shoes lying next to the bottle and realize what has happened. My mother faints, my father does not speak for a year.

One of the most powerful forces of nature.

My parents. Of *course*. I walk flat-footed to the house, holding the bottle like a grenade with the pin pulled, ease through the back door, and enter the living room. Dad's on his couch, Mom's in her chair, chatting like the world is all right. At first, they don't notice me. I grunt to get their attention.

"What's up, dear?"

"*Uuuhhh!*"

"Take that bottle out of your mouth, I can't understand a word you're saying." Mom takes a sip of her coffee.

I point frantically at the bottle and repeat my sound.

"Yes, I notice you've got a bottle in your mouth. Very cute. Are you playing Demosthenes, talking with your mouth full to improve your diction?"

"*UUUHHH! uy uuunk eh uuuk eh uhh ohhtehh!*" I am trying to say my tongue is stuck in the bottle, but they don't get it. I think of the trick we played on Rachel Iverson on the playground, asking her to hold the tip of her tongue and say *Johnny sat on a hot coal and now he has a little red apple*, how the apple became an asshole.

"Mark, how many times have we told you not to talk with your mouth full?" My father thinks this is funny. *Kids.*

If I don't figure out something, the bottle will rip out my tongue right here in the living room with my parents laughing at me. I remember Mr. Gunderson, my seventh-grade history teacher who fought in World War II, talking about adrenaline—how in combat it gives people super strength and ability to make clear decisions in the midst of bombs and blood and death. Everything starts to move in slow motion, silence. I know what I have to do. I march to the desk in the corner of the living room, open the drawer with my right hand while holding the bottle with the left, find an envelope from the gas company and a chewed yellow pencil, and write. I hand the message to my father.

Help my tongue is stuck. Dad reads the note. "Phyl, the boy's tongue is stuck, should we call the fire department?" He thinks it's funny. Mom suggests the hook and ladder. Then Father looks at me and sees the tears.

"I think Mark's in trouble, is that what you're saying?" I nod at my father. I may be rescued yet.

"You're the engineer, Bill. This looks like a job for an engineer."

"But I'm an electrical engineer, not a mechanical engineer. Maybe we should call in the Army Corps of Engineers." Oh no, they still think it's a joke. I start making terrible sounds, like a dog that's been run over and has a broken back. They finally get the message.

My father swings into action, the adrenaline pump. Within a minute and a half, he dashes to the garage and digs up a hammer, pulls two faded towels out of the pantry in the hallway, and snatches a dining room chair. He motions for me to follow him out the back door. I silently obey, tears dripping off my cheeks. With every step the bottle grabs another bite of my tongue. Into the Valley of Death.

Dad marches to the six-foot-high cinder-block wall, the border between our yard and the Burridges'. He places the chair next to the wall, pushes down on it to stabilize the legs in the soft dirt, and motions for me to climb up, a sweep of his arm pointing from my feet to the upholstery of the chair. He doesn't talk—does he think he needs to use sign language because I'm mute? He steadies my elbow as I stand on the seat, the bottle wildly sucking. From the chair I can see over the wall into the Burridges' yard, an eerie quiet, like just before something terrible is going to happen. Maybe I'm going to pass out, people do that from pain, like in the movie when they had to amputate the Civil War soldier's leg. Pain is an anesthetic, puts you out so you can't feel it. Merciful.

The surgeon at work, army field hospital. My father quickly wraps the blue towel around the bottle and motions for me to lay the bottle on top of the wall. Then he takes the yellow towel and covers my head, tucking it down between my neck and the gray block. The sun comes through the towel, but I can't see anything, just yellow haze.

"Close your eyes, take your hands away from the bottle, this won't hurt. Be sure to close your eyes now, one . . . two . . ."

POW! the shatter of glass muffled by the towel. Relinquished by the defeated vacuum, my swollen tongue slips out of the neck of the broken bottle and retracts into my mouth. Like an eel in a tide pool.

"Open up, let's take a look." I open my mouth, but don't want to stick out my tongue. It's dangerous out there. "C'mon, stick it out, I can't see if there are any cuts from the glass." My tongue warily leaves the safety of my mouth, maybe only a half-inch outside, exposed for Dad to examine. It quivers from pain.

"No cuts, but it's pretty swollen. I think I see a big bruise starting to form. Maybe you ought to suck on some ice, take a couple of aspirin." Doctor's advice.

I fall asleep sucking on an ice cube. *Post-op*, as they say on TV.

Dinnertime. "How's your tongue, feeling better?" Mom asks. "Well, then, come have some supper, I made mashed potatoes, that should go down pretty easy. And something cool to drink." I climb into my chair at the table, the same chair Dad used at the fence. Everyone is looking at me.

"*What?*"

"Nothing dear, just enjoy your dinner."

My tongue is still achy. I reach for the glass of cold milk to soothe the swelling. There at the tip of my fork and knife, usual site of the milk glass, stands a frost-dripping bottle of Coca-Cola.

"Very funny. I hate you guys!"

But at this moment I don't hate them at all. I lift the bottle and take a long cold sip.

#47 Blue

A dew-early morning. Sometimes this happens in spring, when the fog settles in after I'm asleep and doesn't leave until burned off by noon's sun. Damp and ten shades of gray; not saddening colors, but the world seems small because you can't see beyond the end of the driveway. On mornings like this Mom used to get up, fix her coffee, look out at the condensed air, and recite the poem about the fog that comes in on little cat feet. My morning ritual: I head up the driveway to pick up the *L.A. Times*, blindly flung with a plunk through the fog by stubbly white-whiskered Mr. Sorenson, who will run his paper route until he croaks. Muffled invisible crow caws echo from the shrouded telephone pole across the street: the deep raspy voice of the old crow that has been strutting around our yard for years, and the screechy broken voice of the juvenile that was born high in the palm fronds last summer.

As I head back to the house with the newspaper, a whistle cuts the fog, air slicing the wing feathers of a mourning dove as it dives from the telephone wire and lands by the boxwood border between the Thompsons' yard and ours. I edge over toward the dove, to where I can see it. The bird goes about its work of combing the dirt for seeds; a flick of its beak tosses junk aside. Doves don't strut like pigeons, with jerky movements and chest leading the way; they glide more when they walk, and lead with their beak. The lines of their body are less angular, more like clay smoothed out with a thumb. I have learned to imitate a pigeon's voice, to curl and vibrate my tongue at the same time while changing the shape of my mouth and vibrating my cheeks—alarm sounds and courtship sounds, aggressive pecking-order sounds. Pretty authentic. But I have never come close to imitating the mourning dove, the purest, most reassuring sound in our backyard or the orchards, maybe anywhere. Especially in the fog.

I have always wanted a dove for my coop. There's a dealer over in the Valley who sells doves, but they're the white kind you find at the Capistrano Mission, church doves without much of a voice. Like the doves they let go at the opening ceremony of the Olympics a couple of years ago, somehow not real. Peace doves, not mourning doves. You don't find white doves in the wild.

I watch the outline of the dove as it pans for seeds, taking its time, not very hungry. I am thirty feet from the bird, on the edge of the driveway. Usually this is a distance that spooks doves, eyeing the intruder, too nervous to eat. They're much jumpier than pigeons. No matter how many seasons they've been in your yard, doves don't take chances with humans. Through the charcoal shades of fog the bird isn't quite sure of what I am. It senses something out there, can see my movement but can't quite make me out. I carefully lay the newspaper on the ground, take a step closer and stop, watch the dove's reaction. Its head jerks up and turns perpendicular to me, eyes straining to bring me into focus through the haze. I freeze in mid-step, all my weight on my right front foot, and hold my position until the dove resumes beak-scratching the dirt. Another half-step as eyes burn through the fog in my direction. Step. Bird neck strains, eyes search fog, relax. Dirt scratch. Step. The bird's turn now. And step. Shadows dancing. I am ten feet away, the closest I have been to a wild dove. Now I see colors in the dove, shades of tan, maroon-tinged breast. It stands at attention, trying to read the intentions of the trespasser that crept in under fog cover. Its head darts side to side, surveying escape routes. Three feet behind her is the boxwood. The dove has two routes of escape: to the right toward the openness of the yard lined with apricot trees and one dying lemon; or to the left, shooting above the twelve-foot red-berried pachysandra bush. We both freeze, hypnotized, focused on any suggestion of movement in the other. I conclude that the dove will most likely fly to the right, to the unobstructed yard, the most space for maneuvering. I breathe in one more time, slowly, then lunge, not at the bird, but five feet to its right, cutting off its probable escape route. The abrupt lurch of my body sets the dove into the air. I have guessed right: the bird streaks to its right at a forty-five-degree angle, toward the light of the open yard.

One motion: I snatch the dove out of the air, the elbow of its left wing hooked in the crotch of my left thumb and forefinger, grab the right wing with my free hand, and collapse both wings against its body to avoid a break or dislocation. A handful of small soft underfeathers, as if the bird shed them to try to slip away. One wing escapes my grasp, thrashing as the dove's feet scratch my palms, and its body expands to force my hands open. Press the frantic free wing down, scissor the legs between my first and second fingers, feet now powerless. That moment when the bird knows it has lost and stops struggling, wild heart beat cradled in my palms.

An hour later I sit ten feet from my pigeon coop and watch. Thrashing metallic sounds of dove slamming against wire mesh. Puffs of breast down hang on the steel strands, some float down and settle in dirt. The bird is disheveled, no pattern to its feathers; many stick out at odd angles from wings and breast, revealing their lighter undersides. Uncombed. The top of the bird's head reveals gray-pink skin with black pinholes, feather sockets. Finally, it sinks to the corner of the fly pen, chest puffing in and out, beak wide open, glaze-eyed. My pigeons ignore all the commotion.

Maybe the dove will settle down in an hour. I eat lunch: ham slices and cheese, white bread and mustard, sloshed down with milk.

I return to the coop. The dove is still in total panic, multiplied each time it slams into the mesh wall. It will destroy itself in desperation. The coop is a refuge for my pigeons, the safe place they return to at dusk after flying in the wild. The dove has no experience of cages, no response except terror. I open the door and head straight for the bird, which thrashes against the cinder-block back wall under the eaves that shelter the nest boxes, slashes out over the feeders, flings its body against the mesh at the far end of the fly pen, loses its grip on the wire and falls into the bathwater. Too exhausted to lift its head, it will drown. I scoop the dove up. Motionless in my hands, I think it might die, the way birds do: their heart beating furiously against the palm of your hand, then the next instant nothing.

I open the door to the fly pen, walk to the middle of the yard, under the dark branches of the overhanging pepper tree, extend my arms and open my hands, palms up. The dove does not move. Shake my hands a little to try to stir the bird, hold it up higher to see the open space, no longer caged. Still no movement. A gray sadness as I sit in the shade of the olive tree, dove dying in the basket of my folded legs, both of us motionless. The dove closes its eyes, I lean against the gray-green trunk of the olive and do the same.

I am awakened by the shift in temperature as the sun dips below the roof of my pigeon coop, maybe half an hour later. The dove's eyes are open, and it is standing, though it shows no intention to fly. We eye each other, both motionless, waiting for the other to move, imperceptible breathing. I slowly reach down between my legs and cradle the bird between my palms. Its eyes are alert now, head calmly swiveling and cocking at various angles. The dove does not resist, even when I loosen my grip to see if it will take off. I ease up to standing.

On the door frame of the coop is a sixteen-penny nail, angling up at sixty degrees. Slid over the nail are seven or eight pigeon bands, numbered, blue, white, and yellow. I slip off the first band—#47 blue—carefully turn the dove upside down, uncoil the band, and slide it over the bird's right leg, move it up and down to be sure it rides free. I blow on the dove's breast and neck feathers; they puff out, revealing no injuries. It's starting to act nervous again, a good sign. We eye each other.

Outstretched arms, palms flat. Immobile, the dove still thinks it's captive. I pump my arms up and down twice, almost a flapping motion, then suddenly drop them. The bird is suspended in air for a moment. Its wings swim, a reflex. With whistling feathers, the dove disappears over the deep green ivy lath house.

Signals

After tennis practice, I'm exhausted in an exhilarated kind of way from hitting a ball all-out for three hours, working on my net game, flattening my backhand, widening the service angles. I'm playing second doubles with Greg Fox—he's a better player, but I've got more fire, so we're a good fit. Sitting on the locker room bench after a shower, I feel a kind of quiet rumble in my body, like something waking up and stretching, the way a butterfly cocoon shakes before it breaks open. I've grown two inches and six pounds since last September, up to five-foot-one and a hundred-five. No giant in the making, but each month a little less puny. Occasionally on the court I have to take a swig from my inhaler and wait thirty seconds for the stuff to take effect, then I'm all set for that deep clean sound when ball meets catgut on my TA Davis racquet following a perfect follow-through. On tennis days my body is my friend.

I walk home on the sidewalk through the new development that was an orchard a year ago, the breeze cooling my wet hair. Dad's car is in the driveway. I open the screen door, and my parents occupy their usual positions in the living room, each puffing on a Pall Mall. Before I can say hello, my father says, "Your mother's having a rough day, Mark, maybe you should go see if Dicky Tostenson wants to shoot some hoops." I am tired and don't want to go anywhere, don't want to be exiled from my own house. I start to protest, Dad grimaces, and the fist in his lap trembles. He's not threatening to hit me, it's something else. Then his fist opens and his hand turns over, palm up, a kind of hopeless resignation. There it is: his Black Dog signal.

"Mother needs you to leave the room. Now." He's trying to talk very calmly, casually, like an usher at a ball game saying *Everyone move along, please.* Part of me wants to make him—them—say it: *The Black Dog is back; your mother wants you to pull down your pants and show her.* Now my father looks so desperate, pleading; I want to hurt her, humiliate her, without hurting him.

"Mark, please don't make me ask you again. Leave."

"But . . ." A feeble protest is all I can muster.

"*Just leave.*"

In my room I listen to her cry, mixed with a flurry of staccato sounds that I try to shut out. But single words and grunts and screeches manage to squeeze under my door:

hospital

    pharmacy

  no   *please*

        dose   *can't*

take   *(sobs)*
       Bill   *no*
               more
(sobs)

For two hours. Eight o'clock. I hate this shit. I should have left the house.

Finally, silence.

My father taps on my bedroom door. "Your mother has fallen asleep. Want something to eat?" I follow him to the kitchen through their bedroom, past my mother splayed out on her back on their bed, head turned to the side, drool trickling out of the corner of her mouth. She breathes with a gurgle.

Dad and I eat our Swanson's TV dinners in silence. Turkey and mashed potatoes and green peas.

"Some days are going to be more difficult for your mother than others." That's all he can say. He really doesn't want to talk. I want to leave him be, *You don't have to make things all right for me.*

"Do you think Mom's ever going to be OK?"

"Sure, sure. She'll be OK. Don't you worry. This is just a hard time. We'll all get through this; your mother will be back on her feet just like new. Her old self. Really."

He answers too quickly. *Really?* I want him to stop talking, trying to make it all right. It's not all right. "Goodnight, Dad, hope you can get some sleep."

Lying in bed now, I wish I hadn't asked him that question about Mother being OK, trying to force an answer. In our own private worlds, we both know the answer: we are losing Mom. We are losing Mom, and will never be able to say that to each other.

Black Bird, Black Dog

Sunday morning, six a.m., Mom's back from her short stint at Edgemont. I am awakened by horrific screeches and chortles, like a thousand car brakes rubbing on metal drums, asbestos pads all worn out. A flock of starlings just landed in the umbrella fronds of our palm. Their stopping-off point used to be the belfry of Our Lady of Perpetual Help, the highest point in Downey. But the priest had the steeple ledges hot-wired with electricity and put an end to the pigeons' and starlings' whitewashing the saints and gargoyles and parishioners on their way to confession. So now the birds use the second highest landmark, the peak of our one-hundred-year-old palm, eighty feet high. They make an incessant racket of shrieks, maybe the ugliest sounds in the animal kingdom, and I am unable to fall back asleep.

A gift of the English, starlings aren't even American. Around 1890 some crazy rich American with nothing better to do decided he was going to import all of the birds mentioned in Shakespeare's plays: English sparrows, European starlings, nightingales, a bunch more. He dumped sixty starlings in Central Park, and sixty years later, eight thousand miles from England, yellow-beaked spotted-breasted stubby-tailed black birds shit all over California and wake me up at six a.m. on Sunday morning. May a thousand owls silently swoop on them. On the old guy who brought them here, too.

For half an hour I lie in bed, praying for the invader flock to desert our tree and move on, giving me peace to sleep. The English Plague is in no haste to fly off this morning, so I have no choice but to get up and read the sports section. The house is quiet, a good sign. I creak open the door to the living room, reach down to turn on the floor heater, and assume my position on the metal grate, my roosting spot until the morning chill burns off. As I lean against the wall and feel the heat rise up through my bare feet, I notice for the first time: Mom sitting in her ugly wooden chair in the corner across the room, staring into the fireplace.

"Good morning, Mom. How was your night?" This has become my ritual greeting, although often I know how the night was without having to ask.

She does not answer.

"Mom, you OK?" Another question in our morning liturgy.

I sit on the edge of the cherry flower-upholstered chair next to the heater and await her reply, not really listening. The sun angles through the gauze curtains behind her chair. The reflection of sunlight on wet cheeks, her well of sadness. What is she crying for, buried in the ashes of the fireplace? Does she remember? After ten sessions of electroshock and five months of painting by numbers and wandering the grounds of Edgemont sanitarium, does she know what she's lost? Does she notice that Eileen Sweet and Harry Cooke and Leota Haas have stopped calling, that The Little Theater now paints flats at the Arnolds', and the annual beach party and grunion run are now at the house rented by the Taylors, rather than ours? That they just produced *Our Town* without her? Can she still recite the garden scene from *Cyrano*, or "The Shooting of Dan McGrew," or quatrains from *The Rubaiyat* ("A jug of wine, a loaf of bread")?

Is she crying for her lost voice?

Her tears enrage me. Can she sense how much I detest her, how I want to bulldoze her into the fireplace and flee this plague, her affliction, her disorder that is consuming us all? Our family's experience, the only thing we have in common: *Mom's not doing well today,* eternal vigilance against the ghosts, medicine bottles crashing onto the floor in slow motion, *If you do that she'll have to go back to the hospital, please leave the room, no I can't come outside I have to stay with your mother, we'll finish the cribbage game some other time, I'm sorry but Mom can't come to your graduation, she's really getting better.*

Is she crying because she's lost me? Does she know? Does she care?

"Here's your coffee, Mom."

"I'm sorry, Mark." Her eyes glance up, then disappear. "Truly sorry." Her pale voice hovers in sadness. I center the coffee cup on the arm of her chair.

"Me, too."

I sit on the couch, bare feet tucked under me. She has returned to the fireplace, her coffee getting cold, and I am alone in the room.

The starlings scatter.

The View from the Pepper Tree

I was ten the first time I ran away. I was protesting some grave injustice that I can't remember now, something I was forbidden to do, or that I was ordered to do. It was the power that my parents exercised over me that filled me with rage and helplessness.

Like all kids, I had threatened to run away before, to go somewhere where life was fair, where parents were fair. My mother would respond to my threats by saying, "Enjoy yourself, send me a post-card." Once, she packed me a lunch to take with me. She had won, again, and I suffered a quiet and minor humiliation.

But this time, I left. Headed up our dead-end street to the Big World. By the time I got to the end of the block, I realized I had no place to go. My parents would surely call Richie Cary's parents or my aunt: *Any chance our young man is over there?* Very funny. So, at the end of our block I climbed a giant pepper tree, close to sixty feet tall, with its weepy branches dipping to the ground. I had been up this tree before, the perfect climbing tree with big branches and crotches to lie back in, easy to get from one to the other, good handles to grab on to. I began to climb and eventually settled myself into a comfortable curve forty feet up. I reached my perch about five o'clock in the afternoon, and was determined to stay until my parents came looking for me.

And come they did, two hours later. I heard them first. *Mark! Mark!* I looked down through the branches. There my father and mother were, checking behind hedges, over walls. They asked the Emersons, whose tree I was settled into, if they had seen me. *No, but I'll keep an eye out, send him on home.* Suddenly I felt a slight thrill—it must have been embarrassing for my parents to ask neighbors about me, admitting they didn't know where their kid was—maybe the neighbors would be talking about that. Give my parents a taste of humiliation.

After they called my name three or four more times, I started to climb down the tree. But then I stopped, suddenly filled with this sense of power I had over them—the power to disappear, to flee. Watching them down through the branches, I felt much older. Then they walked away, and I could hear them talking to other neighbors: *Have you seen Mark? It's starting to get dark, and he needs to come home.* I sat in the tree another hour, until well after dark, climbed down, and walked home. I fantasized that my parents would welcome me with open arms, glad that I was safe, and tell me they had decided they had been unfair—that whatever they said I could not do, or had to do, was null and void.

When I came through the front door, my mother and father were eating dinner with the MacFarlands. They ordered me to bed without my supper. No yelling *you're in serious trouble*, no *we were worried about you*, certainly no repentance on their part. They were trying to show Jimmy and Treva how reasonable they were, how they knew how to use the right kind and level of discipline, *firm, but restrained.* They were trying to show me that of course they knew I would come home, no worry there, that my power play of running away would not get me very far. Lying in bed that night, replaying the power I felt looking down on my parents from the safety of the pepper tree, I experienced a kind of ecstasy: I knew I had won. Sometime, if I had to, I could leave, just leave.

Five years later, at fifteen, I knew I had to escape; and at seventeen did just that, heading for college five hundred miles away. I didn't look back for many years. In her Black Dog state, tempered with Thorazine and jolts of electricity, it's possible that my mother never noticed that I had left. In her more lucid days, sitting in her chair, she might have understood that I was gone, possibly even missed me. Did she ever consider looking for me? Would I have hidden if she had come?

Leave Us in Peace

I have sent my mother to the hospital once, with the help of the Black Dog, and I'm about to do it again. My father is pleading for me to stop.

Last night: Filled with familiar sounds, a more dramatic variation on the theme—Mom's upping the ante to get more Thorazine. She threatens to tell me about Michele and Jimmy MacFarland, or she will lock herself in the bathroom and cut herself. He better believe it—she knows where Dad's razor blades are.

Here we go again. I try to sleep through it, these old stories, this familiar scene of everything falling apart. I flash on *The Glass Menagerie*, which my mother starred in three years ago. Everyone in that play seemed mean or pathetic or controlling, on the edge. When my mother asked me how I liked the play, I said I didn't really get it. She said it was not really material for children. *Bill! Give me the medicine! I can't sleep!* Another layer of rage accumulates within me. I know all about Jimmy MacFarland already. Leave her alone in the bathroom with her razor blade.

It's the next morning now, a Saturday. My father brings my mother her coffee and toast as she sits in her chair, stains on her nightgown, eyes half open, mumbling for him to light up her Pall Mall. This morning her mumbling seems more constant, the Thorazine shuffle. I've fed my pigeons, finished my cornflakes. It is time for my father to drive me to a tennis tournament in Norwalk, three miles away. I pick up my racquet, Dad picks up the car keys, we head for the door.

"Bill, you can't."

"It's OK, dear, I'm just dropping him off. I'll be back in half an hour. You'll be fine."

"I can't. You can't leave me."

I know where this is going, where it's gone before. The arguments about this have gotten shorter and shorter, since my father has learned that my mother will never give in. He puts the keys back on the desk, sits on the couch. End of discussion.

"I'm sorry, Mark. Your mother needs me. You'll have to ride your bike."

"But I'll be late for my match. Come on, it's just thirty minutes. Mom, you'll be OK."

She inhales her cigarette, stares at my father, her way of ordering him. Or daring him. He won't look at her. Or me.

She has won, she always does.

"Do you know what you're doing to our family?" I say to her.

"Mark, please . . ." That's all my father has to say.

I yell with all the rage I can muster. "No! You're destroying our family! Look at Dad, there, cowering on the couch. Nobody will stand up to you. It's all about you!"

"Bill, if this doesn't stop I'm going to have to go back to the hospital."

Dad says, "Mark, please. Please leave."

"Edgemont—that's where you belong!"

"Mark, don't do this, please." My father always asks me to stop, never asks her.

I am amazed at how calm I am when I say this: "I hate you. Go back to the hospital. That's where you belong. Leave us in peace."

Two hours later, our car pulls out of the driveway, delivering her from us, returning her to her rightful place at Edgemont. I feel a sense of triumph as I sit on the front porch and read the sports page of the *L.A. Times*. In their first L.A. home game, in front of 78,000 fans at the Coliseum, the Dodgers hang on to beat the Giants, 6–5.

I never made it to the tennis tournament. Oh well: It's a good day to clean my pigeon coop.

Your Anger Isn't Helping

Dad has had it. "All of this tension and yelling between you and your mother has left me at the end of my rope, Mark. You're making it worse. I can't take it anymore." So I agree to see Dr. Rothenberg, my mother's shrink at Edgemont. Actually, I'm kind of curious—I've never been to a shrink before. Another silent drive to the hospital where my mother is interned, too upset to see me.

Dr. Rothenberg looks kind of like a pharmacist, with wire-rim glasses, a striped tie, shined brown shoes planted firmly on the green carpet, a white cotton coat. A photograph of a perfect four-member family sits on his desk next to a bronze lamp. He leans forward with his elbows on the dark oak desk, trying to capture me with his eyes. I look away.

"Your father says you're pretty angry at home." He waits like he's wanting me to fill in the blanks. I don't take the bait, just sit in silence.

He tries to act casual, like he's talking baseball with a kid over a Coke and fries. "Sounds like you got your mother pretty upset this time, so she had to come back to the hospital."

You got your mother pretty upset this time. I know where this conversation's going. He's trying to buddy-up to me, but I can smell the lecture. I start to say, *You think this is my fault?* But I realize the greatest power I have is silence.

"Your mother is going through a really difficult time. Your father, too. Your anger isn't helping, you know." *Isn't helping: code for you're making it worse, you little shit.*

I shrug. *What do you want me to do about it?* I do know I'm making it worse, but someone has to stand up to her. No way she's going to control me like she controls my father. Ain't gonna happen.

"Do you want to tell me how you're feeling?"

I can't believe my father's paying this guy. "No, that's OK. I'm OK."

"Don't want to talk about it, eh?"

"Not really."

"Well, could you try to control your anger at home? Throwing gasoline on the fire just makes it harder. For everybody—including you. Can you do that?"

I shrug, in a noncommittal kind of way. No way am I going to give this douchebag the satisfaction of feeling like he's contributed to the mental well-being of my family.

"That will be all, then. Thanks for coming in to talk. If you decide you want to talk some more, you know where to find me."

Ten minutes. I close the door behind me without saying a word.

Recapitulation Nightmare #2: Riding the Wild Stallion

My son Jesse was sixteen, a tough year for us. Some days we were in open warfare, shooting words at each other with intent to maim; some days we silently called a temporary truce, exhausted from the fight. He had metamorphosed into a wild stallion, stomping and thrashing behind the door of his second-floor bedroom, his stall. His sullenness hung over our meals, a miasma. We shouted accusations about all things unimportant; doors slammed. It would take us a day or two to let go, to make words not coated in venom. Meanwhile, he thrived outside of our house: his first serious girlfriend, lots of other friends, doing well in school. He hung out with friends whose parents assured me he was a wonderful, funny, gracious kid. After our household conflagrations, which seemed to happen weekly, I would crash. A deep black sadness. I knew where this was going: Jess was preparing to flee, to free himself from our family, from me. I was sure he would make no plans to return.

Forty years after I left home without looking back: payback time.

Jesse was in his Kool-Aid hair phase, wherein he bleached his shoulder-length brown hair surfer blond, then dyed it with packets of Kool-Aid: green one week; then purple; then red. I suspected he was trying to get a rise out of me, but I didn't take the bait. *Very cool, Jess. So far, I think I like the purple best. How about pink?* Actually, I did think it looked cool, my brilliant boy trying on his colors.

About once a month Jess had to prep his hair for the Kool-Aid application, bleaching the natural brown roots that emerged from his cranium. He got out his bottle of bleach, stood in front of the bathroom mirror, and, strand-by-strand, applied the liquid with a special brush. I worried about him getting the obnoxious chemical in his eyes, but warning him would detonate a sound of disgust about how I was treating him like a four-year-old. The pre-primping process took about half an hour. However, there was a problem: standing in front of the mirror he could not see the back of his head to properly detect the devil brown roots. He usually asked his girlfriend to apply the bleach to this hidden area, but tonight she was with her family. Jess came into the TV room where I was watching the Phillies play Pittsburgh, top of the eighth. Bleach bottle in one hand, application brush in the other, he asked, "Hey, would you mind brushing some bleach on the hair on the back of my neck?"

"Sure, why don't you sit here on the floor between my legs and we'll watch the game while I bleach you up." I was working hard to sound nonchalant. A misfired tone of voice could set off a firestorm.

"What's the color this week?"

"Orange."

"Orange. Nice summer tint."

Jess settled his long-legged gangly self down between my knees, and we both watched the game as I carefully, meticulously, almost artistically, dipped the brush into the bleach bottle, inspected the back of his neck for natural brown strands, and applied the liquid until the color was erased. I took fifteen minutes to do a job that should have consumed no more than five. Neither of us seemed impatient for me to finish.

"Thanks."

"Sure, anytime."

The Phillies won, 4 to 3.

God, I loved this kid. Maybe, just maybe, we would be OK.

Dangerous Dan *Redux*

In my forties, my mother sent me a remarkable birthday card with a long note, which I have saved. She told me that she'd been thinking about me a lot, how proud she was of me, that she was missing me terribly, and hoped I would come home soon. The note was chatty and affectionate and filled with longing. She had come looking for me. I was searching for a way to connect with my mother, any way would do. I came across a beautiful children's illustrated version of "The Shooting of Dan McGrew," and remembered her recitation thirty years before at the cast party for *The Solid Gold Cadillac*. I bought the book and wrapped it up for her. I had visions of her unwrapping her present, embracing the book, then embracing me. Then we would spontaneously recite in unison:

A bunch of the boys were whooping it up in the Malamute
   Saloon . . .

Or maybe I would read it to her. Then we would begin to talk about books, after all these years. She would be glad to know that as an adult I heeded her call to read. I didn't expect her to jump on the coffee table and gesticulate; but I hoped to uncover her buried love for books, to have a real conversation.

When I walked through the door of our California house, wrapped book in hand, there she was, sitting in her old chair. She didn't get up, but smiled and told me she liked my hair shorter. I bent down and hugged her, then sat across from her on the old divan. She was tired, said she needed to go to sleep. The next morning, I presented her the present. She unwrapped it with Thorazine-ized pill-rolling hands.

"*Dan McGrew* . . . Nice."

"A bunch of the boys were whooping it up in the Malamute Saloon . . . ," I incanted.

She put the book down on the side table, next to her ashtray and cold cup of coffee. "Mark, please call your father. I need him."

"Shall I read it to you?"

"Maybe. Later. Bill! I need you! Where's your father?!"

The next morning Dan McGrew was on the mantel, stashed between Agatha Christie and John Steinbeck.

OVER THE YEARS my mother would occasionally send out such signals that she was looking for me, she had noticed I was gone and missed me. I would return to the house where I grew up—not with great expectations, but with hope that I would find her at home. And every time, she had disappeared, again and again. After so many years, was she still haunted by guilt for what might have happened with Jimmy MacFarland or her sexual fantasies about me? Had the mega-doses of ECT, Valium, and Thorazine left her forever unable to connect with the outside world, with her son? Did she notice the sadness in me as I said good-bye? Was she no longer capable of such sadness? The mother I had grown up with was nowhere to be found.

Poem with Forgotten Title

In tenth grade, Ms. Haas—Leota Haas—encouraged her English students to submit a poem to the annual California Scholastic Federation poetry contest. Selected winners would be published in the Federation's annual collection. My poem was one of five or six poems from our high school that were published that year.

Over five decades later, I can still recite the poem from memory, though the title escapes me. Pretty awful poetry. But there it was: a mantra, a self-fulfilling prophecy.

(Forgotten Title)

Find no friend that so engrossed
You become in him
That if that friend should
Be a friend no more
Your future would be dim.

For if that friend so dear to you
Should be a friend no more
You'd find yourself
All alone
In this living worldly war.

Recapitulation Nightmare #3: 1975, Ten Years to Go

I had just ended a relationship with Susan. I'd been with her for three years and loved her very much. She wanted to continue, but I froze with fear, convinced that I could never be happy with her. Or anyone.

So I broke her heart, and mine. Once again, my loving was venom, I was dangerous like a serpent. I was the most depressed I had ever been, desperate to love without fleeing, to believe I was not dangerous, but sure I would never learn that. I tried on suicide—how soon before I started making plans? I was running out of time.

Time to see a therapist.

"So, what brings you here?" he asked.

"I'm thirty-two, and have ten years left before I go crazy like my mother."

Mr. Rainey's Polo Shirt

Bob McLennon is rich by Downey standards. His father is a doctor, and they have a sprawling ranch house on two acres with three wings and a sliding glass door in every room that overlooks the pool. But his family doesn't act rich—they're Seventh Day Adventists, and evidently acting rich is not considered Christian. Until last year he had giant elephant ears. Seems even Seventh Day Adventists can be vain, so Bob had his ears trimmed down to normal size, the first time I'd ever heard of an ear job. Oh, yeah: he's a champion golfer, ranked in the state. He's the perfect package now: tall and good-looking, humble in a way that makes everyone like him, rich, and a champion. Not the kind of guy who would normally hang out with me. We became friends this June because I mowed the lawn of his rich neighbor, and saw him over the fence in his swimming pool. We started playing tennis on their tennis court, swimming in their pool, going over to the junior high school for some pickup touch football.

Bob's mother is beautiful. When I come over, she says I look like I could put some meat on my bones and offers me peanut butter and jelly sandwiches, keeps filling my glass with lemonade. This afternoon she and Bob are going down to Rainey's Department Store to buy some clothes for school. Would I like to come along?

Recently I have become quite the dresser—got to look sharp for high school. Always, before, my mother shopped for me, bringing home new sets of back-to-school clothes from Bullock's in August and spring clothes just before Easter. I've decided I want to buy my own clothes from now on, I like going down to J.C. Penney's to pick out my stuff, don't want my mother deciding what I should wear. She doesn't take me shopping anymore, anyway. I've saved up my lawn-mowing money to buy clothes. My favorite purchases so far: a pair of white bucks and a brown-striped button-down short-sleeve shirt.

So of course I say yes to Mrs. McLennon's offer.

"Do you want to call your mother, let her know where you'll be?"

"No, that's OK. Nobody's home right now. I just need to be back by six-thirty, when my dad gets home."

Mr. Rainey's Department Store is old-time: big square bins of clothes, scuffed wooden floors, two old ladies following behind you folding the clothes as fast as you can unfold them, a general store kind of smell. Mrs. McLennon heads for women's wear and leaves Bob and me in sportswear. A half hour later, we are in checkout. The same old lady who followed us, folding with a sigh, is at the cash register. I pull out my wallet to pay for my first polo shirt, red with black stripes and a tight elastic band around the short sleeves.

Mrs. McLennon tells the register lady, "I'll take care of it." Then she waves her hand at my wallet and says, "Put that thing away, Mark. This one's on me."

Will you marry me? I think to myself.

"How about a Dairy Queen, guys?" says Mrs. McLennon.

Back at their house, I notice the clock, time to go. I don't want to leave. I want to stay in this house where everything seems normal, where I'm offered PB&J sandwiches and lemonade, where we go shopping for clothes and stop off for soft ice cream at the Dairy Queen on the way home, where I'm asked about my day.

"Would you like to stay for dinner? Lasagna and salad, nothing fancy. We're vegetarians, you know. But you're welcome to join us."

"Thanks, but I should head out. My father will be home soon."

Dad calls shortly after I get home. He has to drop by the hospital, Mom's upset about something, needs to see him right away. Go ahead and scramble up some eggs, there are some frozen French fries in the fridge, just put them in the oven at 350 for ten minutes. He'll catch a bite on the way home, no need to wait for him. Jeannie will feed Michele and drop her off by bedtime.

After dinner I put on my new polo shirt and stand in front of the bathroom mirror. *Damn*, I do believe I see some pecs. I flex my biceps—is that a bulge beneath the elastic?

Tenth Grade Report Card

Fifteen and a half now, a year of high school under my belt. Here's my report card:

Friends: I'm spending less time with Richie Cary, who goes to the other high school, across town. I haven't seen him for three months, and am surprised that I don't miss him so much. I feel like maybe I'm getting this social thing at school. For the first time I have some friends, besides Richie, whom I hang out with. The Hoffpauir twins, Robert and Richard, just got their driver's licenses and get to borrow their mom's black and red '55 Ford Fairlane; sometimes they pick me up in the morning and we drive to school or cruise Harvey's Broiler. They're really smart, but not asses about it. Their mom is divorced. We don't talk about that; but we don't talk about my mother, either. Bill Tweite is big and burly, gruff and teddy-bear at the same time, a real outsider—almost a hood, but not quite. We're sort of a Mutt and Jeff. He always calls me *Lyons*. I kept calling him *Twat*, and couldn't understand why he got so pissed off—then he explained to me what the word means. Danny Finley seems lost, even though he smiles a lot. I think he hangs with us because he hopes we'll keep him out of trouble. Karl Lehman is sad in a kind of sweet way, like he has trouble starting his motor and keeping it running; but he makes me laugh. He took me to his garage last month and showed me his father's set of playing cards with photos of naked women doing some weird shit. I'm not part of the cool beautiful set, the kids who have swimming parties in their new homes over in east Downey. No, thanks, I like the friends I have.

Academics: My grades are up. I got an A– in English from Miss Haas, who really busts your butt. My mother, home for the time being, was pleased with that; but she wasn't tempted to call Leota Haas and give her a hard time for going easy on me.

Extracurricular activities: I wear my new tennis letterman's jacket, wool with leather sleeves, even when it's eighty-five degrees out. I plan to practice tennis all summer, work on my ground strokes. I was elected head cheerleader in the spring, and in July our squad will go to cheerleader camp at some college up in the mountains where we'll work on our backflips. In June, I'm spending a week in Sacramento at Boys State, the model legislature thing. They sent just one kid from our school—pretty cool. And I'm keeping up my lawn-mowing business.

Physical: I'm still growing. Quarter inch by quarter inch. Way over five feet: five feet two inches, to be exact.

So, yes, I'm looking forward to eleventh grade. And to spending much less time at home.

Father Who?

My high school buddies—the Hoffpauir Twins, Karl, Danny, Tweite— like hanging out at my house. More to the point: they like hanging out with my mother. They think she's kind of eccentric, irreverent. She swears a lot—swearing's not allowed in their houses. *Damn, Ike may be a good general, but he sure as hell can't run a country. Half of the teachers at your school don't know their ass from a Shakespeare sonnet.* She asks questions. *So, who has a girlfriend? Any of you guys going to the prom, or are you just going to sit on your thumb while everyone else is having a good time? Any of you chums read a book lately, other than what is assigned by your teachers? Who's your favorite teacher? Why's that? What are you doing this summer?* She gives advice. *Robert, you should get yourself a haircut, you're starting to look like a goddamn juvenile delinquent—you're not Elvis Presley, you know. One of you guys should ask June Schildhauer out—she seems like a hot ticket.* She tells off-color jokes (that's the word she uses, like *You guys want to hear a joke?—It's a bit off-color.*). Here's a joke she tells them, sitting around our living room eating PB&Js:

> These two nuns are sitting on a bench discussing how big a fish they should buy for Friday night's dinner. Nun #1 says, "I think it should be about this long" (my mother holds her hands about twelve inches apart). Nun #2 says, "No, I don't think that's big enough, I think it should be this long" (my mother holds her

hands about twenty inches apart). Nun #3 walks in on the conversation and says, "Father Who?"

It's like she turns on a switch and kicks the Black Dog out of the house when they come over—time to chat it up with the kids. She's *On*, like on stage, entertaining the troops. My friends love it.

Karl: "Your mom's kind of cool, how like she can talk to us."

Robert: "If my mom swore like that, I'm sure she'd spend the next two weeks in confession."

Tweite: "Lyons, your old lady's outrageous, I can't imagine getting down with my ma like that."

It's like they think I'm lucky. Mark goes home to his cool mom every day. And today, for a moment, for an afternoon, they are right.

When they leave, my mother turns the switch back to *Off*. Let's the Black Dog in the back door.

SCHOOL JUST GOT OUT, late June, and my mother is back at Edgemont. A tune-up, as my father calls it. The twins and Danny are bored, cruising around town in their Fairlane. *Let's go hang out at Lyons's.* They pull up in the driveway just as I get back from mowing the Warners' lawn. We sit on the front porch chugging down some Cokes.

"Where's your Mom at?"

"She's away."

SUMMER 1958

Hang Down Your Head, Tom Dooley

Early summer heat starting to percolate. L.A. heat wipes me out. I feed my birds, water down their fly pen to keep the dust down, spray them while they roost on their perches, then open the door so they can get in their morning flight before it's too hot. I realize I'm missing Richie Cary, so I head over to his garage.

"Hey, I got something to show you, something I'm working on." Richie pulls two large plywood dollies off the wall, each with four roller wheels, and places one on each side of his Studee, now up on blocks. He instructs me to lie on my back on one of the boards, then disappears around to the other side of the car. We roll ourselves under the car, he from the driver's side and I from the passenger side, and meet in the middle, head to head, looking up at the frame. Richie takes me on a tour of the parts of his car that nobody sees. The new glass-packed mufflers dripping itchy fibers. The red-painted gas tank with the line running forward to the gas pump. The steering rods, the shock absorbers. He pats the crankshaft affectionately, then turns it with both hands. The shaft enters the universal, which hums quietly as it turns over the rear axles. The rear wheels move.

"Cherry," I say, trying to talk car talk. "She's in mint condition."

"Guess what?" he says. "I talked with the people at Warren Vocational Tech. They've got this serious auto mechanics shop there. Most of the graduates go on to the GM auto school and get great jobs. I'm transferring."

Lying under Richie's car, I have this ominous feeling, a dreadful sadness, which hangs over me like the fumes from his Studee gas tank. I reach up and jiggle the muffler.

"That sounds great. When?"

"It's all set, I start in a couple weeks—they got a summer course on ignition basics. Want to help me clean up my tools?"

I spend the rest of the day with Richie, preparing his tools. We soak the wrenches and screwdrivers and sockets in kerosene and wipe them clean with a rag, sand the handles of the ball-peen hammers, oil the pliers so they won't stick. Then we arrange his tools by size and carefully stack them in his red-and-black metal Snap-on tool box. We latch the box shut. I feel like I am packing Richie for a trip from which he will never return.

A couple of weeks later I come home from mowing the Thompsons' lawn, Richie Cary calls me up, says come on over, his Studee's ready for a spin. Still some work to do under the chassis, but she's almost there. The engine runs tight, turns over with one crank, and the tappets hum (*tappets*—another onomatopoeia). The clutch pops with a ping. He's painted her himself, with a spray gun, a metallic blue—but not ugly like the brash blues the gangbangers paint their lowriders with. We do our test runs with her, short forays, tune-ups for the Big Trip: to Thompsons' for pigeon feed and chicken mash; then up Firestone Boulevard to cruise Harvey's Broiler and order chocolate milkshakes from the waitress on roller skates; a five-mile trip over to Norwalk Park to watch the Fourth of July fireworks.

"So, what happened to our trip to New York?" I ask.

"Next summer. We'll save up some money by then, leave the day after we graduate."

"Yeah, next summer."

"But we gotta do something big before school starts, some kind of serious road trip."

"How about cruising the Boardwalk at the Pike?" That's the Long Beach Pike, sort of the Coney Island of L.A.

"Hell, yes! The Pike. Let's do it."

So, we head up Lakewood Boulevard to where it meets the Pacific Coast Highway, turn north. Richie spins the dial of his radio. "You gotta hear this song, just came out. Some group called The Kingston Trio, never heard of them."

Hang down your head, Tom Dooley,
Hang down your head and cry
Hang down your head, Tom Dooley,
Poor boy, you're bound to die

By the second chorus we're singing along, windows down. *Poor boy, you're bound to die.* Amen.

Long Beach Pike, Keep Right. We pull into the parking lot and ease ourselves out of the Studee like we're dismounting from a horse. A sign hanging over the arched entrance to the boardwalk announces that we're entering *The Home Away from Home for the U.S. Pacific Fleet. Welcome Sailors!* The Church of Divine Intervention people march back and forth dressed in black with spit-polished shoes, handing out salvation cards: *Beware! This is a den of sin! All who enter will get a glimpse of Hell! Save your soul!*

"You ever sinned?" Richie asks me, loud enough for the soul-savers to hear.

"Oh yeah, bunch of times."

We enter at our own risk. A woman in high heels, a short skirt, and a big cleavage greets us at the entrance and asks if two young boys would like to have a good time. "We're already having a good time, thanks." We smile, like real men. First, we tour the freak house, populated by Zuzu the Monkey Girl, Stone Man, the Mermaid, Blimp Lady, Tiny Tina, a guy who has tattoos on every inch of his body. The freaks never look at us, they don't talk. Like being at the zoo, except the freaks just sit there—they never pace back and forth looking for escape.

The sun sets on the Pike, pink and purple settle on the waves that lap the cement abutments. The lights come on, colored like it's Christmas, and the boardwalk fills with perfectly shaved skinny sailors in white round caps and spit-shined shoes, looking good with cigarettes hanging at a cool angle from their mouths. "How about a hot dog?" We head over to the arcade to shoot some ducks, try our luck at pinball and Skee-Ball. We ride the Cyclone Racer wooden roller coaster until I almost puke. I'm not feeling too good, need to find a bench. Nine-thirty: "Wha'dya say we head for home?" We follow the Exit signs, which lead us past the tattoo parlors, blinking green and red neon signs in the shapes of naked women and navy insignias. Richie and I stroll up to Zeke's Tattoos, #1 Choice of the Navy, lean against the open doorway while sucking some saltwater taffy, and eye the sample tattoos on the wall.

"My uncle George has a tattoo on his arm, right here." Richie points to his right forearm.

"Yea? What is it?"

"It says *Guadalcanal, '42.*"

"That's all? What's that mean?"

"I dunno, exactly. George just says something important happened to him there, something he never wants to forget. He also has another tattoo on his left shoulder. *DG*. That's all: *DG*. He says that one's for somebody he always wants to remember."

Richie and I contemplate the tattoos, listening to the hum of the artist's machine drilling indelible memories on the forearm of a sailor. We're getting excited, sharing the same idea: just a small tattoo, maybe high up on a shoulder, under the sleeve of the tee shirt where our mothers won't notice.

"Double dare you."

"What would you get?"

"Hey, you little assholes! Get the hell outta here, or the cops'll bust my ass! See the sign up there? *Eighteen!* Eighteen, not fifteen-year-old pimply virgins who never saw a damned razor! Outta here!"

We ride home in Richie's Studee with the windows down and *Tom Dooley* blasting on KPOP again, our faces lapped by the cool air, relieved that Zeke rescued us from our own fantasies.

Where Did You Go, Richie Cary?

Richie and I never went on our cross-country trip. Those powerful forces that we feel, but can't name or see, spun us into different orbits. Richie's world became populated with auto mechanics, welders, machine operators, and technicians; my domain was filled with confused discussions of careers and majors, SAT scores, and college essays. Though we continued to live only three blocks from each other until I moved away to college, the distance between us stretched slowly and irrevocably, and our passion for each other was silently dissipated by differences we had no name for.

I was home after I graduated from college, packing up for my move to the East Coast. I had not seen Richie Cary for five years. I walked over to his house on La Reina, past Our Lady of Perpetual Help. His house was gone, replaced by an eight-unit two-story apartment complex with curved palm trees in the front and balconies big enough for one beach chair and a hibachi on a cinder block. Richie and his parents were not in the phone book.

I never spoke to Richie again. Writing this, over five decades later, I realize that he was the first person whom I trusted just to be who he seemed to be, trusted that he wanted me to be his friend just as I was. The spaces we made together—working on his Studee; talking pigeons; shoveling rabbit shit; him teaching me the ropes of mowing the lawns he willed to me; singing *Tom Dooley* as we tooled home from the Pike; planning our great escape; eating dinner with his old-timey parents—came as close to home as I could imagine. Of course, I loved Richie, though I had no way to know what love was, and certainly had no way to tell him.

I made it to New York City, where I lived for two years.

Fifteen-Four

My mother's back from her Edgemont tune-up, and the family has returned to Sunset Beach for our annual vacation, one more attempt at normalcy. Maybe the beach will reset our family foundation and patch the leaks. I want to find the lazy rhythms we've had in past beach summers, to believe that last summer was all a mistake, an aberration.

This summer, I tell myself, will be like the good old days: Early in the morning I'll squeak open the screen door before there are colors in the sky, feel the silent beating of the sea breeze, and find a wadded-up newspaper filled with empty cracked mussel shells on the front porch—a sign that Dad has prepared his bait and is already down below the sandy ridge surf casting for whatever. I'll squeeze a glass of orange juice, sit on the night-cooled ridge, and watch the silhouette of my father and his pole working the glassy low tide. When the sun is high enough to turn the water from silver-gray to blue, I'll walk up 21st Street to the Bayside Market to buy fresh glazed sweet rolls and the newspaper, barefoot because the blacktop is still cool. Then I'll read the sports over breakfast, body surf in the furious waves, and dry off in the perfect late morning sun. Michele and I will play some catch, each day increasing our distance a little further. Afternoons will be filled with more rounds of the same, usually ending with surf casting into the pink sky with the land breeze at our backs. We'll have visits from inland friends, dinners at Sam's Seafood, and night fishing off the Belmont Shore pier. All the while Mom will sit in her striped-back canvas beach chair with her straw hat on, a pile of books in the sand, alternating her "blessed trash" with a book that Leota Haas would approve. This summer: a return to the good times.

Just four days into our vacation, there is no doubt what this summer is going to be like. Dad is often exhausted in the morning because he has been beaten up all night by Mother, the battle of the medicine bottles. This morning I find my father collapsed in a beach chair planted in the sand, a cup of coffee in his hand. The sun is all angle and color, no warmth, just above the horizon of the Pacific Coast Highway. The heat has not yet thinned the air, which hangs thick and low with a salty taste, and the morning sand is too cool for heat waves to distort the view of the pale flat surf forty yards away. I start to say good morning, but realize I am talking to closed eyes. I hunker down next to my father's chair and feel the breeze begin to shift as the sun rises behind us.

In a few minutes Dad jerks awake and sits up, almost spilling his coffee.

"Well, good morning. Guess I fell asleep."

"Want me to heat your coffee up for you?"

Dad blows over the cup and watches for a puff of steam, sips, frowns in disgust, and hands it to me.

"That tastes foul. Thanks, a fresh cup will definitely improve the situation."

He's asleep again, breathing through his gaping mouth. I watch him folded up in the beach chair, legs crossed, eyes collapsed shut, and try to imagine his exhaustion. Father doesn't like to talk about the night world that he and Mother inhabit after we all go to bed; he wants to protect Michele and me from the after-dark. He is half-successful: I think Michele sleeps all night, but I am not sure. I hope so.

A half hour later I bring my father a steaming cup of coffee and a sweet roll. He blows on the cup and observes the steam, then slurps contentedly.

"How about a game of cribbage?" I ask. "I think this is the summer I finally wrestle the championship from you." I produce the cribbage board, tap the sand out of the holes, and set up the pegs—my father has no choice in this matter. We cut the cards for first deal.

Dad and I have been playing cribbage since I was eight, a tradition begun at the beach. Bill and I had been diving under the waves at high tide, but after ten minutes my scrawny body tiptoed out of the mocking Pacific Ocean, shivering uncontrollably. As I lay thawing, blanketed between the warm sand on my belly and the sun on my back, I heard the gunshot sound of the beach house screen door slam. Soon I felt a shadow block out the sun and opened my eyes. Dad looked down at me as I squinted.

"Want to learn a new card game?"

I didn't like card games, and had never bothered to learn. Whenever Dicky Tostenson would challenge me to a game of rummy or keno, I found an excuse to go home. Cards are for old people. Or prisoners.

"What kind of card game?" I wished I hadn't given him an opening.

He lowered himself beside me with his spindly legs bent out to the side, like a giraffe might try to sit, and pulled out a piece of light varnished wood, three inches by ten inches, drilled with hundreds of holes in four perfectly straight parallel lines. The work of woodpecker engineers.

"It's a cribbage board. Your grandfather taught me how to play. The game's English, maybe four hundred years old."

Great, a card game played by old Englishmen. I felt trapped. When Mom asked me to read a book, I could say sure I'll try it and take it to the bedroom until she had forgotten about it. But my father wanted to play right now, there was no escape. Learning some silly card game was no vacation.

So with my indulgence he began to teach me the intricacies of cribbage: fifteen-counts, single and double runs, flushes, the strategies of cribbing, the odds of inside and outside draws, discards, the dealer's crib hand, reading your opponent. I realized, with some secret embarrassment, that I was enjoying learning this old game of old people.

Dad and I would hunker down on our towels, my back to the waves to shelter us from the sea breeze, and deal our cards. My father was a whiz at card games; they matched his electrical engineer's logic. Before my mother's memory was short-circuited by electricity, they were a serious bridge team, matching his methodical play with her unpredictable daring. Over those summers, he taught me the science of cribbage.

"Look at this crib here: When I played my four, you should have considered that I might be holding a run with a five in it. When you played your six for ten, you set me up to add a five for a run of three plus fifteen-two, for a total of five. Next time, if you have it, play a more neutral card like a face card, so I can't build some runs. I'm killing you on the crib."

I gradually learned to count the fallen cards, neutralize my father's crib, intuit the chances of inside and outside runs or fifteen-combinations, build conservative strategies for keeping my lead, and play against the odds when I was behind. By the end of that summer I could almost hold my own against my father. For six years our cribbage season began on the second day of our vacation at Sunset Beach and ended a month later when we packed up and headed for home. A secret place we shared for at least an hour a day.

We are midway through our first game of the morning. "Fifteen-two, fifteen-four, fifteen-six, a pair makes eight." My father carefully spreads the cards on the orange-and-white striped beach towel for me to see, each card slightly overlapping the edge of the card under it. The sun has begun its arched ascent toward noon, and the breeze has picked up, drying the sweat on my back.

"A pair of sixes for two." I toss my cards down on the sand in resignation.

Dad is about to skunk me in cribbage. We both know it, but you can't tell by looking at his face. The only thing he does differently when he is about to humiliate me is shuffle the cards with a little more noise. He deals out six cards to each of us, twelve flicks of his wrist, picks up his pile, quickly sorts them, and discards two into the crib. He moves with the sureness of a player who already has a good hand and doesn't have to calculate the odds of getting the right card on the cut. I sort my cards in and out, trying different combinations, figuring out how to get the twelve points I need to avoid the skunk. I have the possibility of a double run, but will need to draw into the middle of the run, a jack. Enough for eight points; if I play a good crib, I can pick up four more and avoid the skunk.

I cut the deck and Dad turns the card over: The eight of hearts. We play out the crib and count our hands. My father pegs out and I am thirty-four points behind: skunked by four. He writes the double score down on the back of an envelope.

"Master defeats student again, retains title," he says matter-of-factly, as if reading a headline from the metropolitan section of the *Times*. His eyes glance up with a playful satisfaction.

"Shuffle up, Father William. Haven't you learned when you're being hustled? I just wanted to spot you some points so you'd get cocky and I could come from behind and whup your butt." In those infrequent times when we can be silly, I call my dad Father William, from a limerick (apparently tracing back to Lewis Carroll) that Mom used to recite around the house. It's about an old man who stands on his head for fun. His sons tell him to

Stop, for you might injure your brain.
To which Father William replied
Now that I'm perfectly sure that I have none
I'd do it again and again and again.

"Be back in a minute. Got to check my line." Dad takes a short break after he skunks me, heads to the edge of the surf to reset the line on his fishing pole. I watch him surf casting, his light blue Dacron pants rolled up to the knees, pale tan golf shirt revealing his bony clavicles, a painter's hat brushing a shadow across his face. He runs twenty yards down into the hollow temporarily molded by the receding waves and swings his ten-foot bamboo pole behind him, rotating like a discus thrower. In one motion he sweeps his entire body in an arc, points his arms out over the six-foot waves crashing toward him, and retreats up the bank as the nipping waves soak his pants. The line hums from the reel as the two-ounce pyramid-shaped lead sinker and baited hook sail sixty yards out and plunge into the surf. He sets the drag and places the pole in the eroded stainless-steel stand, sits down on the sand with his arms wrapped around his knees, and watches the dance of the line: rhythmic movements of the charging and receding waves, subtle nibbling of bonito, impatient chomping of barracuda, jerking ravenous movements of sand sharks and baby hammerheads.

Michele stumbles out the front door of our beach house, carrying a plastic shovel and bucket, and sits on my blanket. She's still sleepy. I smear some suntan lotion on her arms, shoulders, nose, and cheeks. We take turns filling the bucket, pack it down tight, then turn it over to make turrets, the four corners of a sand castle. She gathers some clamshells and we put them between the four turrets to outline the walls. She pulls a cracker out of her pocket and offers me half.

I realize I am going to lose my father to fishing. "Dad! I want another shot at beating you!"

He saunters over the crest of the beach and we deal up another round of cribbage. Michele plays with the cards that we're not using for that hand. Halfway through the game, a Sprite in my right hand and a perfect set of cards in my left, I am on a roll. Dad is helpless.

"Seven for twenty-six. Or is that a go?" I wave a card in the air, knowing his answer. I have figured out that my father has all face cards and I have control of the crib.

"Go."

"And six for thirty-one and three big ones." I slap my six of clubs down and move my peg three holes to increase my lead to twenty with my crib coming up. I look at him with gleeful defiance. I love this game.

"*Bill* . . ." Was that a faint voice calling or just a breeze down the narrow alley between the beach houses? Dad and I perk up our ears. Whatever, it's gone. It's Dad's crib and we carefully sort our hands in search of an advantage.

"*Bill!* . . . *BILL!*" Now my mother's distinct voice flies down the hallway from her bedroom and bursts through the screen door. Dad and I look at each other and at the cards we are holding. We deposit our two cards into the crib.

"*BILL!!!*"

I cut the deck and eye my father, squinting because the sun is behind him. He turns over the crib card, a queen of diamonds. I listen for more sounds coming from the house. Silence. Maybe she has fallen back asleep. My father leads with a ten of clubs.

"And five for fifteen-two." I peg my two points.

"Eight for twenty-three." Dad looks toward the house, distracted.

"*BILL, I NEED YOU!*" Her voice shakes the house.

My father starts to fold his hand; his eyes ask me to understand.

"But, Dad, this is our last game before lunch, it's down to the wire. *Please . . .*"

"*BILL . . . NOW! I'm hungry!*"

She has won. My father folds his cards, tosses them on the cribbage board, maneuvers his legs beneath his body, rises to his feet. He opens his hands to me in resignation. As if he has no choice. All I see are deep craggy lines in his palms, going in every direction. A fortune-teller's dream.

"Sorry. Your mother's calling."

I say nothing. I look at Michele to see if she gets what's happening. She seems not to—still innocent. It won't be long.

My father disappears behind the screen door on the porch, easing it shut so it won't disturb my mother. I sort the cards, blow off the sand, and slide them into their blue Bicycle box, count the pegs to be sure none is missing, place them in their hatch on the back of the cribbage board. Michele and I walk back to the house, and I dust the board with my tee shirt and place it in the shade on the porch. Michele lays her shovel and bucket down on the steps.

I have to get out of here. "Want to go for a walk, Little Sister?" Michele loves time alone with her big brother. She takes my hand and we run over the sandy ridge, out of sight of our beach house. We walk north along the wet, packed sand toward the Navy Yard. I try to let go of my rage, my face stretched tight, eyes narrowed to slits that see only shadows. *Bill! Bill!* Every day now that shrill sound echoes through our lives, penetrating and paralyzing everything; every night it marks the beginning of our sleeplessness. I despise my mother, screaming from her bed, the Queen ordering her subjects to come. I despise my father, who always comes.

Michele and I find an abalone shell and use it to scoop up sand crabs. She snatches a skittering crab and holds it in both hands, laughing as the tiny feet tickle her. Finally she releases the crab, and it buries itself immediately, kicking up flakes of sand. A shadow of a gull hovers overhead. "Got another cracker in your pocket?" I ask. She pulls out a cracker, and I show her how to toss it in the air to the gulls—first, fake an underarm toss to get the gull's attention; then, when the gull starts circling, toss it straight up and watch the gull snatch it out of midair. She loves this, her screeches of joy matching the gull's screeching demand for more crackers. Fortunately, she has three more crackers in her pocket. She helps me find some flat rocks, and I teach her the art of skipping—a bent-over sidearm throw of the rock into the surf just as a five-foot wave charges us. The trick is to make the rock hit the surface perfectly flat so it jumps over the wave. Michele wants to try it; I stand behind her and sweep her arm through the motion. She gets a couple of short skips and wants more. This kid's got a good arm. A few more tosses, then it's time for lunch.

I don't want to return to the beach house. Mother will always invade the small spaces Father and I share and demand that he choose. He will always choose her. I pick up a golden-green slimy float of giant sea kelp and smash it against a flat gray granite boulder, a hollow sickening sound, like a smashed skull. I lick the wet salty taste that has settled on my upper lip.

I have to sit.

I know, I just know: our cribbage games will never be safe again.

Michele has found a clam on the beach and tosses it to a swooping gull. We both laugh. She takes my hand and we head back to the house.

Shooting the Curl

This is it, I'm sure: the last night of our last vacation; our family will never return to Sunset Beach. I try to fall asleep in the silent damp air. Listen to the waves *lap-lap* the hard-packed sand slanting down to meet them. Then the sounds I dread: the click of the light in the kitchen, the click of pills on the tile counter. Sobbing night shadows.

Something I am learning: to shut out the shuffling night sounds of my parents. Sometimes, pulled into their humiliation of begging and chasing and pulling at pajamas, I cry, *Please don't do this to yourselves.* Other times I feel rage at the pathetic night figures who once were heroes to me. But tonight I feel nothing, matter-of-fact: they're up again, the light's in my eye, it's a little chilly. I take a swig from my asthma inhaler, roll over out of the light coming down the hall, pull the blanket up to my ears, and fall asleep.

THE LAST DAY of vacation. I wake up early, jarred by the crashing sounds of waves. Unusual activity on the beach, where most mornings are calm and the waves pick up as the winds move in during the day. Mornings are my favorite time, when the house and beach are just mine, space and light and sounds with no interference. I heat up a cup of hot chocolate, wrap myself in a sweater, and quietly slide out the front door, not letting the screen door slam. A howling cold gray day, more like winter, canvas beach chairs blown against houses, dried seaweed rolling down the sand like tumbleweed. Clouds swirling. I pull my sweater over my head, walk down to inspect the water. The waves are angry. Three hundred yards off shore they swell up, at first just a rhythmic deep green mound, then begin their takeoff. Growing deeper and wider, they slowly pick up speed in their rush to the beach, the green turning to black and blue. Then, very suddenly, about sixty yards from me, they rise up in fury, straight up, at least ten feet in the air, white fuming froth raging at the shore. No longer able to sustain their menacing posture, the waves collapse over, thunder as they implode upon themselves, pushing a gust of wind onshore. Then they limp to the sand at my feet, rage spent.

A loose flock of seagulls heads north, flying into the wind, fighting the storm. Now I know where they go: back to their secret nesting colony behind the *No Trespassing* sign. But they aren't getting very far. Quickly exhausted by the winds, they have to stop flying and go into a glide, only to be pushed back down the beach. Losing ground. Many of the birds give up, their breast muscles cramping, refusing to pump their wings. Then they settle onto the sand to wait out the storm on one leg, head pointed into the wind. Twenty such gray and black weather vanes planted in the sand patiently and passively twist in the wind twenty yards up shore from me, some with head tucked under the leeward wing. As I approach, they nonchalantly hop to the edge of the surf on one leg and circle around me. Offshore I watch one mature herring gull defiantly struggling against the wind, hovered over the trough where the giant waves are breaking. The bird peers into the froth in frustration; I am sure he will join the other birds on the beach. The gull spreads its tail feathers and slightly tips them, causing its body to dip downward. The black-tipped wings at first are arched wide, its torso at a forty-five-degree angle. It's going into a dive. As the bird picks up speed the tail narrows and wings fold into the body; it streaks directly into the very peak of the giant breaking wave. Just as it reaches the top of the wave, which has now curled over, the tail flicks and wings open as the angle of the body flattens out, and the bird disappears into the spume. I am on my toes, following the wave as it rolls over and over, the curl hurtling toward me. No bird appears.

Suicide.

I feel a little desperate and helpless as I imagine the gull thrashed by the furious wave, the sadness of a seabird drowning. I hate the wave, its power, its noise, the arrogance as the curl moves up the beach. Then I see: Just as the last crash of the curl folds over before the wave meekly flattens out, two hundred yards up shore, the gull glides out of the end of the tube, spreads its tail, and rises skyward on the updraft created by the dying wave. It cocks its eye down at the froth, dips its left wing, and flaps as it heads out to sea to catch another wave. The gull is a surfer, waiting for the right wave, then diving into the breaker, shooting the curl as the wave moves in, gliding up shore in the calm of the tube. The wave pulls the gull two hundred yards up shore, against the unbeatable wind. I walk up the beach for fifteen minutes, face into the whistling wind, following the seagull as it hovers and dives, shooting curl after curl, patiently gliding its way home.

Nobody will believe what I have just seen. I will keep this secret.

Sixty yards up the beach, something thrashes at the edge of the spent waves licking at the shore. Probably a beached sand shark. Anticipating the discovery, I approach on my toes to find an immature herring gull being tumbled over and over by the surf, trying to right itself to keep from drowning. The receding wave sucks the bird with it, a target for the next incoming wave. I watch a new wave roll the helpless bird over four times, beating it against the slanted beach, then pull it back out with fierce undertow. The bird is trapped. I run twenty yards into the sandy hollow of churning shells and sand crabs created by the retreating wave and snatch the gull with both hands, holding it just above the snapping incoming wave, which soaks my sweater.

The bird seems dead in its limpness and shredded feathers. Still eyes. I wrap it in my sweater and carry it back to the wooden porch of our beach house. Seated cross-legged, I hold the gull in my lap, my thumbs arched over its back and my fingers under its breastbone, like I hold my pigeons. I put pressure on its chest. Saltwater dribbles from its smelly nostril, but no movement, so I press more firmly, a desperate pressure. Suddenly the neck whips with a guttural sound as the throat clears and water sprays my face. Calmly the gull cocks its head to get a good look at me with its now fiery orange eyes. I am always amazed at how unterrified birds are when I catch them; they almost never struggle and seem to look at me with a kind of curiosity. I am sure they think I am going to kill them, but they seem resigned, knowing when it's useless to fight. I spread the right wing open to its full thirty-inch span, checking for broken bones along the leading edge, feeling the movement at the base where it connects to the chest to examine for a dislocation. Shifting hands to hold the bird, I check the left wing, which also is uninjured. Now the legs. One of the webs on the left foot is torn, slightly bleeding. I move the legs in all directions and look for a reaction in the gull's face, which reveals no pain. Now I feel along the shafts of the upper and lower bones for ridges as I put torsion on the legs: no evidence of a fracture. The knee joints are in place. The bird is just exhausted, near-drowned. Probably trying to shoot curls and got caught by the wave and thrashed to the bottom of the surf. Too impatient to wait out the wind on the beach.

My parents are up now, calling me for breakfast through the wind. "Come on, Mark, we have to pack so we can be out of here by noon, vacation's over." Again I feel desperate, we can't go yet, I have to be sure the bird's all right.

"What've you got there?" Dad has found me out.

"Just a bird I found. I think he almost drowned."

"He's OK? Let's go, you should start packing, don't forget your baseball stuff."

"Let me put him in the backyard. I don't want to return him to the beach until he's got his strength back." I wrap the gull in a dry towel, feet pinned to its chest so it won't struggle and hurt itself, and carry it to the small patio between the garage and the back porch. Most of the patio is already shaded by the house, but in the far corner by the cactus is one spot of sun. I carefully unwrap the bird and lay it on the warm red brick, slide back on my butt and watch from the shade ten feet away, arms wrapped around my knees. The gull is alert, cocking its neck to the unfamiliar surroundings. Curious, it hunkers down on the brick, absorbing the heat. It pecks twice at the grass growing between the bricks.

Packed, I return to the gull in an hour. It is standing now and shuffles away as I approach, still easy to catch, but refueling with energy from the sun. The one thing I have left unpacked is my Brownie Hawkeye camera, which I unstrap from my shoulder, and down on my knees I take four pictures of the keen-eyed gull, unafraid in its uncertainty, having realized no harm will come from me. Everyone is in the car now, I feel the impatience.

"C'mon, Mark, we're waiting. Pack your camera and let's get the show on the road."

I reach down with the palms of both hands and pick up the gull, which does not resist. Along the side of the house toward the beach, past the spot where I buried the seagull egg from the *No Trespassing* beach, I carry the bird to the ridge of dry warm sand just before the drop-off of beach to surf, and set it down. It is now standing. The bird and I both back off ten feet and stare at each other, waiting for the other to take off. Neither does.

"Mark! We're all waiting!" I traipse back to the car, climb in.

I stare out the Chevy window moving north on Highway 101. The parking lot of Sam's Seafood is starting to fill up with lunchtime customers, high tide in the lagoon, phragmites grass picking up the breeze in the salt marsh. We rumble over the bridge that crosses the channel to the Navy Yard. Far off, the rusted blue stack of a navy destroyer rises behind an abandoned beach guarded by chain-link and barbed wire. A flock of seagulls turns in the wind, their backs reflecting the sun.

Monsters

When I was five, we bought our house on the unpaved dead end of Stamps Road. Our first house, our half-acre of pepper, pine, and palm trees, olives, apricots, lemons, and honeysuckle. The guy who had owned it was a bit weird—he built a croquet court, a four-hole miniature golf course with a bridge going over a stream, and a lath house covered with ivy. At one time, our barn-red house had been a real ranch house. In the front yard we raised goldfish in a round cement pond where a windmill had been. Our neighborhood was surrounded by orange groves, mostly Valencias, a few navels. The Van Couverings lived in the middle of a forty-acre orchard just over our fence; Dr. Steere owned four hundred or so acres along Cherokee Drive; another thousand acres were across Lakewood Boulevard—thousands of orange trees all within half a mile of where we lived.

My favorite grove was Dr. Steere's. Richie Cary took me there first, after I met him in first grade. I started to walk home with him from school, down Downey Avenue.

"Want me to show you a shortcut?" he says.

"Why not?"

At the edge of the orchard, Richie stops. "Better roll up your pants first. They're irrigating."

Spring was the best time, when the green John Deere tractors plowed two-foot dikes around each tree, then one of Dr. Steere's men cranked open the rusty valves inside four-foot-diameter cement pipes. *Whoosh!* We watched the water gurgle from tree to tree until the entire grove looked like a giant's rice paddy. Nourished now, the trees bloomed millions of small flowers. Richie and I climbed down to the base of the cement pipes and searched for crawdads and black widow spiders and green snakes and frogs. We didn't play in the orchards much during winter, though we walked the now-flattened dikes to get to school. In January the groves were the quietest. But there was this oily winter smell, like the derricks on Signal Hill: an army of stinky black smudge pots burning all night to beat the frost. They looked like little guard gnomes, standing sentry over the trees. When they stopped burning the pots, I knew that spring was coming.

The big mystery of the orchard was where the hundreds of crows went to roost at night. At dusk, you could see them all returning from feasting at ball fields, lawns, schools, and parks. They formed a giant cawing flock, circled above the orchard, then suddenly went into a dive and disappeared into the trees. In a few minutes all was quiet. Richie and I were determined to find the crows' roosting place, but at night it was too dark to enter the grove, and by the time we got there in the morning, they had already taken off to forage for food. We never cracked the secret of the Crows' Roost.

I SHOULD have seen it coming when they started construction of the Stonewood Mall a year and a half ago. It's the new rage: *malls.* Stonewood is going to be the mother of all malls, located at the intersection of Lakewood and Firestone—they say it's the busiest intersection in all California, the crossroads between downtown L.A. and Orange County. They say the mall will be a *destination place.* All you can buy or eat, one-stop shopping at forty brand-new stores: J.C. Penney's; Woolworth's; W.T. Grant; Thrifty Drugs; Hardy Shoes; Miller's fine clothes for men; Downey Music; Hollander's Cafeteria; Downey Community Bank, in case you run out of money; a bunch more. Great place for kids to hang out after school. Plenty of parking. All on a hundred acres that was once a beautiful orange grove.

And now it's happening everywhere. When I get back from what I am sure is our last Sunset Beach vacation, I call up Greg Fox, my doubles partner, and ask if he'd like to hit some balls. *Sure, why not?* I grab my racket and a can of balls and head over to take the shortcut through Dr. Steere's grove that separates our neighborhood from the high school courts, over past Seventh Street.

First, I smell the smoke. Then I turn up Cherokee and realize that the orchard—all four hundred acres of it—is gone. In the month that I have been away, the orange trees and dikes and irrigation pipes have disappeared. Nothing. Black ugly earth, muddy after last night's rain. Criss-crossed twelve-inch tire ruts, footprints of giant machines. A few branches of broken trees sticking out of the mud. Like photographs of Hiroshima after the Bomb. Signs along the edge of the scorched fields warn:

No Trespassing
Private Property
Keep Out

Then a giant sign, ten feet wide, five feet high:

Cherokee Groves
Residential Properties for Sale
Quarter Acre Lots
$10,000
Thompson Developers

Humongous moaning yellow Caterpillars roam the wasteland. Stump pullers yank the few remaining trees out of the ground, roots and all. I can almost hear the trees screaming. Bulldozers herd the trees, still green with oranges hanging on them, into fifteen-foot-high piles. Men douse the trees with something, toss a match. *WHOOSH.* Like a funeral pyre. Trees burned at the stake. I feel like crying. I want to throw rocks at the machines and the men manning them.

In one month, my trees have all disappeared. Gone. Developers have turned the groves into a wasteland. Like a horror movie, an army of giant gnashing munching monsters roaming the countryside and destroying everything in its path. Subdivide and conquer.

Welcome to Southern California.

I do not recognize this place, I no longer feel at home here.

I go home and call Richie. "Do you know what they've done?"

Lo-BOT-o-MEE

A new word floats out of the August night sounds that I try to ignore: *lobotomy.*

I know this word, from the *Saturday Evening Post* article I read about depression. They cut out part of your brain, the part that has feelings. No feelings: no pain. The treatment of last resort.

Lo   BOT   o   MEE

Iambic. Like a heartbeat.

Please!   *Bill!*

My mother is begging for a lobotomy.
May he grant her wish and put us all out of our misery.

1990: The Night My Mother Died

I was forty-seven. Three a.m. in Philadelphia, the phone rang. "Mark, this is Dad. Your Mom had a massive heart attack an hour ago. We're not sure if she'll make it." My mother had never had heart problems. I consoled my father, asked if he had called Bill and Michele, who lived close by him in L.A. He would call me if there was any change.

"You OK?" Jeane Ann asked.

"I am."

I was unable to go back to sleep. It was like Christmas Eve, all of the presents awaiting me under the morning tree. Please. Please die. The biggest gift of all.

The next morning my father called. She had died. I went through the motions of saying she died in peace, seventy-nine years is a good long life, etc. etc., and made plans to fly to California to help make funeral arrangements.

I was not embarrassed by the ecstasy that I felt. Nor surprised.

On the plane I was already making plans for things I could do with my father now that he was free, that we were free: he could come to Philadelphia for Thanksgiving; we could go to the Air and Space Museum with the kids; we could all go to Catalina Island, fish off the Belmont Shore pier, take in a ball game; he could teach the kids about stamps and coins.

The only people at the funeral were my father, brother, sister, plus a cousin and his family who had not seen my mother in years. Also, twenty members of the Long Beach Police force—my sister's co-workers had a tradition of showing up for each other's family funerals. None of the people whom my mother had locked out of her life thirty-three years before were present—the crew from The Little Theater, the families that grew up together after migrating from the Midwest, neighbors she counseled and consoled. Not even her hairdresser. My brother gave the eulogy. I did not recognize the woman he spoke of with such affection. Did we have the same mother? I had nothing to say in my mix of rage and relief, my impatience to move on. I held my thirty-five-year-old sister's hand, not to console her, but because we both shared the same joy.

Two Questions

I continued to frequent therapists into my late thirties, searching for someone who could shake me loose, free me from my family and help me find a way to stay—just stay—in a relationship. A new therapist asked me two questions that startled me: how clear they were, how simple, yet demanding and profound. Questions that I had never been able to ask myself:

Question #1. (Upon hearing the details of my mother's Black Dog fantasies about me, her prying into the intimate details of my dates with Ann Hegardt, hanging on to my curly hair, Napoleon's big penis): "There's a word for that, you know. What is that word?" I did not answer. "You need to say it out loud," she said.

Question #2. "Was your father ever there for you when you were a kid?" She wanted examples.

Answer #1. It took me an entire session to say the word. I am still unable to write it.

Answer #2. I had few memories of really being with my father as a child, just the two of us together, doing the father-son thing. Here is what I could manage to remember:

Father Memory #1: When I was twelve, Dad came to a baseball game, the only time he watched me play. I was in seventh grade, just before I temporarily retired from baseball because my body was on the disabled list, a victim of awkwardness and asthma. Earlier that season I had almost been beaned by a ball, and my batting average plummeted below .200. My hitting and fielding were so pathetic that the coach saved me for the end of losing games when my play didn't hurt the team. But that June Bobby Cochran, the starting second baseman, went away for a two-week vacation, and I had second base to myself. Over breakfast I mentioned to Dad that I was going to start Wednesday night's game. Then I did something I had never done before:

"Can you come and watch me play?"

"Come watch you play? Hmm . . ."

Dad went to the kitchen to refill his cup of coffee. Buying time to think of an excuse.

He returned. "I think that might be possible, your mom's rehearsing her play 'til ten o'clock, and Jimmy MacFarland can bring her home. The only thing is, that day we may be flying the C-124 with the updated electrical system I'm responsible for. If anything goes wrong, I'll be stuck at work."

For three days I had visions of trotting out to second base, taking infield practice, beautiful moves and pivots, swinging away to smack stinging line drives. An hour each morning I practiced against our brick chimney, throwing scorchers to my left and right, digging out grounders and making perfect pegs to the square marked with chalk. I rode my bike down to the batting cages on Firestone Boulevard, popped quarters into the pitching machine, and swung away at a hundred fastballs. There was no way I was going to bunt in front of my father. The rest is history, as they say, but it's true: the new improved C-124 flew perfectly on its first test run, Dad showed up during the second inning, and I played like I used to play, hitting a triple and two singles, cleanly snatching three grounders. For one night I loved the game again.

"Say, you were pretty hot out there tonight," Dad said matter-of-factly as we slurped a root beer float at the drive-in. He had no idea how terribly I had played all season, how I had decided to get out of baseball.

"If you came to every one of my games, I'd be on the all-star team."

Father Memory #2: In the fall of 1958, Clyde Walker gave a clinic to our tennis team. Over seventy years old, Clyde was the coach of Billie Jean King (*née* Moffitt), who was then ranked #1 nationally among sixteen-year-old tennis players. Clyde mentioned that he gave private lessons, and I begged my father to drive me over to Long Beach for just ten lessons. He agreed, and found someone to stay with my mother every Sunday afternoon that fall. Riding back and forth with my father felt easy, natural—this is what fathers and sons do. My biggest memories of those lessons: Clyde said, "I have a friend who is practicing on the next court, said she'd work with you on your net game." His "friend" was Darlene Hard, the U.S. doubles champion (and soon to be singles champion), who played a great serve-and-volley game. Another Sunday he suggested we work on my doubles game, and he introduced me to one of my opponents—Billie Jean. (I did manage to return a few of her serves, and made one great drop shot. The final score was irrelevant—I knew I had a story to tell for the rest of my life.)

Father Memory #3: Our cribbage games.

Other Father Memories: Working in the garden together; going to a Hollywood Stars minor league baseball game; an occasional round of pitch and putt, watching a U.S.-Russia track meet at the Coliseum.

That's it.

"That's it?" said my therapist. "You aren't pissed at your father?"

It took a few more sessions for me to allow myself to be angry at my father, at the way he had cowered before the demands of our mother, always choosing her over me and Michele. It was difficult to allow myself to feel that anger—it felt disloyal to my father, ungenerous, selfish. After all, he had stayed with my mother, while I had fled.

Ordinary People

Approaching forty. I went with my wife-to-be to see *Ordinary People*. The film was about a family brought to its knees by a tragedy—the older, favorite, son drowned in a boating accident. Mary Tyler Moore, the mother, tries to stay afloat but finally succumbs to her grief. As she sinks, she grasps at her husband and remaining son: she will pull her family down with her. Timothy Hutton, the younger brother, filled with guilt for not having saved his brother, teeters on the edge as his mother announces that she wishes he had been killed rather than her older son. Donald Sutherland, the father, tries to hold his family together, to be an anchor for his child and wife who are drift-ing away, drowning. Finally, the mother makes her husband choose: go down with her in her ship of grief, or rescue his drowning son.

The father chooses his son, cuts the tether to his wife, lets her float away.

When we left the theater and got into my car. I drove a block, then broke down. Made it to the curb, turned off the engine. I sobbed uncontrollably for ten minutes, my own tears of grief.

My mother made my father choose: her, or my sister and me.

He chose her.

Fall 1996: Our Last Cribbage Game

That last beach summer of 1958 took the spirit out of our cribbage matches, as a cloud settled over the ritual my father and I had begun when I was eight. I don't remember playing with him during those last two years before I left home. When I moved away, my father occasionally would travel for work and leave my mother with Jean-nie. On these visits he might be in my neck of the woods—Berke-ley or Atlanta or New York—and spend a day or two. Our visits often began with an awkward dance, two very different species trying to find a common language. Then he'd dig into his suitcase and pull out his father's fold-up cribbage board and Bicycle cards, the same board we had played on at Sunset Beach. After a couple of rounds we loos-ened up, on familiar territory with a familiar language.

After my mother died, I visited him more regularly, visits that began and ended with our cribbage game. Fifty-two years, a thou-sand cribbage rounds. Even match.

When he turned eighty-five, Father William's sight and powers of concentration began a race to see which would finally end our rit-ual. I bought him a mammoth cribbage board, with bigger holes and pegs, and playing cards with large numbers and primary colors. Our games became longer as he shifted the cards of his hand in and out, trying to find combinations that he had previously scanned instanta-neously. Occasionally I threw away game-breaking combinations to keep the game close, as I suspect he had done when I was eight. Ten-game marathon sessions were shortened to two. Often when I visited, he would start to disappear into his private cloudy regions, and I would pull him back with a request—not a challenge any more—for a couple of hands before he went to sleep.

A year before Dad died, during a few hours when he was especially alert, I suggested we go a round of cribbage.

"Your deal," he said, "but just one game."

I dealt the cards and sorted my hand, then picked the two cards to discard into my father's crib. I looked up and watched Dad finger his cards, eyeing them in deep concentration. He must have a good hand, I thought; he's trying to decide which combinations to keep. He lowered the cards and looked toward me, but not at me. His eyes were desperate, unfocused. He folded his cards and put them on the table.

"I can't, Mark. I can't."

We sat in silence, taking in the meaning of what had just happened.

"It's OK, Dad, it's been a long day. Let me help you get to bed."

My father and I shuffled down the hallway to his bedroom, arm in arm.

Father William

My father died at eighty-seven, I was fifty-five. He lived seven years after my mother's heart attack. During that brief time together, without Mom, we created a new list of memories.

The first years:

Dad went on a kind of rampage, a man cut loose. A month after his wife of sixty years died, eighty-year-old Father William announced that he was going to China on a three-week tour. He took a newfangled camera with him—a gigantic VHS recorder, the first-generation kind that was fourteen inches long and eight inches high, the kind you hoisted on your shoulder like a TV cameraman. He did it all: the Forbidden City, the Great Wall, Tiananmen Square, the Terracotta Army, the Yellow River. He sucked duck feet for dinner, slurped slimy tripe soup for lunch. When he came home, he said he couldn't understand why he used up so much VHS film. Then, when we all sat down to see the video of his Great Adventure, we understood why: on several occasions he had forgotten to turn off the recorder, photographing many minutes of the ground and his size twelve feet as he walked with the camera slung from his swinging arms. His own Long March, documented.

Three months after Mom died, Dad came east for Thanksgiving—the first time he had visited our family. We took more photos in ten days than we had taken in three decades of my visits home: Dad sitting with sixteen-year-old Jess, looking over a gift to his grandson—my father's first stamp collection, begun in 1922, when he was twelve. Dad sunning himself in the backyard. (Ten minutes after he came inside for a drink of ice water, we heard a *Crack!* and a *Crash!* We went outside and a nine-inch-diameter limb from our maple tree had broken off, completely crushing the beach chair he had occupied— he had come within minutes of an early demise.) Dad walking along the beach on the Chesapeake Bay, our dog Maya trailing after him. The kids and I playing hearts with Grandpa on the Amtrak train to Washington, DC. Grandpa being our own personal tour guide in the Air and Space Museum, introducing us to Donald Douglas (whom he had worked for) and other pioneers of aviation, showing us the first commercial aircraft, which he had traveled on in 1933 between Chicago and Milwaukee, reminiscing about the age of space while pointing out the satellite rockets he had put electrical systems in. And the best photo of all: my father, my kids' grandfather, riding the carousel on the Washington Mall, wearing a giant shit-eating grin.

The next year our entire family visited Dad in Southern California, where we were joined by Michele. We walked the pier in Seal Beach, the same pier where he had caught an octopus when we night-fished in the early fifties. Michele had brought some gloves and a softball. *Snap:* a photo of my eighty-one-year-old father playing catch with his kid and grandkids in the sand. Better late than never. Another photo: Dad sitting on an inner tube, hanging on for dear life, being towed at twenty miles per hour by my sister's speedboat on the Colorado River.

And more photos: Grandpa dressed in a *rasta* wig and cap, mouth all awry, trying to look Bob Marley cool. Father and son in their plaid cotton summer jackets and Panama hats, arms on each other's shoulder, looking very thirties and a bit dangerous. My proud father sitting in the front row of a conference room in the statehouse in Trenton,

watching his son give testimony about why New Jersey's farmworkers needed a law to provide them water, toilets, and hand-washing
facilities in the fields where they harvested blueberries, peaches, and
tomatoes.

After my mother died, I called Dad three times a week, just checking in. He was living alone now, though mobile; but hearing each
other's voice without interference was a gift to both of us. Small talk,
unencumbered.

The last years:

When Dad was eighty-two, it all began to fall apart. Jeane Ann
noticed that he walked with a very slight shuffle, occasionally catching his toe on the rug. We suggested he get evaluated: early Parkinson's. The disease progressed rapidly and he became a full-blown
Parky: terrible bruising and hip-breaking falls (both hips), expres-
sionless face, unable to concentrate enough to finish (and eventually
to begin) a cribbage game. Caretakers came for a couple of hours a
day, then all day, then twenty-four hours a day. He awoke in the night
terrified of the demons lurking in the corners of his bedroom, who
conspired to burn him or stab him. He would not talk about advance
directives, so we had to decide what to do when he stopped eating.
Feeding tube? Yes (Bill); no (Mark); I don't want to be involved in
this decision (Michele). So, with tubes in place, he withered for eight
more months in the hospital bed we put in his bedroom, eyes gazing
upward, each night assuming a fetal position, each day his caretaker
un-ratcheting his legs and arms. Morphine to ease the breathing.
Then his heart start stopped as his lungs flooded with fluid.

During the last two years of my father's life I called him every
night at 8:00. I planned my days to be at a phone at that time (no cell
phones then). He and his caretaker waited for my call, which usually
lasted no more than five minutes. I talked about my day, the kids; he
said he was fine, could be worse. Then we hung up, me in a haze of
sadness, my father now ready to sleep. Eventually he made only guttural sounds—at the beginning of our conversation when I asked if
he could hear me, at the end of the conversation when I said I loved
him, sleep well. Once I forgot, or was unable to call. When I called
the next night, Dad's caretaker said he had insisted on staying up

until 9:30, expecting my call, then finally fell asleep. I never missed another call. Another photo: of me in the Chiricahua Desert, thirty miles north of the Mexican border, after watching hummingbirds and trogons all day, standing at a pay phone, Dad on the other end of the line.

In his last year, the slope of my father's downhill demise became very steep, so I flew out to California for three or four days each month to be with him. On the plane I kept a notebook to help me enter and leave his world. I made a list of stories I would tell him at night to ease him to sleep: playing pitch-and-putt golf, his love for his yard, fishing in the troughs of Sunset Beach, him teaching me to swim in the lagoon along Highway 101, his visits when I lived in Berkeley, Atlanta, NYC, our pool games and ongoing cribbage competition, playing catch at Seal Beach, him rescuing my tongue from the Coke bottle, his stamp and coin collections, his coming to my baseball game the night the C-124 flew, tennis lessons with Clyde Walker. At night we had a ritual. I washed the crust from his forehead and mouth with a cool washcloth, then rubbed cream into his arms and hands, slowly kneading his flesh until it relaxed, fingers uncurled. Finally holding hands with him, I would start: "Remember when . . . Often he fell asleep before I finished the story, and I sat awhile longer, often stirred up by the parts of the stories I did not tell—of how our cribbage or fishing or catch in the yard came to be interrupted by Mother, of the times we should have made together. How he always chose her over Michele and me. How he didn't stand up for us, or for himself. I felt sad more than angry. I wanted to leave my father and myself in peace, I would find a way to deal with our stories' complicated endings some other time.

When my father died, I gave his eulogy, based on an African string letter I had read about many years before. I tied objects to a cord that was attached to the end of Dad's bamboo fishing pole—the pole that he had put in the rafters of our garage forty years before, after our last summer at Sunset Beach. I talked about his fishing pole, how as a kid I loved to watch him in the private place he went to cast his line over the early morning waves. I then told stories about each of the objects hung on the string letter. A coconut—my father, durable but hard to crack, to get inside; how in so many ways I had no idea who he was, but he was gentle and I loved him. Of course, the folding crib-bage board, our ritual which brought us together, our private place. A rocket ship. Coins and stamps. A Coke bottle. A basket of fruit: a banana (Michele), a softening mango (Bill), a hot pepper (me)—the makings of a salsa, a mix of unlikely ingredients. I spoke about how we all loved Dad; but we wanted more, much more, leaving us frustrated and at times angry about lost opportunities, missed intimacies. I returned to the fishing pole, how it works because it is forgiving.

Family Photo

In the last decade of his life, before his Parkinson's made his hands shake too much, my father decided to make a gift for his children. He got out the boxes of family photos and made five albums: William Louis Lyons II, Phyllis Teague Lyons, Bill, Mark, and Michele. The albums would be distributed to his children after he had died. I got the Mark and Mother albums, Bill got the Bill and Father albums, Michele got Michele.

I looked through my mother's album two years after my father died, about a decade after her death. There were a few photos of The Little Theater group: Hanging out in the snow up at Eileen Sweet's cabin in Big Bear Lake. A cast picture from a play. And there: a photo of sister Michele, who looked about one, sitting on Jimmy MacFarland's lap. Her blue eyes and blond hair matching his. Both smiling.

How could my father have put this photo of my sister and the man my mother insisted was her father in our family photo album? What was he thinking?

Explanation #1: Dad did not believe that Jimmy MacFarland was Michele's father. My mother's claim was a delusion—as he had always insisted to me. My father was Michele's father. I wondered if this would be a relief to my sister or not. The good news: Dad was her father. The bad news: if he was her father, why didn't he take better care of her? Why did he farm her out to Jeannie all those years? Why wasn't he there for Michele when her mother had disappeared?

Explanation #2: Dad knew Jimmy MacFarland was Michele's father. He had denied Mother's claims vociferously to protect his children as he made the decision to never leave their mother. But, finally, he had decided to tell the truth, to reveal the secret after he and Mother had died. There, in the photo staring out from the album: Jimmy Mac-Farland and Michele, father and daughter. Now you have the truth. If you're still wondering, if you need to know.

Both explanations seemed reasonable; both were inadequate.

I never showed the photo to my sister.

The Lists

Found in my father's desk drawer after he died, four decades after my fourteenth year: the warp and weft within which my memories are woven.

Dates, Places and Lengths of Stay That Phyllis Was Hospitalized, from March 31, 1957, to April 1, 1970. (Number of days in hospital is in parentheses; dates were included as well.)

Grandview Sanitarium (5)
Edgemont Hospital (13, 150, 4, 16, 7, 49, 19, 58, 31, 73)
Long Beach Hospital (4)
Whitney (5)
Santa Barbara (10)
American Rivera (1)
Compton Foundation (7)
Cedars of Lebanon (8)
Norwalk Metropolitan State Hospital (88, 168, 5, 167)
Brea (10)
Studebaker Hospital (2, 2, 3, 3, 5, 3, 5, 14, 2, 3)

Father did the math: *Total:* 940 days, or 2 years and 7 months, in mental institutions in a 13-year period.

Psychiatrists Seen by Mrs. W.L. Lyons. The complete list, over a thirty-five-year period.

Medicine Prescribed for Mrs. W.L. Lyons for Her Nerves. This list included all dates from 1957–1970, and names of doctors who wrote the prescriptions. The bracketed descriptions of the class of medication and indications for treatment are mine.

Trilafon [phenothiazine/antipsychotic]
Pacatal [phenothiazine/antipsychotic]
Tuinal [barbiturate/sedative]
Doriden [hypnotic sedative]
Tofranil [tricyclic antidepressant]
Carbital [barbiturate/sedative]
Pyribenzamine [antihistamine/sedative]
Chloral hydrate [sedative]
Paraldehyde [sedative]
Thorazine [phenothiazine/antipsychotic]
Librium [benzodiazepine/sedative, anxiety]
Valium [benzodiazepine/sedative, anxiety]
Stelazine [phenothiazine/antipsychotic]
Atropine [anticholinergic/cardiac]
Phenergan [antihistamine/sedative]
Ritalin [stimulant]
Elavil [tricyclic antidepressant]
Marplan [monoamine oxidase inhibitor/depression]
Compazine [phenothiazine/anxiety, schizophrenia]
Placidyl [sedative]
Vistaril [antihistamine/anxiety]
Parnate [monoamine oxidase inhibitor/anxiety, depression]
Mellaril [phenothiazine/antipsychotic]
Beta-Chlor [sedative]
Dexamyl [barbiturate and amphetamine/anxiety, depression]
Prolixin [phenothiazine/schizophrenia]
Quaalude [synthetic barbiturate/sedative]

According to my father's notes, between 1957 and 1970 my mother's doctors wrote prescriptions for twenty-seven different medications to treat her depression. Seven of these drugs were phenothiazines, which were (and still are) a primary drug for treating schizophrenia—they were never indicated for depression. Thorazine and its relatives were given to my mother for their "calming effect," and often left my mother stuporous. As a fourteen-year-old, I observed this state as *gorked out*.

Doctors prescribed twelve different sedatives, several of which were barbiturates. As soon as Librium and Valium came on the market in the early sixties, the psychiatrists added these benzos to their armamentarium.

The apparent goal of treatment, with its multitude of antipsychotics, sedatives, and anti-anxiety medications, was to tranquilize my mother. No doubt: they succeeded.

My father's catalog did not include the number of electroshock treatments.

The Box

Thanksgiving, 1997. I flew home for my monthly four-day visit to hold eighty-seven-year-old Father's hand, stroke his forehead, sponge his cracked lips, and pump Ensure through the feeding tube extruding from his belly. I breathed with him in his quiet Parkinsonian hypoxia, as oxygen flowed from his nasal cannula. Fetal, cachectic, he was beyond speech, mostly beyond understanding what I said. But not beyond soothing voice and touch. So that's what I did, again and again, until his eyes closed and we breathed on the same beat.

Tired and restless after putting Dad to sleep, I resumed the late-night ritual I had begun on my monthly visits to tend to his dying— exploring the bookshelves and walls and drawers and closets for things to take home with me to Philadelphia. Like an archaeologist on a dig, collecting shards to reconstruct a life I had run away from but now needed to make sense of. Shards: seven of my mother's books, carefully selected from the hundreds stashed on the mantel and hallway bookshelf (*The Le Gallienne Book of English and American Poetry* [1925], *The Snow Goose*, *The Shooting of Dan McGrew*, *The Glass Menagerie*, *A Treasury of Damon Runyon*, *The Rubaiyat*, *Cyrano*); her collections of Sarna bells, bone china cups, and ruby red glassware; my father's folding cribbage board and a few tools; *Willie Nelson, His Very Best*—the CD I had given him ("Stardust," "All of Me," "Georgia on My Mind," "Help Me Make It Through the Night"); photos of my parents that had hung on the walls for fifty years, unnoticed; a box of high school mementos buried in the closet of my old bedroom; *Record*, my pigeon diary; letters I had written home for forty years, bound with rubber bands, almost hidden in the back of the desk drawer.

As a child, my father's closet had always been a mystery. Open the door, and it looked like a regular old man's closet: polished Florsheim shoes for work (brown and black), cleated golf shoes, blue canvas shoes for gardening, all aligned perfectly on the floor; suits (light tan, dark tan, charcoal gray, no stripes, no tweed); dress shirts (all white) and casual shirts (Hawaiians and checkereds) on hangers; ties on a special rack (all one color, to match his suits); plaid Bermudas on a hook. Above and behind the hangers was a shelf—too high and too deep for me to reach. The shelf seemed hidden, secretive, tempting. Once, when I was about ten, I could stand it no longer. I parted my father's shirts, slacks, and coats, pulled up a dining room chair, and stood on it. There behind the clothes, surrounded by unpainted walls, was a cardboard box, about the size of an orange crate. Before I could act on my impulse to reach back and pull the box down, I was discovered by Mother. She gave me a short lecture about "respecting people's privacy," and extracted my assurance that I would never invade the back of my father's closet again. And I didn't, until the week of Thanksgiving over four decades later, my mother long gone, my father finally, fitfully, sleeping in the next room.

As my father was dying, I completed the task I had begun at ten: I climbed up on a dining room chair—the shelf in the back of the closet was still deep and high—and parted my father's clothes. There it was: the cardboard box. I lowered the box down, carted it to the living room, and began to explore its contents. I lifted out a large manila interoffice envelope from Aerospace Corporation, my father's last employer. He had written *Phyllis' Patched Poetry* on the outside. I opened the envelope: at least seventy-five poems, written in my mother's perfectly angled script; another batch of letters between the two of them, written when they were in their thirties, when all was possible. I began to read one of her poems; but, no—not now. I would need more time for this. I replaced the papers in the manila envelope and stashed the envelope in the bottom of my suitcase.

My last morning before flying home, near dawn, I packed my

clothes and went to my father's room. His helper and I stretched his trembling arms and legs, slowly un-ratcheting them, and sat him in his rocking chair. He breathed easier when he was upright.

"It's time for me to go, Dad," I said. "I'll be back for Christmas, just a month."

He looked up at me. His brown eyes had turned to blue, returned to the color of his infancy. A small quiet tear sledded down the furrow of his right cheek.

It broke my heart.

"I have to go, Dad. I have to go. I love you."

Eighteen hours later, my father's caretaker called 911 and he died alone in the hospital. Heart failure. I was three thousand miles away. My brother and sister arrived at the hospital the next morning.

WHEN I RETURNED HOME, I put the envelope in a drawer without reading one poem or one letter. The envelope sat in the drawer for almost two decades. At seventy-two I pulled out the envelope, dusted it off, and began to read what my mother had written seventy-five years before.

Phyllis' Patched Poetry

When I was six or so, Valentine's Day crept up on me, and I didn't have a card for my mother. She was completely distraught and ran into her bedroom crying dramatically: if her son loved her, he wouldn't have forgotten. As my father watched, I sat on her bed and tried to console her, repeating, "Mom, I love you, I really love you," over and over. She wouldn't stop crying. My father turned off the light, and she fell asleep. As Dad and I sat in the living room, I began to feel angry: *Come on, I just forgot to give you a card.* We finally got her to come out and have dinner with us.

The next morning, I found some papers in a box with writing on them—words that I was too young to read. I took several of the papers and cut them into hearts, belated Valentine's cards. About fifteen in all. When I presented them to my mother, she took a quick look and started to yell at me, a mix of rage and tears. The papers were a stash of her poems, written a long time before. She was heartbroken. My father carefully pieced the poems back together with Scotch tape, put them back in the box, and placed the box in a safe place: his closet.

The poems of Phyllis Miriam Teague (PMT), and Phyllis Teague Lyons (PTL), written in her twenties and thirties:

Many of my mother's poems were filled with naturalistic metaphors—trees, sky, wind, stars, gardens, twilight. Growing up, I remember her hating the outdoors, no way was she going to hike or camp. Her idea of an adventure was spending three days at the Sands Hotel in Las Vegas. Some poems were about death and loss, emptiness—most likely following the early death of her father. She kept reworking a poem about throwing dead purple asters into the yard, "the bowl is empty now." Several of her poems were carefully typewritten with a return address, prepared for submission. One rejection slip.

She had also typed poems of some of her favorite poets: Dorothy Parker, Carl Sandburg, Sara Teasdale, Robert Frost, Rudyard Kipling, Louis Untermeyer, Amy Lowell, Edwin Markham, Anna Wickham, Margaret Widdemer, Clara Shanafelt. Before the Black Dog, without any encouragement, my mother would recite her favorite poems, the way some people break into song: "If," "Fog," "Birches," "The Road Not Taken," "Invictus," "Fire and Ice," "The Man with the Hoe."

In school, when given a choice of poems to memorize, I chose those poems, whose verses never left me. At fifteen I memorized Edwin Markham's "The Man with the Hoe." A foretelling of the remaining thirty-five years of my mother's life?

Who made him dead to rapture and despair,
A thing that grieves not and that never hopes.

Dearest Bill—Mom's letters to Dad:

The letters were written in the thirties, around the time that my parents were married. Her letters were filled with gentle caring and encouragement, reassuring my father when he was having doubts and insecurities about working as an engineer for his rich uncle who had paid for his education. She was optimistic about the tensions with my father's Jewish mother, who found it difficult to accept a *shiksa* into the family. She crafted her letters with care and sentiment. A sweet love letter to my father: "You have come closer to some hidden me," saying the sound of winds carried his voice. No doubt: my mother was there for my father. She was in the world.

Dear Phyl—Dad's letters to Mom:

Ever the engineer, my father's letters were filled with practical details— exact mileage traveled, times of arrival and departure, price of fixing flat tires, amount spent on gas. He reassured her that his Jewish mother would come around, she would grow to love her *shiksa* daughter-in-law (she did). "Promise me you'll never change," he said.

Did my father ever, in his darkest times, when he felt most alone as my mother slept in her Thorazine haze, go to that box of letters and poems and read them? To remind himself of this woman with whom he had fallen in love, to hope that buried somewhere in that haze was that same woman? Did those letters help him stay, if he ever thought *I can't do this anymore?*

What did it mean to me to read these poems and letters, to see the woman my mother had been before the fall? Who could have predicted, reading her vibrancy, her passion, her being-in-the-world, that within twenty years she would become a recluse, a chair-sitter who needed frequent visits to the sanitarium for electrical jumpstarts, who would watch her children flee from her and not know how to—or possibly care to—pull them back into her orbit? Possibly, if I had pulled down that box earlier, and read her poems and letters when I was twenty, or thirty, or forty, I would have been reminded of who she had been, what she had lost—what we had lost. Would that have calmed my rage? Would I have been able to care for her more, to want to find a way to be there for her instead of flee? Would I have been able to ask her to read me a poem?

Twenty-five years into my mother's illness, my father sent me a note filled with the usual news: sister Michele has been promoted in the Long Beach Police Force; I am working on my stamp and coin collections; your brother just took a new job; Mother's reflux is acting up, and her knees are bothering her so she just sits; some days are down, some are manageable, we just keep going; nothing to complain about. Oh, here's a poem your mother wrote when she was thirty, for her father who had died that year. She got up this morning, asked for a pen, and started writing—she wrote the poem from memory.

The poem was forty lines long, her penmanship now shaky. Where had she gone to find it? What was it like to go back to that place where she was a poet, where she was capable of grief and passion, when she wrote and read and all was possibility? What was it like for her to return from the place of her poem to her chair, to stare into the fireplace again?

I never asked.

I found the original of the poem in the envelope containing *Phyllis' Patched Poetry.*

Windmills

In college, when I got particularly lonely, I would wander into Moe's bookstore on Telegraph Avenue in Berkeley and browse through the stacks of used books, askance and unordered by author or subject. The first book I bought at Moe's was *The Prophet* by Kahlil Gibran, a hardback buried in a pile with its cream-yellow book jacket Scotch-taped together. I was certain I had discovered a unique poet that nobody else had heard of. I took the book home and committed Gibran's poems of love, children, joy, sorrow, and self-knowledge to memory. In my senior year, still grieving over my breakup with Ann, my first true love, I headed to Moe's. There on the counter sat a huge book, close to two inches thick, with a gilded cover: *The History of Don Quixote de La Mancha, with Illustrations by Gustave Doré.* For half an hour I turned the pages and ran my fingers over Doré's engravings: el Don astride his bedraggled horse Rocinante on his first sally forth; Sancho and his master engaging in philosophical reflection, then setting out to defend the world from evil dragons; Quixote famished and yearning for his lady-love Dulcinea. Over one hundred plates.

Sometime—possibly during a lucid spell between her earlier hospitalizations—my mother had told me about Doré, who in the nineteenth century illustrated books that I had never read—*Rime of the Ancient Mariner, Paradise Lost, The Divine Comedy.* She described how, when commissioned to illustrate *Don Quixote,* Doré retraced the twelve-hundred-mile voyage el Don had made through Spain two hundred years before in his quest to revive chivalry and bring justice to the world. The artist absorbed the dust and wind of La Mancha, sketched horses and mountains and gardens and plains, then visited museums to learn how the peasants and aristocrats of seventeenth-century Spain dressed, what armor they wore, what weapons they carried. Then he sat down to make engravings that forever defined readers' images of Quixote and his squire Sancho and the world they set out to make right.

There in Moe's, for a moment I felt proud of my mother. Another one of those things she just *knew*, that she cared about when she was still capable of caring and passion. When she had wanted her son, too, to know about important books, about *literature*. Five hundred miles from the home I had fled, I had wandered into a moldy used book-store seeking refuge and found an old gilded tome that reminded me of my mother, who had stopped tilting at windmills.

Did I feel sad for her? I don't remember.

On my bookshelf rests a Dover book: *Doré's Illustrations for Don Quixote*.

Silence Makes You See More

"Careful when you do that, pigeons have been known to break your finger when you mess with them on the nest." That's what Richie Cary told me four years ago when I first inspected the pigeons in his coop and tried to push a hen aside to see the two eggs hidden in the straw. "Homers, especially—all that long-distance flying really builds up their breast muscles. When you reach in there, they snap their wing at you and that big bone on the leading edge catches your finger. *Pop!* Pigeons'll die defending their nest." I always believed everything Richie Cary said, he never gave me a reason not to.

Something I have noticed about pigeons, watching them nest in my coop. When they first lay their eggs, they aren't so protective of the nest; you can reach your hand under them, pick up and look at the eggs, move them out of the nest box without any resistance. If you mess with them too much, the birds will just abandon the nest box, start over in another box three or four days later. Sometimes when the eggs are only a few days old, both the hen and cock will leave the nest and eat and bathe together for fifteen minutes before one of them returns to brood. But something happens around day twelve, seven days before the eggs hatch. The parents become rabid protectors of their nest, changing shifts in a careful side-by-side maneuver that leaves the eggs uncovered for no more than five seconds. Then one stands guard outside the box while its mate incubates. Even my oldest birds, who have known me for almost three years, go crazy if I reach into their nest after day twelve, pecking and flailing their wings at me, staccato sounds, more barks than coos. When their eggs are close to hatching, there is no way you can get a pigeon off the nest. "Hey, Lyons, I was cutting through your backyard on the way to the basketball court and I saw a big black dog coming out of your coop, maybe a Labrador. Might want to check it out." Art Dever and I used to be sort-of friends, he even had a few pigeons for a year or so. But he lost interest in pigeons and me when he discovered basketball and girls. He was tall and popular.

"Thanks, I'll check it out."

I half-jog down the block and turn into our backyard. From a distance, the coop looks in order. The fly-pen door is open, the way I left it this morning so my birds could free-fly before it got too hot. Fifty feet from the coop I realize I hear no familiar sounds. No courting, no splashing in the bath, no fights at the feeders. Like somebody turned off the volume, a silent movie.

Something I discovered five years ago, the first time I ever watched television: silence makes you see more. A bunch of us kids used to go down to old Missus Sample's on Sunday afternoons—she was the only one on the block who had a TV back then, a twelve-inch Emerson. She'd fix us popcorn and we'd watch *Hopalong Cassidy*, maybe six of us. Sometimes I'd cover my ears so I couldn't hear what the cowboys were saying or hear the hoofbeats or gunshots. Just watch and not listen. What I saw was much more vivid, the way William Boyd's eyes met the eyes of the girl whose farm he had just saved—you can love but you can't touch; then he slowly mounted his horse and rode away, the dust and the clouds becoming one, heaven and earth. Or the muscles on the calves of the horses as they raced across the prairie, the steam from their nostrils that tells you it's morning. Or how Hoppy would catch the thief in a box canyon and the next scene would be a prison cell.

I can see things you can't, that's what deaf people say.

Silence. I discover Roger face down in the bath sink, the water streaked with blood oozing from his neck. One bird glides to the safety of the roost inside the nest house as I enter the coop. The sandy floor is a no-man's-land, like World War II photos of the Battle of the Bulge. Bodies everywhere, a bird with blood dripping from its beak, another with a missing leg, a chest ripped open, a head missing. At least ten dead. I enter the nest house. Two of the nest boxes are sprawled on the ground, broken eggs, a line of boxes still against the back cinder-block wall. A jagged bone juts through bloody feathers of a white wing, hanging over the edge of a nest box. Pinky, my favorite bird. When they are fresh-killed, the necks of birds twist and hang in an unnatural way, warm and limp, spineless. I move Pinky aside with the back of my hand. Two unbroken eggs.

Eleven birds are dead, three more are alive but gasping for air, lying on their sides, eyes starting to shade over. Two four-day-old squabs are under Arthur's stiffening breast, too young to survive on their own. This is the part I hate the most. I can't find the hatchet in the garage, so I get the shovel out of the old, unused chicken coop, sharpen the edge with a file. I find some hard flat ground out of sight of the coop. One by one I hold the injured adults and squabs with my left hand, put the shovel blade over the neck with my right, and thrust down on the handle. Usually the head doesn't come off, but the neck breaks. Pigeons don't make noises like chickens.

Too many birds to bury. I'll have to cremate them. I shovel the ashes from our upright cement incinerator into a trash can to get a good draft. Then carefully stack the birds on top of each other inside the incinerator, a pyramid with five birds on the bottom and one on the top. Reaching down inside, I gather soot on the inside of my arm, along the white part above the elbow that never gets tanned. The red gallon gas tank we use for the lawn mower gurgles as I bend the spigot and dip it into the incinerator, basting the birds. Strike a wooden match against the cement and toss it inside. *WHOOSH*, air being sucked in.

The sound has been turned back on. I sit on the grass ten feet away and feel the heat from the fire, curious that burning pigeons don't smell.

I rake up the feathers in the fly pen and hose down the dirt; the blood disappears. Scour the bath with Dutch Cleanser, stack up the nest boxes. The surviving birds are shell-shocked and voiceless, hiding in the rafters of the coop. I toss a handful of feed on the ground to try to coax them down. Close the door to the pen, let the birds come to their senses. I return to the incinerator, stir up the ashes with a stick, and detect solid parts of pigeon carcasses. Pour on some more gasoline, toss in a match, a burst of heat.

I open the back door of our house, call into the living room, "Mom something's happened in the coop, a dog." Silence. I forgot: Mom's back at Edgemont, a week now. Dad's at work. Michele's at Jeannie's.

I wash the soot off my hands and sleep. Three hours later, the drop in temperature wakes me and I return to the pigeon coop. The remaining birds are down eating now, and one whose mate was killed has returned to incubate the eggs in their nest. She'll sit on the eggs twenty-four hours a day for a couple of days, then abandon them. I hear the powerful flap of James as he drops from the pepper tree to the roof of the coop. He escaped the dog and disappeared until it was safe to return home.

Big Bear

It's been almost a month since the Lab visited my pigeon coop, now fifteen birds, down from twenty-nine. Except for James and my Johnny Otis fantail, who survived, I burned all my favorite birds. Shoveled their ashes into a trash can that I put on the curb for Tuesday trash pickup. I still feed and water the birds that survived, rake the pen twice a week, open the wire door so they can free-fly, make sure they're all in the coop by nightfall. I don't lie under the pepper tree to watch the flight circles they make, expanding then contracting against the sky. Most of the nesting pairs were broken up in the massacre; the remaining mates abandoned their nests and I threw the eggs out. One pair, Ivan and Harriet, continued to incubate their eggs and have a new clutch.

Mom's home from the hospital. She doesn't cry much; but she doesn't remember much either, and sometimes goes all day without talking. Father is more frantic when Mother is home, eyes nervous as he hovers over her in the nest of her living room chair, trying to protect her from any disturbance that will send her back to Edgemont. Brooding. My father and I have learned to communicate with almost invisible head signals when I enter the living room, like at an auction: a slight up-and-down movement of his head means it's OK, I can join them; an upward glance toward the door to my bedroom signifies Mom's in bad shape and I need to move on, go outside or to my room; a barely perceptible side-to-side means it's touch-and-go, have a seat but be prepared to leave. I sleep through the night more. Sometimes I am still awakened by the bathroom sounds of my mother and father arguing over the medicine bottles. When I realize what the disturbance is, I roll over and fall back to sleep. The arguments seem shorter now; I think Dad goes through the motions of saying *no, you've had too much already*, then gives Mom her medicine so he can get some rest. When my mother sleeps 'til noon, deep guttural snores, Dad says, "I shouldn't have given in, it's my fault, I was just too tired, I'm worn out, Mark."

Yesterday my father found me hanging up my clothes on the clothesline. "Listen, I'm going up to Big Bear Lake for a three-day meeting, they're bringing in some people from Grumman's in Georgia to talk about how we can work together on this new project. I wouldn't go if I didn't have to. Mom will be OK. Jeannie's going to sleep over, take care of her and Michele, cook your meals." I can tell, by the way he carefully folds his shirts and underwear and pats them into his suitcase, that my father's trip to Big Bear is a vacation.

Early Wednesday morning, the sun still hasn't appeared over the church parking lot that used to be the Van Coverings' orchard; there's dew on the grass. Dad leaves today for Big Bear, before Mom wakes up. Jeannie is already here setting the table for breakfast—why does she always have to make so much noise?

I've been awake all night deciding what to do. "When do you have to go?" I ask my father now.

He checks his watch and taps the face. "Forty-five minutes or so.

I've got a little more to pack, pay a couple of bills. I want to get an early jump, beat the traffic."

Big Bear Lake, maybe 110 miles up in the mountains, plenty of sky. Where The Little Theater used to have weekend parties at Eileen Sweet's cabin. But it gets cold in the winter. I've seen pigeons feeding in the snow along the lake in front of the village. They seem to survive the cold fine.

On the top shelf of the garage are four empty cardboard boxes that Dad picked up at the liquor store for storing stuff. I knock the boxes off the shelf with the end of a rake handle and punch holes in the tops and sides with a large greasy screwdriver. For air and cross-ventilation.

The coop is still quiet, the birds in the nest house huddled together under the warmth of the rafters. They're used to me catching them for banding or administering their monthly dose of louse powder; it doesn't take long to put my pigeons inside the boxes. James is the easiest to catch; with his training I've handled him the most. I fold down the tops of the Seagram's, Absolut, and Budweiser boxes, apply masking tape on the seams, and drop some pigeon seed into the air holes. The birds coo in alarm and their feet shuffle on the cardboard as I lower the boxes into the trunk of Dad's car. I close the trunk door, then put my ear against the cold green metal and listen. The pigeons are silent in the dark, not panicked.

"So where do you want me to let them go?" Dad gently taps the trunk door. He's a little uncomfortable with the responsibility of disposing of my birds.

"Anywhere, somewhere in the village, maybe by the grass in front of the hardware store. There are lots of pigeons there, and people throw them popcorn. I saw an old guy who lives up there and feeds the pigeons every day. He sits on a bench, sort of like he owns it. That way they won't have any trouble finding food right away. And they can drink out of the lake."

"You're sure you want to do this? They won't come back, you know, this'll be the last time you see your birds."

I feel a little awkward, nudge an apricot pit off the driveway with the side of my foot. Dad and I have never talked about my pigeons.

This is the first time I realize that he knows how important they are to me.

"Yeah, I'm sure. They'll be happy up there."

"Pigeon heaven," my father says. "I'm sure they'll be fine." He touches me on the shoulder.

Dad's car backs down the driveway and rolls up our street, I watch the trunk door turn up Cherokee Drive and disappear around the corner.

The sun warms me as I scrape the bird shit off the roosts and nest boxes, scour the porcelain bath, and rake the sandy floor of my coop. Latch the wire mesh door. Lie on my back staring at the skeleton of the pepper tree against shifting morning sky. I turn on my transistor radio, hold it to my ear. Johnny Otis's new hit song, *Willie and the Hand Jive*, is blasting away.

> I know a cat named Way-Out Willie
> He got a groovy little chick named Rockin' Billie
> Do you walk and stroll with Susie Q
> And do that crazy hand jive too?
>
> Papa told Willie, "You'll ruin my home
> You and that hand jive have got to go"
> Willie said, "Papa, don't put me down
> They're doin' that hand jive all over town"

I imagine Blanca, my white fantail, against the blue sky above Big Bear Lake, and fall asleep.

EPILOGUE

· · ·

Family Legacy

IN MY MID-THIRTIES, perusing Renninger's, a giant flea market in rural Pennsylvania. I came there every year or so to buy something to give character to wherever I had moved: a 1920s Morris chair, a counter stool and jukebox from a diner, an art deco mirror or oriental rug. I thumbed through old magazines at a stall, two dollars each. On page twenty-three of the July 3, 1939, *Life* I saw an image that froze me: a photo of a short pudgy balding man in a dark suit. He was launched, mid-jump, perhaps ten inches off the ground, feet crossed, arms outstretched. Behind him, his shadow danced on the wall. The headline: "The Great Nijinsky Dances Again in a Swiss Insane Asylum." Nijinsky, the premier dancer of the twentieth century, stopped dancing at twenty-nine, retreated from his friends and family and art into a silent shadow-life, spending his last thirty years in and out of mental hospitals. He barely spoke, enough to say, "Don't touch me."

In 1912 Nijinsky crossed his feet ten times in one leap while dancing *The Rite of Spring*, as the audience rioted in disgust or pleasure at his androgynous persona. Ten times: no dancer had ever accomplished that. And in that *Life* photo, not having leapt once in twenty years, the great Nijinsky, coaxed on by a younger dancer who had come to visit his idol, managed one inelegant leap, then made a deep bow and returned to his near-silence until he died eleven years later.

In the upper left-hand corner of the article was another photo: Nijinsky as a young man dancing in *Le Spectre de la rose*, ethereal, torqued on his heels, feral, deep in a forest.

Those photos haunted me. I bought the magazine and have opened it many times over the last thirty-five years, staring at the ghost-shadow of a man taking one last leap to a place he had loved, where he had been most alive, but had retreated from forever. Then mute, lost somewhere he could not be found. I have often thought of my mother, mute in her chair, having fled from her husband and children, her world of theater and friends. She occasionally would arise and attempt a leap—send a thoughtful note to the outside, tell a dirty story, talk about a good book she was reading, play a game of contract bridge, invite her grandchild to sit on her lap—then retreat back into her chair, eyes inward. Did she mourn, being sucked back into her melancholia after having again felt the sensation of being air-bound? Did she hope that she might find a way back, could she imagine the path? Was it too exhausting?

My mother lived twenty years after the last time she was institutionalized. Perhaps she ran out of sufficient feeling to sustain the pain that would require *putting her away*, as they used to say. She was never alone for thirty-five years, cared for by my father or hired strangers who sat with her in our living room or orderlies who ordered her stays in hospitals. Never alone, yet completely alone. At seventy-nine her heart stopped; but in a sense that was a formality. She had lost heart many years before.

After my father released my pigeons into the clear altitudes of Big Bear Lake, I lost all interest in birds. My redwood coop was converted into a woodshed, time to put away childish things. James, whom I had trained to home, returned from the mountains in two days, strutted through the trapdoor of the empty coop, and waited for me to bring him feed. I gave him away three times before he stopped returning. Seventeen years later, I lived next to a pond on the north shore of Long Island, a recent migrant from Philadelphia. The fall migration brought hundreds of birds to the pond—loons, black ducks, widgeons, gadwalls, green-winged teals, shovelers, mute swans, sand-piping shore birds. I attempted to rescue a mallard with a broken wing. I bought a bird guide. In a phone call home, I mentioned that I was surrounded by flocks of redwings and Canada geese, yellowlegs and plovers. A week later I received a package in the mail with a note from my mother: a pair of binoculars. Like Nijinsky, my mother had become momentarily air-bound, responding to a memory and an image, a brief connection to the outside world, to me.

I learned to love birds again. Not long after my mother sent me my binoculars, I went to the Arctic Circle on a research trip to band snow geese, phalaropes, and ptarmigans. Because the geese are precocial, like baby chickens, they wander off with their mother as soon as they are hatched, and thus are difficult to band. The solution: to band them *in utero*, while still in their egg. I learned to use a pipping hammer, small and pyramidal, and to hear where the almost-hatched goslings were tapping their way out of the egg. In the egg, the chicks are in a fetal position, their feet and head touching. Listen for the pip, then tap there with the hammer and chip a small triangle from the shell. Pull out the foot and the leg that is attached, place a numbered band on the leg, and tuck it all back inside. Within twenty-four hours the egg will be an empty shell, the chick long gone with its identification that will be logged in a computer. After pipping and banding my first snow goose chick, I sat by its nest, contemplating the small miracle I had just been part of.

Birds of America, and the memories of the day my mother gave the book to me, sits on a shelf five feet from where I write this.

I did not go crazy. At forty-two I learned to love Jeane Ann, to tackle being with someone without recoiling, destroying everything, and returning to the black hole of loneliness. Of course, it was not easy; but I never left and never will. I do not for a moment take for granted the miracle of my connectedness with my two sons, Jesse and Seth. My children did not need to run from me to free themselves. My favorite family photos are of my kids with birding scopes and binoculars on the Delaware Bay or in the Maine woods or the rain forest of Costa Rica. The scent of my mother's Black Dog has not completely disappeared; but it is very weak, an occasional whiff of what might have been, a reminder of who I did not become. I do have paroxysms of loneliness at predictable intervals and spend a day or two finding a way back to my current life. I have learned to embrace my loneliness—or rather to embrace the boy who grew up lonely, the boy who in some ways I will always be.

Possibly I can finally finish this story because, looking back on my life, I can see that I have been free of the terrible ending that was my mother's story, that neither I nor my family inherited her sad fate. Possibly, finally, in being free of her I can care for her.

After writing about my teens for four years, I found myself wanting to embellish the stories, bend the facts to make them more interesting, add a twist of excitement to an event that might seem mundane to anyone but me. But that was betrayal, shaving and polishing the pieces, dressing them up. So I put the stories away for seventeen years, unfinished, in disarray, disordered. But true. My solution: to become a writer of fiction, which demands made-up stories that tell their own truth.

This is the irony, perhaps ultimately the greatest gift of my mother: Over two decades ago, hiking on the Algonquin trail of the Adirondacks, where I began my catalog of memories of my fourteenth year, I was not a writer. My mother's melancholia, her retreat from the world and from me, is what started me on this journey as I searched for words to reclaim the buried part of my childhood—not only the rage and loss and fear of foundations crumbling, but also the magic: a pigeon flying a hundred miles to return home; holding a hummingbird up to a honeysuckle; befriending my puny body; the seduction and terror of hunting; the way theater invites eccentricities in non-eccentric people; the intimate communication of a cribbage game; the first boy I loved; the secrets of the orange groves, iambic pentameter, and onomatopoeia. As I wrote this story, I learned the power of words, learned to love them, to become a writer.

Over the years, as I've written and published, I have occasionally fantasized about sending my stories to my mother, dead before I had begun to write. She reads them and awaits my next visit. After I've been home a day or so, we hunker down to business. She sits in her chair with a cup of coffee, my marked-up manuscript in her hand. We talk about word choices, images, subtleties she has discovered, parts that hit the mark, parts over- or under-wrought.

I refill her cup, and she says, "I think you're on to something."

"You know where I got my love for words," I say.

ACKNOWLEDGMENTS

Twenty-five years ago, Judy Zimmerman was the first person to read short pieces from what became this memoir. She made me consider that I might be on to something, and should keep writing, just keep on writing. I kept sending her more drafts and she took me seriously, providing critical, writerly support. In all ways, she has been a true friend.

Over the last forty-five years, Arthur Veen and I have shared our stories of love and loss, family disappointments and trauma, road stories, wanting to do it right for our children, dreams surpassed and dreams denied. We have demanded and received honesty from each other, with long talks that continue to deepen. In a sense, in Arthur I found my adult Richie Cary, except now we know how to talk about our feelings and to say we love each other. Arthur knows this story as much as anyone.

For the last sixteen years the Working Writers Group has been my writing family. Once a month we meet and critique each other's works-in-progress with honesty and sensibility and perspective. *Homing* abounds in changes in point of view and voice, jumping back and forth over a fifty-year time span. When my WWG friends read the first draft, it was a tangle of confusion. Three drafts later, they had helped me navigate structure and voice, deepen my narrative and tell the story I needed to tell. A thousand thanks to David Sanders, Ann de Forest, Miriam Seidel, Douglas Gordon, Debra Leigh Scott, Louis

Greenstein and Nathaniel Popkin. Special thanks to Miriam, with whom I went back and forth to design the cover of *Homing*, until it reflected the story within. And special thanks to Doug, the artist in all things related to typeface, headings, and making a book visually beautiful. Often the cover and layout are what make us want to hold a book, to embrace it.

To Richie Cary, to whom I never said goodbye: I'm not sure I was as important to you as you were to me. Likely not. I'm sorry that you'll never know.

To those folks who have given me encouragement and support along the way: Joy Stocke and Kim Nagy, publishers who believed in my work and became great friends; Lin Backiel; Ned Bachus; Connie Garcia-Barrio; Eli Goldblatt; Hal Sirowitz; Annie Steinberg; Harvey Feldman; Suzanne Daub; Sandy Dempsey; and Irv Ackelsberg.

To my family of origin: For too long, it was not easy. Then I found a way to let go and come home. Unfortunately, you were both long gone. This book is my way of returning home one more time and saying good-bye.

Finally, to my family of choice: Thirty-five years ago, I believed that I was incapable of being with someone, that I was trapped in the loneliness I experienced as a teen. Then there was Jeane Ann. We leaped into each other, embraced each other's fears, dared each other to stay, then realized we were going nowhere—that this is where we belonged. Our being together is the sequel to *Homing*. The connection I have to my sons, Jesse and Seth, is an unimaginable gift. They did not have to flee to save themselves; we are all in this together.